Memoirs of the Church of Scotland in Four Periods. I. the Church in Her Infant-State, from the Reformation to the Queen Mary's Abdication. Ii. the Church in Its Growing State, from the Abdication to the Restoration. Iii. the Church in Its Persecuted State, from the Restoration to the Revolution. Iv. the Church in Its Present State, from the Revolution to the Union. With an Appendix, of Some Transactions Since the Union. by D. Defoe
by Daniel Defoe

MEMOIRS

OF THE

CHURCH OF SCOTLAND,

IN FOUR PERIODS.

BY

DANIEL DE FOE.

WITH A PREFACE AND NOTES.

BY THE

REV. WILLIAM WILSON,

CARMYLIE.

JAMES DEWAR, PERTH :

W. WHYTE & CO., JOHN JOHNSTONE, ROBERT OGLE,
EDINBURGH ; WM. COLLINS, GLASGOW ;
WM. MIDDLETON, DUNDEE.

MDCCCXLIV.

46.

11.

9.

1.

PRINTED AT THE WARDER OFFICE, DUNDEE.

EDITOR'S PREFACE.

The "Memoirs of the Church of Scotland," though published anonymously, are well known and universally admitted to have been the production of DANIEL DE FOE.

Of the authorship of the work a strong evidence is to be found in the time of its publication, when viewed in connection with the fact that it is avowedly written by an Englishman who had made a visit of some considerable duration to Scotland, and taken pains to inform himself of the character and history of the Scottish Church. It is well known that De Foe was one of the Commissioners sent from England to promote the Union between the two kingdoms—that he was, immediately previous to the Union, resident for a considerable period in Scotland, and that his wonted activity was not slumbering during the time of his visit. The Memoirs were published shortly after the Union, and their author could scarcely be mistaken.

A more striking evidence still is to be found in the style of the Memoirs. It is impossible to read many pages without detecting the hand of the author of Robinson Crusoe. We find in the Memoirs the same lively and vigorous style, the same captivating interest, the same inimitable art of simplicity, which has made Robinson Crusoe one of the most fascinating and popular books of any age or country. The writer of such a strange and truth-like fiction could not feel himself much out of his element in giving the matter-of-fact history of the Church of Scotland. Truth is often stranger than fiction ; and the Church of Scotland, during the period of her eventful history, presents to the view scenes of more stirring interest than the imagination ever painted.

The most conclusive evidence of all is to be found in the spirit and sentiments which pervade the work. De Foe is no cold-hearted chronicler, who gives a detail of facts, without manifesting any interest in his theme. He does not seek to disguise his passionate admiration of the Church of Scotland, and his indignation against the men who, from time to time, have sought to corrupt and to enslave her. De Foe was an English Dissenter, and hated the Stuarts, one would almost think with the violence of personal animosity. He had not sought to disguise what he felt ; and at a time when the Ministry of Queen Anne were looking with too favourable an eye to the restoration of the exiled family, De Foe wrote against them with a bitterness so severe, as to bring upon himself heavy punishment. He was subjected to the pillory, and to fines which utterly ruined his fortunes. To a man entertaining such sentiments, no subject could have been more congenial than the Memoirs of the Church of Scotland. It was against her that the Stuarts had, generation after generation, displayed the whole extent of their treachery, malignity, and tyranny. If De Foe had been desirous of frightening the nation from the apostacy and folly of recalling the exiled race, nothing more appeared needful than to shew how they had dealt by the Church of Scotland. Everywhere, accordingly, throughout the Memoirs, we find this hatred of the Stuarts exhibited. It appears as the Author's reigning passion ; not so much, indeed, in its odious aspect, as hatred to the men, but to the atrocities of which they were guilty. And, assuming this aspect, it presents itself often in the character of a generous sympathy with undeserved injuries, an enlarged love of liberty, and, above all, of that highest liberty, which is the foundation of every other, the liberty of worshipping God as he has himself directed.

There is also running through the work an undisguised dislike of Prelacy. It had shown itself too much the friend of absolutism to be a favourite with De Foe. On the other hand, he glories in eulogising the Church of Scotland. He grows eloquent in detailing her various excellencies. He desires, in the Memoirs, to present her to the world as a pattern to other Churches, especially in her two great characteristics as a Church free from controul in her internal administration, and in her Presbyterian constitution. The work, indeed, might be properly entitled, an historical plea for Presbytery, and against Erastianism.

Alas ! that it should be true of the " Established Church of Scotland " now, that she has entirely destroyed the foundations of De Foe's eulogy. She is no longer a free Church, and she is no longer a Presbyterian Church.

It is to be regretted that the Memoirs of the Church of Scotland should be so little known in this country. Several causes have conspired in consign-

ing this work to comparative oblivion. Scotland was
the field where alone it could be expected to acquire
an extensive and enduring popularity; and its circulation in Scotland was from the first hindered by
very natural, though, I am convinced, very unjust
prejudices.

It was written by an Englishman. This, in our
day, would scarcely tell against the popularity of a
work, even on Scottish Church affairs. Indeed, there
is a likelihood of its telling the other way. It was
not so till long after the Union. The Scottish people
believed very cordially that the English did not like
them, and they were by no means unwilling to reci-
procate the feeling. They could not believe that a
book of any value upon their Church could be written
by an Englishman, and hence the Memoirs have
never become widely known. They never constituted
one of the books of the people, and yet they are not
unworthy of such a place.

But the Author was a Unionist as well as an Englishman. He had laboured in promoting one of the
most unpopular deeds which was ever accomplished in
Scotland. The Union was especially dreaded by Scottish Churchmen, as opening a way for the overthrow
of their ecclesiastical liberties. De Foe was not, therefore, likely to be an acceptable person, nor his work
an acceptable offering, to those who were most of all
interested in, and would have formed the readers of,
the History of the Church of Scotland.

Besides, De Foe was a novelist, and it but seldom
happens that a writer of fiction makes a trustworthy
writer of facts.

De Foe, moreover, was a very voluminous writer,

and it was not likely that his Memoirs should be otherwise than ill-digested and hastily-arranged.

The two last of these feelings which I have supposed as operating against the circulation of the Memoirs may be presumed still to exist.

That the Author is not trustworthy in his facts is a groundless prejudice. I have examined the whole work with considerable care, and have often been forced to admire the diligence with which the Author has collected his materials, and the faithfulness with which he has used them. The few errors I have detected are very trifling in their character, and are corrected in brief notes at the end of the volume. Almost all the facts I have been able to verify by a comparison with our best accredited historians. The only exceptions to this, indeed, are in the third part, where many statements are made that do not occur in any other historian. Here the Author's guide was, to a considerable extent, the traditions existing among the people, of the sufferings under Charles II. But to his credit be it said, that he visited the scenes of the Martyrs' sufferings, both in the south and west of Scotland, and endeavoured to gain the best information which was then accessible, and I have seen no reason to distrust his fidelity.

That the facts are ill-digested, and the narrative confused, is an objection to which I cannot give so decisive an answer. It should be remembered, however, that the work does not profess to be a History, but Memoirs. Though frequently there is not a narrative of the facts in the order in which they occurred, they are connected together as illustrations of some common principle. This renders the work all the more interesting, and certainly not the less instructive.

While some may distrust the Author's impartiality, from the strong leanings he exhibits and glories in, on the other hand I acknowledge the conviction that no man can write a true history of the Church of Scotland without a full and hearty sympathy with the principles on which that Church is based, and for which she has been honoured so often to contend. An honest man without this could give a dry chronicle of facts. These are but the bones of history. If it is to have flesh, and blood, and animation, it must come from a sympathetic heart. This is what constitutes the great charm of the following work. This is what will tend to make it truly useful.

WESTHAVEN, 29th April 1844.

AUTHOR'S PREFACE.

~~~~~~~~~~

The following Work seems to have as little need
of a Preface as any of the kind that has been published in this age. It is hoped it is itself but a preface or introduction to some larger and fuller history,
that may, by better hands, some time or other, do
justice, not to the Church of Scotland only, but to the
memory and families of the particular sufferers and
confessors who have sacrificed themselves in defence
of religion in that part of Great Britain.

It is a moving reflection, that these larger and
fuller accounts have been so often promised, and so
long ago undertaken by several able and worthy
hands, and that yet nothing has been finished, in a
cause wherein history is so much in debt to truth.
We see no full account yet given, and, it is to be
feared, will not be given in our age.

This consideration has made an officious stranger
concern himself in the work; he could not bear to
think that the memory of the most glorious scene of
action and the most dismal scene of suffering which
the Church of Scotland has passed through, should lie
buried in their own ashes, and not a man to be found
who would effectually employ himself, and set seri-
ously about the work of ransoming things of such consequence from the grave of forgetfulness.

For this reason he has applied himself, by books,
by just authorities, by oral tradition, by living witnesses, and by all other rational means, to make him-

self sufficiently master of the matters of fact ; at least, to furnish out memoirs, though not a perfect history, of these things ; and to endeavour to restore the general knowledge of these great transactions to the use of posterity, till some more large and particular account of these things shall appear.

I shall say nothing to the performance but this, that I have endeavoured carefully to adhere to truth of fact, and to have it told so evidently and clearly, that it may not be misunderstood by the ignorant, or misrepresented by the malicious part of mankind in ages to come.

The Author recommends the work to the candour of impartial readers; and if any mistakes are to be found, though he has been critically careful to avoid them, he desires they may be placed to the account of a disinterested zeal to do justice and service to the people of Scotland, and to a cause which he had too much at heart to let lie neglected any longer, how many imperfections soever might happen in his performance.

CONTENTS.

MEMOIRS

OF THE

CHURCH OF SCOTLAND.

PART I.

OF THE CHURCH IN HER INFANT STATE.

WHOEVER enquires narrowly into the subject I am now entering upon, I mean the Church of Scotland, will find it a mere *terra incognita*, a vast continent of hidden, undiscovered novelties; and will find himself surprised, to the last degree, that things so near us should be so entirely hid from us.

Not that there is anything monstrous or unheard of in the constitution or circumstances of this Church, much less in her profession and practice; but that she has been represented to the world in so many monstrous shapes, drest up in so many devil's coats and fool's coats, charged with so many heresies, errors, schisms, and antichristianisms by the mob of this slandering generation, that when a man comes to view her in her original Reformation, her subsequent settlement, her many revolutions, convulsions, and catastrophes, in her subjected, persecuted state, and now in her glorious restoration and establishment, nothing can be more wonderful in human affairs than to see

A

how mankind has been imposed upon about her, and with what front the absurdities charged on her could be broached in the world.

When we view the soundness and purity of her DOCTRINE, the strictness and severity of her DISCIPLINE, the decency and order of her WORSHIP, the gravity and majesty of her GOVERNMENT: when we see the modesty, humility, and yet steadiness, of her Assemblies—the learning, diligence, and painfulness of her ministers—the awful solemnity of her administration—the obedience, seriousness, and frequency of her people in hearing, and universally an air of sobriety and gravity on the whole nation—we must own her to be, at this time, the best regulated National Church in the world, without reflection upon any of the other nations where the Protestant religion is established and professed.

I am not comparing the constitutions of Churches, neither shall I enter into an invidious comparison here between the circumstances of this Church and the Church of England. Let them fight that quarrel out with the pen and ink by themselves.

But this, I believe, I may challenge the nations for, in the name of the Church of Scotland, that as to obeying their constitution, as to preserving the purity of doctrine and worship, as to enacting good laws, and maintaining a strict observance of them, no body of men in the world come up to them.

I know the Church of England have canons and injunctions, which, when people defend her, they argue from; and those canons and injunctions are far less liable to objection than those who only guess by her practice may imagine: for, when they come to examine how her ministers obey those canons, and how they are punished when they break them, *hic labor, hoc opus*, this is the most monstrous thing in the world, and confirms what was said by a divine of the Church of England, viz., that no nation or church, in these parts of the world, have so good laws so ill regarded as they.*

Nor shall I examine here whence a thing so justly scandalous to the Church of England proceeds ; it is not the work of this piece, in which the state of the Church of Scotland, not of the Church of England, is my theme : but when I have shewn therein the advantages which the Church of Scotland reaps by a strictness of discipline peculiar to herself, and that discipline exactly executed in every part ; and how by this she seems qualified to be the church in the world, the hardest to be invaded by errors and schisms, and perfectly invulnerable by heresies and corruptions ; we must be very blind in England, if we do not see, that the slackness and remissness in discipline is the only door at which all the notorious errors and heresies, now swarming in the English Church, have crept in ; such as Arianism, Socinianism, Arminianism, Scepticism, Atheism, Deism, and the new ridiculous corruptions, notions, and novelties of Dodwell, Coward, Asgill, and others, who call themselves of the Church of England, and are daily filling the world with absurdities in religion, not fit to be suffered in a Protestant Church or Government.

Did the Convocation of the Church of England do their duty, who often times sit long and do little ; did they, in time, check the growth of these things ; did they call in the aid of the civil authority, to curb the exorbitance of the press, and exercise their ecclesiastic authority in that of the pulpit ; in short, were they as exact in their discipline, as grave in their censures, and as strict in the pursuit of such things as the Church of Scotland, errors and heresies would creep, like other venomous creatures, upon the ground, grovel in the dust, and come out but in the dark ; such crimes would be acted as crimes, and the guilty

* See Dr Edwards' Testimony to the Discipline of the Church of Scotland, in his sermon on the Union.

would hide themselves, like Adam, among the bushes; and not bully religion, and affront God Almighty to his face; laugh at Church discipline, and banter civil justice, as now they do every day.

But in Scotland, I take upon me with boldness to assure the world, it is not so; no error broached lies brooding like hot embers laid among dry buildings, neglected till it sets all in a flame; no ignorant person can gain admitance to, no immoral person obtain connivance in, the pulpit; no error there escapes censure, no censure dies there for want of protection. If any breach be made, the Church judicatories never fail to keep it in the stated forms of proceeding, where it cannot sleep; the guilty person must be brought either to repentance or to punishment.

If there is any breach in this order, any stop in the free exercise of their authority, or any interruption to the full extent of the Church's power in censure, it proceeds either, 1st, from the exorbitant power of the gentry and nobility, who, often especially when their own guilt is the question, stand out to extremity against Church censures, and think themselves too great for the authority of the ecclesiastic judicatories; or, 2d, from the looseness of the Episcopal Dissenters, who, as they separate in worship, so they would be understood to be excused from discipline. Of both which I shall speak at large in their place, and only note it here, that even in both these cases, there are instances wherein the highest and most obstinate have thought fit to submit to the discipline of the Church, either convinced of its justice, or loath to have the just reproach of the opposition entailed upon their posterity. In which case Scotland is not without instances, where her noblemen have accepted a rebuke for the breaches of their morals in the open congregation. But of all this I shall be more particular in its place.

In these judicatories, the admirable order of proceeding is such that it seems impossible any man can be oppressed; for he is able to appeal so often, the cause shall be heard so often, and by such different judges, that he cannot fail of justice. On the other hand, the subordination of judicatories is such, and the proceedings so nicely accounted for by the Kirk-sessions to the Presbyteries, by the Presbyteries to the Provincial Synods, and by the Synods to the General Assemblies, that there can no mistake pass unobserved, no complaint pass unheard, no grievance unrectified.

I shall not insist on the particulars here; because I shall give it at large in the scheme I purpose to draw of the state of these Judicatories in this Church, to which I refer.

But what I am upon here is, that by this means you have the fewest breaches made upon this Church by the defection or degeneracy of either ministers or people, among themselves, of any Church in the world; and this, I believe, will very remarkably appear in the subsequent sheets.

To give a true and concise scheme of the state of this Church, it will be needful to go back to its original constitution, which I shall only abridge, and take no more of it than is needful to hand down a right understanding of its circumstances to the present time. And this is the design of these memoirs.

It began to reform from Popery in the year 1557, being sometime before the Reformation in England. Not but that the seeds of the Protestant religion were sown, and the Protestant doctrine spread very far in private even before that, as may appear by the several confessors for the truth, who were put to death under the administration of the Queen-Regent, by the assistance and particular fury of the Cardinal Beaton, of which presently.

But this will be farther evident by entering into an examination of matters in England. For after the death of James V., Henry VIII., King of England, sending ambassadors openly to treat of a marriage* for his son with the Queen of Scotland, the said treaty and marriage being proposed in Parliament, was so openly contradicted by the priests in general, with the Queen Dowager, a French woman, and Cardinal Beaton at the head of them, that the Cardinal was confined till the question was put in the Parliament.

And though when the Cardinal was thus removed the matter was soon concluded, yet the Cardinal making his escape out of prison, he and the Popish faction so ordered affairs that the articles could never be executed, nor the hostages agreed on obtained.

A cruel war followed on this, the King of England resenting all these indignities; which war, and the calamities it brought with it, together with the confusions in the Regency of the Earl of Arran, occasioned by the policy and cruelty of the Cardinal Beaton, gave the people a greater liberty than otherwise they would have had; so that the Protestant religion, then particularly called Lutheranism, got a great deal of ground; and not only were the common people inclined to it, but a great many of the nobility and gentry of Scotland favoured the Reformation: Nay, so far had it obtained, that some towns began to own it in bulk; and Buchanan records it, and from him I hand it down to posterity for the particular honour of the town of Dundee, that they were the only town in Scotland that was then addicted to the Protestant Religion :†   Or, which the sense will very well bear if the history of the time be examined, the town of Dundee was the first

* See Buch. lib. 14, fol. 63.
† Ibid, lib. 15, fol. 157.   Sed Cardinalis, parum tutum ratus duos homines nobiles, et factiosos, et bene comitatos in opidum recipere, unum instauratæ religioni addictissimum, egit cum prorege, ut Pertham rediret.

Protestant town in Scotland, and therefore the Cardinal would not venture to receive the Earl of Rothes and Patrick Gray, who, it seems, favoured the Reformation in that town, but fled to Perth.

This was the time when, at Perth, they burnt a woman and her infant, because she would not call on the Virgin Mary when she was in travail. And having vowed the destruction of the reformed, they came to Dundee, to search for such as read the New Testament. And then it was that they raised a report among the poor people, that the New Testament was written by Luther, and therefore to be rejected as an heretical book.* But it seems the honest people of Dundee, like true Bereans, enquired farther into the matter, and have retained their better knowledge to this day.

That the Popish clergy apprehended a general revolution in the affairs of religion, and saw a strong inclination to that change in the people, was apparent from their vigilance and subtilty in rejecting the offer of an intermarriage with England, first made by King Henry VIII., in the time of James V. of Scotland, and afterwards their running headlong into a war with England, rather than consent to match their Queen, then an infant, to Prince Edward, afterwards Edward VI., King of England : the true reason of which appeared to be, lest the English Reformation should be imposed upon them.

This obstinacy was so great, as that, had the English pursued their design with force, after the battle at Pinkie, they might have ruined Scotland very much, their Queen being a child, and the nobility much divided among themselves. And yet the Scots, though their army was overthrown, and their country over-run by the English, rejected the match,

* Tantaque erat cœcitas, ut sacerdotum plerique contenderent, Novum Testamentum nuper a Martino Luthero fuisse scriptum. Buch. fol. 157.

and privily conveyed their young Queen into France, and all this for fear of a reformation.

This was all from the subtilty of the Popish clergy, as is evident through the whole course of the histories of those times. The priests had in vain opposed the growing reformation with the unprevailing remedies of fire and faggot. The burning of Patrick Hamilton at St Andrews, a gentleman of noble extraction, was rather a help than a hindrance to the Reformation, of whom George Buchanan says, he died by the conspiracy of the priests.* And the story of the Dominican friar, whom he having convinced of the truth of his doctrine, afterwards betrayed him, and witnessed against him, is very remarkable; for, when Patrick Hamilton, at his death, appealed to his conscience that he believed, and was convinced of the truth of what he persecuted him for, the friar, struck with the conviction, ran distracted immediately, and died mad. This, says the same author, much terrified the minds of the people.†

Afterwards, in the year 1539, five more were burnt at St Andrews, many persecuted to banishment, and some recanted. Among the banished, George Buchanan‡ says himself was one, but that he made his escape out of prison.

How the priests managed King James V., a prince, as Buchanan says,§ naturally superstitious—

---

* Buchanan rerum Scotarum, lib. 14, fol. 146. Eo quoque anno, Patricius Hamiltonius e Johannis Ducis Albani sorore, ex fratre Comitis Araniæ, natus, Juvenis ingenio summo et eruditione singulari, conjuratione sacerdotum oppressus, ad Fanum Andreæ vivus est crematus.

† Ibid. Animos hominum conterruit Alexandri Cambelli mors See the story in Buchanan, fol. 146. Is erat e sodalitio dominicanorum, ———— to mortem obiit ————

‡ Ibid, fol. 150 Initio anni proximi qui fuit M. D. xxxix., Lutheranismi suspecti complures capti sunt. Sub finem Februarii; quinque Cremati: Novem recantarunt: Complures exilio damnati. In his fuit Georgius Buchananus, qui sopitis custodibus per cubiculi fenestram evaserat.

§ His velut machinis admotis cum regis animum superstitionibus obnoxium labefactassent, tum corruptis, qui plurimum poterant aulicis, magnam per eos regi pecuniæ vim polliciti, penitus cum a colloquio averterunt, Ibid. fol. 149.

how they corrupted his courtiers—how they flattered him on the giving to them the books sent him by the King of England—how they, by the mere force of money, prevailed upon him first to delay, and afterwards to break off, the interview appointed between him and the King of England—and how all this was for fear of the growing reformation in England, and the introducing it in Scotland, is so plain in history, that I need only refer the readers to the particulars which they will find in Calderwood, Spotswood, and Buchanan, the last of whom (viz., Buchanan) speaks it plainly, that the priests* had this in their view.

And yet in all this, Scotland had an unforeseen advantage, viz., that having been obliged, by these things, to defer the Reformation, I mean as a public action, they had leisure thereby to see the defects of the English Reformation, which happened in the meantime, and going a step farther, to leave out some things which the English retained, and which, by the error of the times, got such deep root there, as never to be altered to this day ; such as the supremacy, prescribed rites and ceremonies, and, which they esteemed also a defect, Episcopacy ; which things, as they began now to be objected against in England by several of the best and most eminent for piety in the First Reformation, so they obtained not at all in Scotland ; but John Knox, whom, for this, I think I may call the Father of the Church of Scotland, going over to Geneva, and there conferring with the most eminent Protestant divines concerning the model of church government, which should be most agreeable to Scripture institution, he brought over the figure of a church as to worship, discipline, and government, the same which we find now established.

---

* Demum Sacerdotes, qui pro aris ac focis sibi certandum videbant. Jacobum Betonium Fani Andreæ Achiepiscopum et Georgium Crichtonium Caledoniæ Episcopum, senes invalidos, ad aulam pertraxerant, fremere religionem, hoc congressu prodi, &c. Buch. lib. 14, fol. 149

It would be too long a work for these Memoirs to set down here the beginning, progress, manner, and issue of the First Reformation.   It may be sufficient to note here the heads of it, and withal, the different manner of it from that in England, which produced that effect mentioned above, viz., a differing form of settlement.

In England the reformation, as to the settlement of it, began in the Crown, the several kings put the first hand to it : As, 1st, King Henry VIII., by dethroning the Pope's supremacy, demolishing the religious houses, forbidding appeals to Rome, and the like.   2d, King Edward VI., by a general overthrow of all the Popish hierarchy, casting their images out of the churches, their mass, and all their Romish innovations out of their worship, dethroning their whole authority, and rooting out the remains of their ceremonies from the nation.

But this had two effects.

1. That when King Henry VIII. abolished the Pope's supremacy, his principle at that time being rather politic than religious, he set his own authority up in the stead of it, calling himself supreme head of the Church in all things, whether ecclesiastical or civil ; a thing since made very ill use of, and improved to a tyranny, which neither in the divine or human original of it could find any legal foundation.

2. That when King Edward rejected the Pontificate of Rome, he yet erected a Protestant Pontificate in its stead, which, being soon opposed by some of the most eminent for piety and wisdom in the Reformation, quickly begot a division in the Church, which has since been carried on to that height, and increased to the magnitude which we see this day.

3. King Edward, and the first Reformers, when they came to the matters of worship, did not wholly destroy the model, but reformed it only ; and though I am willing to believe they, to the extent of their

light, honestly designed to leave out all that was superstitious and idolatrous in the former, and did really believe it was so; yet they thought themselves obliged to retain a similitude of form.

Nor do we since so much object against the form, less against a form in general; but against prescribing that form as a term of communion.

These are the three heads which have since caused so much dispute in England, made unhappy breaches in the common charity, and risen up to such divisions as we see at this day.

But, to return to the Scots, their Reformation began quite in another manner. The knowledge of the Scriptures began the first step to it, and the English Bible got in among the people very quickly: Some, eminent for learning, even among the Popish zealots, began to be enlightened by the reading the Word of God: and as knowledge is naturally diffusive, so this kind, having an invisible instructor to second it, I mean the Holy Spirit of God, spread secretly, but swiftly, through the nation.

Among those whom it pleased God to make use of as the first instruments in this glorious work, was George Wishart, and several others, who became eminent. They were bold and steady preachers of the Reformation, and the people of all sorts became so addicted to the Protestant religion, by their instruction, that after the Regent, by the instigation of Cardinal Beaton, had consented to the martyrdom of that great and good man Mr Wishart, Buchanan* tells us the whole nation began to disrelish his government.

---

* Buch. lib. 15, fol. 163. Ob hanc imperitiam Regni gerendi, totiusque vitæ segnitiem, cum animos etiam vulgi prorex offendisset, tum ob alia indies fiebat vilior: Præcipue post sublatum Georgium Sophocardium, maxima parte hominum secutas calamitates in religione vertente: Sed iis maxime, qui non modo puritatem doctrinæ et vitæ totius moderationem in Georgio suspiciebant: Sed qui multis et ejus veracissimis predictionibus persuasi vim futuri perspiciendi divinitus ei inditam credebant.

It would be endless to recite the names, lives, and death of the many preachers who, at first, with the extremest hazard, and with a constancy, even to martyrdom, spread the reformed doctrines through Scotland. It suffices to note, that in a few years it had such success, that in general the whole kingdom seemed to be touched with the sense of the true religion, and not the common people only, but the nobility and gentry embraced it with great zeal, eagerness, and resolution ; and in this case the affairs of the Church of Scotland stood, when the Regent was persuaded by the French court to demit, and to resign his government into the hands of the Queen Mother.

This lady being wholly French, and acted by their counsels, set herself, with more heat than discretion, to suppress the reformed religion, and, as she flattered herself, to extirpate the beginnings of it out of Scotland : but she found herself mistaken, it was now too late ; the thing had taken too deep root in the hearts of the people for her to master it.

However, for two years, matters of religion slept, the Queen being married to the Dauphin of France, the Regent taken up by a war with England ; and the clergy, though cruel and bloody enough, yet being baulked by the murder of Cardinal Beaton (who was slain in his bed-chamber, as George Wishart had predicted, and cast out of a window by Norman Lesley, son to the Earl of Rothes, and his followers), they wanted a head to prosecute the reformers to blood, and a power to protect them in it.

All this while the reformed held their private assemblies, where they had their worship in their own language, and had frequent conferences upon religious matters ; for as yet they had no public preaching. However, by this means the work of reformation still spread itself, and took deep root in the nation.

The first popular discovery this made in the minds

of the commonality was in the city of Edinburgh, when the shrine of St Giles, the patron of that city, was robbed of its relics, which they had in so much veneration.

The 1st of September, it seems, was the festival of this tutelar saint, when his image was to be carried in procession about the city, and the Queen Regent resolved to be present at the solemnity. But when they came to look for the saint, he was pleased to suffer himself to be stolen away, to the great confusion of the clergy, who had pleased themselves with the expectation of the procession, and the honour done them by the Regent to grace the show.

However, to make up the matter as well as they could, they made another image to set in the pageant, and began their procession in the usual form. After the show had passed the principal parts of the city, and the Queen Regent was retired, the mob rose upon the priests, and put an end to their pageantry : for they pulled St Giles out of his throne, which was erected on the shoulders of the priests, threw his saintship into the dirt, and, in short, the sacred image suffered immediate martyrdom. But the priests had no mind to die with their deity ; for they fled every man as he could. And yet this they need not have done, for the rabble offered no body any injury but the wooden idol, which they broke all to pieces, and so departed.

This, however, might give the Regent a taste of what posture the affairs of religion were in, if she had pleased to have taken notice of it. However, she countenanced the priests to go on with all the persecuting methods they could, though everywhere they met with insults, slights, and contempt from the people. As particularly when citing Paul Meffan of Dundee before them, and he not appearing, was intercommuned ; that is, every one was forbid to harbour or relieve him, or converse with him, on severe penalties; which yet the brave citizens of Dundee openly disregarded, and protected him, entertained him in their houses, and sued to the Regent to remit his banishment.

But things were now coming to a greater height; for the asserters of the reformed religion resolved not to bear any longer the oppressions and invasions of the clergy, but to demand their liberty in a different manner from what had formerly been done.

They had calculated their right first, and then their strength. They found that, if they were proceeded against by law, they could not be hurt, for they had offended no law; and if their enemies had recourse to arms, they were more numerous than they, and would defend themselves. Upon these resolutions, several were sent abroad by their brethren to concert measures, and to form themselves into something of a body.

These were eminent persons, as Buchanan observes,* which may serve to answer those who allege that the Reformation in Scotland was the effect only of the fury of the rabble. They went severally to the remotest parts of the kingdom,† moving the gentlemen and towns to adhere to the mutual defence of religion, and to stand by one another.

These carried with them tables,‡ as Buchanan calls them, for those that were willing to join with them, to subscribe their names. I take this to be something in the nature of an Association,§ for their mutual defence, in case they should meet with any more

---

* Buchan. lib 16. fol. 167. Inter hæc quidam viri nobiles e Fifa maxime et Anguaia, ac aliquot opidorum cives illustriores.
† In omnes Scotæ prefecturas dispersi hortabantura universos ut sinceram divine legis prædicationem amarent, Ibid. fol. 167.
‡ Quibus hæc placerent Tabulas ea de te confectas quibus subscriberent offerunt. Ib. folio ut supra.
§ John Knox, in his History of the Reformation, calls it, in his marginal note, the First Covenant of Scotland, and gives the copy of it, lib. 1. p. 110; but I conceive it was not properly so called: for that the Covenant was not formed till some time after, and this was therefore only called a common Bond.

violences, as they were sure to do. And to this was added the Assurance, as it was called, which some called the First Covenant, and is as follows :—

THE FIRST COVENANT OF SCOTLAND, 1557.

"We perceiving how sathan in his members, the antichrists of our time, cruelly does rage, seeking to overthrow and destroy the Gospel of Christ, and his congregation, ought, according to our bounden duty, to strive in our Master's cause, even unto the death, being certain of the victory in him : The which our duty being well considered, we do promise, before the Majesty of God, and his congregation, that we (by his Grace) shall with all diligence continually apply our whole power, substance, and our very lives, to maintain, set forward, and establish the most blessed Word of God and his congregation : And shall labour according to our power to have faithful ministers, truly and purely to minister Christ's Gospel and Sacraments to his people. We shall maintain them, nourish them, and defend them, the whole congregation of Christ, and every member thereof according to our whole powers, and waging of our lives, against sathan and all wicked power that doth intend tyranny or trouble against the foresaid congregation. Unto the which holy Word and congregation, we do join us ; and so do forsake and renounce the congregation of sathan, with all the superstitious abomination and idolatory thereof. And moreover, shall declare ourselves manifestly enemies thereto, by this our faithful promise before God, testified to this congregation, by our subscription of these presents. At Edinburgh the third of December, anno 1557. God called to witness. Sic subscribitur

A, Earle of ARGYLE.
      GLENCARNE.
      MORTOUN.

ARCHIBALD, Ld. of LORNE.
JOHN ERSKINE of Dun,
Et cetera.

Soon after this they sent their proposals to the Queen Regent by Sir James Sandilands of Calder, which contained in short these particulars.

1. " That the worship of God, prayers and sacraments, might be had in the vulgar tongue.

2. " That scandalous ministers might be removed.

3. " That the people might have the choice of their own ministers."

This was called the oration and petition of the Protestants of Scotland to the Queen Regent, and is at length printed in the said history of the Reformation, *lib.* 2. *p.* 127, 128, 129; but is too long to recite here.

The Parliament soon after this sat down, which was in December, Anno 1558, and the Reformers presented a letter to them also, including their requests, and annexed to it a solemn protestation, which they demanded to be registered at the same time that they delivered it.

The Regent's answer to this protestation was mild, and such as deceived the Reformers for a while. Her answer was thus—" Me will remember what is protest. Me sal put good order in all thing that now controverse."*

The Regent all this while dealt cautiously and subtilly; for she guessed wisely that the people who durst make these demands, must have some prospect of power to support them; and she dreaded the tumults of the rabble. She therefore consented, in show, to some things, as particularly, to let them have their worship in the vulgar tongue, on condition it should be without tumult, and that they should not preach publicly in Leith or Edinburgh.

For some time, it seems, the Reformed contented themselves with this, and kept the injunctions of the

---

* The Regent was a French woman, and spoke broken English.

Regent exactly ; but the priests were furious to the last degree at these things, and made all possible opposition, till at last they drove things to the extremities which followed, and paved the way for their own overthrow.

They held their meetings to consult for the suppressing the reformed, and had all the assistance underhand that the Queen Regent could give them ; but she still carried it fair to the Reformers, and answered them mildly, leading them on in hopes.

At last she threw off the mask, and openly professed her resolution to destroy them ; that she would not suffer the majesty of the Government to be debased, but would restore it to its ancient veneration by some remarkable thing.

I am content to acknowledge I follow Buchanan in these notes upon the affairs of those days ; because, though other historians are more particular than he, yet the enemies of the Reformation are not without objections against the reputation of their writings, whereas Buchanan's reputation, as an historian, is unquestioned, even by his greatest enemies. I find them also all agree in substance with him. He is also concise, and more pertinent than some of them ; and all sides acknowledge him to be authentic and faithful. But this by the way.

The Queen, as I have noted, dealt for a while mildly with the Reformers, but it lasted not long, for they were obliged to come to a point with her ; and, therefore, not to be wanting to themselves, as well as at the same time to behave decently to the Regent, they sent the Earl of Glencairn, Hugh Campbell, Sheriff of Ayr, and others, to entreat her favourable answer to their desires.

The Queen Regent, now casting off the mask, gave her passion a full vent, and told them, in so many words, that they had nothing to expect from her. They calmly reminded her of her promises to them, but in vain. She told them in effect *princes were not*

B

bound by the promises which they were obliged to make in the exigence of their affairs.   The Protestants finding such usage as this, and knowing as well what they were to expect, as their own strength to resist it, boldly defied her, and told her to her face, that they then renounced all obedience to her, and advised her to consider the consequences of it.

Now the fire was kindled, and the flame began to burn out, and though the Queen Regent was rather enraged by their boldness than made thoughtful, yet she soon found the differences of things; she found her authority to decrease, and her commands every where slighted.   For example, she commanded the Provost of St Johnston, now called Perth, to suppress the innovation of religion there; he answered, that he had no dominion over their consciences.   She commanded the Sheriff of Dundee to send Paul Meffen, their Protestant minister, bound to her, instead of which the Sheriff sent to Mr Meffen, to tell him that he might secure himself.   She wrote to the neighbour assemblies to observe Easter as usual, after the Roman way, but not one of them obeyed her.

Upon this she cited all the ministers of Scotland to appear at Stirling on the 10th of May 1559; but they came there with such attendants, and so numerous, though unarmed, that it frightened the Regent out of her design, and made her entreat John Erskine of Dun, a lover of the religion, and that could influence them by himself, that he would disperse the people, giving her promise at the same time to act nothing against the Reformers.   But see the faith kept at that time with Protestants.   As soon as on those promises the honest men were returned home, she held the meeting intended, called over the names, and outlawed those that were absent for contempt.

The nobility and gentry assembled with the ministers, finding in what manner they were to be used, that the Queen was wholly bent for their destruction, and neither to be bound by promises, or any other obligation, and that their ruin was absolutely determined, prepared for force, resolving to defend themselves.

And now began the fury of the people to break out a little beyond the bounds which the better sort designed ; for the mob at Perth, says Buchanan, on Mr John Knox's preaching a sermon to them against idolatry, took fire at the hint, and immediately fell to breaking down the images in all the churches and monasteries at Perth. Other historians say, this was upon the laird of Dun's giving them an account of the falsehood and injustice of the Queen to the ministers at the meeting at Stirling, and give a very particular account, introduced thus : " The laird of Dun coming to St Johnston, exposed the case even as it was, and did conceal nothing of the Queen's craft and falsehood, which being understood, the multitude was so inflamed, that neither could the exhortation of the preachers, nor the commandment of the magistrates, stay them from destroying the places of idolatry."* Be it which way it will, whether by Mr Knox's sermon, who, it is true, did preach at that time against idolatry ; or by the Laird of Dun's giving them an account of the Queen Regent's behaviour, this is certain, that here the demolishing of images, &c., began ; the Franciscans, Dominicans, and Carthusians were immediately pulled out of their houses, and all they had was plundered and wrecked. The nobility and armed men, with an unusual moderation, avoided all appearance of enriching themselves by this work, and let the priests go away loaden with gold and silver. But as for the buildings, they not only demolished them, but caused their soldiers to carry away the very stones and rubbish ; so that in some places they hardly left any remembrance of them to posterity.

And now the war was begun in earnest ; for the

---

* Vide Knox's History of the Reformation, lib. 2, fol. 136.

breaking down of images and pulling down monasteries began to spread over the whole country. The town of Coupar followed that of Perth, and the friars and ecclesiastics began everywhere to shift for themselves, all the rest being apprehensive, and not without good cause, of the same fate.

The Regent, exasperated to the highest degree, solemnly swore she would be revenged on the city of Perth, that she would have the blood of the citizens, and burn their city down to the ground. But she reckoned without her host; for the people let her see how little they feared her; for the very same week several other towns did the like. In order, therefore, to put a stop to this sort of work, she raised an army, and marched directly against the Protestant nobility, who, by the way, had, ever since the Association I mentioned before, been called the Lords of the Congregation; and the Protestants in general, as then united, were called the Congregation.

The Lords of the Congregation, for so I shall now call them, far from being discouraged at the Regent's preparations, sent messengers to all their brethren to come and stand by what they had begun, and not to desert so good a cause in its last extremity. And this had such an effect, that they had soon a very good army, and it is recorded, to the honour of the Earl of Glencairn, that he brought with him 2100 men, well armed, to their assistance.

The Queen Regent had rather more forces than the Congregation, including her French auxiliaries, but yet she was loath to venture a battle; but sends two gentlemen who were in her army, and who were favourers of the Reformed, to treat with them; these were the Lord James Stuart and Gillespie Campbell, and they, to shew their willingness to hearken to reason, readily appointed two of their number—viz., Alexander Cunningham and John Erskine of Dun, to treat with her.

These made, says Buchanan, a temporary agreement; for, indeed, it was no more. It amounted to a disbanding the troops on either side; the Queen was to be admitted into Perth, on her promise not to injure any of the townsmen; her French troops were not to come within three miles of the town; and all religious differences were to be left to the next Parliament.

Thus the war, which was just breaking out, was seemingly stopt for a while. But the Queen Regent kept not one of her articles; for she brought her Frenchmen into the city, she exercised all sorts of violence on the citizens, and fell on them by fines at pleasure, change of their magistrates, banishment of some, and murder of others, and, at her departure, left a garrison of mercenaries in the town,

This treatment of the citizens of Perth finished the ruin of all the Regent's affairs, and this was the last day of her prosperity; for now her friends began to forsake her; the Lord James Stuart and Gillespie Campbell, after Earl of Argyle, deserted her; for that, having employed them to bring the Lords of the Congregation to an agreement, she had dishonoured them so much in breaking her word.

The same Lord James Stuart, with the Earl of Argyle, joined themselves soon after to the Congregation. The Regent, thinking to revenge herself on Coupar and St Andrews, as she had done on Perth, they raised the country again, and sent about to all the Reformed for help; nor did they fail of assistance, for the country came in to them in great numbers, and so a second army was raised for the Congregation, and, as Buchanan observes, they were so enraged at the perfidious dealing of the Regent, that they resolved to trust her no more, but to overcome or die.

It should be noted here, that at the breaking up of the meeting of the Lords of the Congregation at

Perth, when that city was yielded to the Queen Regent, there was another writing subscribed, which Mr Knox calls the Second Covenant, and was for mutual assistance.   And to this the Earl of Argyle and Lord James Stuart signed, having before promised, if the Queen broke her word to the citizens of St Johnston, they would join with all their power with the Congregation, as now they did, together with the Lord Ruthven, the Earl of Menteith, and Lord Tullibardine. The Queen sent after them, requiring them to return, on pain of displeasure ; but they boldly rejected her, sending her word plainly, that, with safe conscience, they could not be partakers with her in so manifest tyranny as was by her practised, Knox, lib. 2, p. 152. The Second Covenant was as follows :—

THE SECOND COVENANT AT PERTH, 1559.

" At Perth, the last of May, the year of God 1559 years, the congregations of the West Country, with the congregations of Fife, Perth, Dundee, Angus, Mearns, and Montrose, being convened in the town of Perth, in the name of Jesus Christ, for setting forth of his glory, understanding nothing more necessary for the same than to keep a constant amity, unity, and fellowship together, according as they are commanded by God, are confederate, and become bounden and obliged in the presence of God, to concur and assist together in doing all things required of God in his Scripture, that may be to his glory ; and with their whole powers to destroy and put away all things that doth dishonour to his name, so that God may be truly and purely worshipped.   And in case that any trouble be intended against the said congregation, or any part or member thereof, the whole congregation shall concur, assist, and convene together, to the defence of the same congregation or person troubled ; and shall not spare labours, goods, substance, bodies,

and lives, in maintaining the liberty of the whole
congregation, and every member thereof, against
whatsoever person shall intend the said trouble for
cause of religion, or any other cause depending thereupon, or lay to their charge, under pretence thereof,
although it happen to be coloured with any other
outward cause. In witnessing and testimony of the
which, the whole congregation aforesaid have ordained
and appointed the noblemen and persons underwritten
to subscribe these presents. Sic subscribitur.

ARCHIBALD, ARGYLE,   JAMES STUART,
R., Lord BOYD,   MATHEW CAMPBELL of Tarma-
Lord OCHILTREE,   ganart.
GLENCAIRN,

The Queen was now in Fife, marching to Coupar,
and from thence intending to St Andrews, where the
Lords, having designed to go on with the Reformation,
had brought Mr John Knox to preach against idolatry;
but the Bishop, terrified with the thoughts of reformation in his Cathedral Church, hasted thither with
100 spearmen, and came into town the evening before.
The two Lords and their friends had no soldiers, only
their mere household servants, and the Queen with
her army was but twelve miles off, viz., at Falkland,
nor was the town yet confirmed in the reformed religion ; and, to complete all, the Archbishop, who had
before caused John Knox to be burnt in effigy, sent
them word by Mr Robert Coldwell, laird of Clesse,
that, if Knox dared to present himself to the preaching
place in his town and church, he would cause him to
be saluted with a dozen of culverins, the most part of
which should light upon his nose. The Lords deli-
berated on the matter, and most were for not exposing
Mr Knox ; but when they came to consult him he
valued no threats, but boldly resolved to preach, and
did preach, and preached against idolatry from that
text in Matthew of the ejection of the buyers and sellers

from the temple.* In this sermon he showed the duty of magistrates and people to pull down idolatry; and this he did with such vehemence, and it had such an effect upon the people, that not only the common people, but the provost, bailies, and magistrates resolved to remove all the monuments of idolatry in that place, and performed it accordingly; the bishop taking sanctuary with the Queen, who lay with her army then at Falkland, as before. The Queen, though she had no great kindness for the bishop, yet heard him upon this occasion with great concern and attention, and resolved immediately to advance with her army to St Andrews, to punish the offenders with the utmost severity, and accordingly ordered her army to march.

As the Queen was drawing towards them with her forces, so they, as before, had sent about to all the rest of the Congregation, desiring them with all possible speed to come to their assistance; which they did with such speed, that, by the next day, they increased from about 300 men, horse and foot, to above 3000, well mounted and accoutred, and among them were some of the most eminent of the nobility, such as the Earl of Rothes, the Lord Ruthven, the Earl of Argyle, the Lord James Stuart, Earl of Glencairn, and others.

The Queen's army marched all night to surprise them, but found they had intelligence of her march, were drawn up ready to offer her battle, and resolved to give her a warm reception. The Earl of Ruthven led the gentlemen of Fife, Angus and Mearns, who made a thousand spears on horseback. The towns of Dundee and St Andrews made a good brigade of foot, and were drawn up by themselves.

When the Queen's men saw the order the Lords appeared in, and that they were so posted as that

---

* Knox's History of the Reformation, lib. 2. fol. 153.

they could not be attacked but with great hazard, she had recourse to her old subtilty of treating with them ; but they were not to be taken twice in one snare.   They refused to treat with her, and prepared to fight.   She sent messengers again, who pressed them to treat, to prevent the effusion of blood ; but they still declined it, and stood ready to engage, bidding her fall on with her French cut-throats when she pleased, alledging there was no safety in treating with her.   However, at length they consentéd to come to a treaty on this preliminary first settled, that an assurance should be signed by the Duke of Hamilton that all the French should be sent away over the Firth.

This was done, and is called in Knox's Histoy the Assurance,* and is signed by the Duke of Chattelerault (Hamilton) and Dosell, a French lord.   This Assurance was, that, in eight days, messengers should be sent by the Queen to treat of a full peace ; but the Queen, who never regarded her engagements in such cases, never sent any body to treat as she had promised, nor, it seems, did she intend it, but thought that, upon this treaty, she should have an opportunity to convey her French troops safe out of Fife, and perhaps bring the Lords, in confidence of her treaty, to disperse their men.   The first of these she gained, but not the last.

The Lords waited some time, but, finding nobody come, they, as reason good, concluded the treaty broken ; and, from this time forward, they depended no more upon the faith of treaties, but upon their arms.   Many of the principal nobility came in to them every day, and, instead of dispersing, they grew very strong ; and first they marched to St Johnston, to deliver it from the oppression of the garrison which the Queen Regent had placed there.   The town was

---

* Knox's History, p 155.

surrendered after some difficulty, and the Bishop's house at Scone rifled and burned, his servants unadvisedly provoking the multitude, whom the Lords had prevailed with to let it alone.

From hence, fearing the Queen should intercept their advancing, which she was about to do, by marching herself to Stirling, and putting a garrison into the Castle, they resolved to prevent her; and, marching all night, they took possession of Stirling, and stopping there but three days, in which the churches were stript of their Popish ornaments, and the Abbey of Cambuskenneth demolished, they marched on the fourth day for Edinburgh.

The Queen might, by this time, have perceived, if her eyes had been opened, that the whole nation was bent upon the Reformation, and that there was no resisting it; but God had hardened her heart, and she would not understand what was visible to all the world; for the people of Edinburgh, hearing the Lords of the Congregation were marching to them, did all the work to their hands, and left no remnant of Popery in any of the churches, even before the Lords got thither.

It was now the year 1559, when the Lords marched to Edinburgh. In their passage, they took Linlithgow, and were joined by Duke Hamilton, who now came over to them; and, wherever they came, the images, altars, pictures, and other ensigns of Popery, went to wreck.

I think it is a piece of justice to God's Providence, which no one ought to pass over, that, in this beginning of the Reformation, the awe of the work was on the hearts of the Popish party; for, had they made the least regular opposition, the Congregation might at first have been easily suppressed.

Bishop Spotiswood,* in his History, tells us, the

---

* Spotiswood's History, lib. 3, fol. 126.

Lords had but 300 men in all their company when they marched from Stirling to Edinburgh, and the Queen had nearly 3000 French soldiers, besides the Popish party and their adherents, who clave to her; and yet, at the first news of their approach, she fled to Dunbar with all her forces, and durst not look them in the face.

The Congregation being now masters of the capital city, and the Queen and her foreign troops fled, they began to act in behalf of their country's liberty, as well as in religious matters. This, even by the accounts which all the historians of that time give of it, will clear the first Reformers from the slander that is so diligently cast upon them of making a *tumultuary* Reformation, or that it was only a rabble of the meaner sort, who were for plunder, and who, to enrich themselves with the spoils of the churches, ran into the Reformation merely to justify their robberies and indemnify the depredations they had made upon the Church; for now they had not only Duke Hamilton at their head, but a very great number of the nobility and gentry were professed managers of the Reformation, and the common people having, except in their excesses about demolishing idolatry, had little hand in it but as directed by their superiors.

Another thing worth noting here is, that having now gotten possession of Edinburgh, October 17. 1559, they appointed the reformed ministers to preach publicly in Edinburgh, which had not been openly done before in any place, save just where their army was assembled; but they saw an eminent hand was with them, and, as the Scripture says of Jacob when he journeyed from Succoth, the fear of them fell on all the cities round about.

Things standing in this posture (after consultation in council), says Calderwood,* though he does not note

---

* Calderwood's History. fol. 12.

that there was yet any stated council of the nation established on their side, they sent several messages to the Queen about the settling matters now in so much disorder. The Queen had published a proclamation, wherein she professed to be willing to refer matters of religion to a free Parliament, to meet in January next following, and gave liberty of preaching, &c., till then; but reproaches the Lords of the Congregation with rejecting all reasonable offers,* shewing, that it is not religion they seek, but the subversion of authority, and the usurpation of the crown. The Lords confronted this with letters to the Queen, and by open proclamation to the people.† In both they called God to witness, that their only intention is, to banish idolatry, advance the true religion, and defend the preachers thereof, promising to continue in all duty towards their sovereign and her mother the Regent, provided they might have these things secured to them, and offered, in the meantime, to give assurance of their loyalty.

Several messages and returns passed between them, and a meeting was appointed of one hundred of a side, to see, if possible, to accommodate matters. The chief on the Reformers' side were the Earls of Argyle and Glencairn, Lord Ruthven, Lord Boyd, Lord James Hamilton, Lord Ochiltree, &c.

These could come to no conclusion, and parted; and the Queen, on her part, prepared to attack the Congregation. They kept together in Edinburgh, and prepared to defend it. The Duke of Chattelerault and the Earl of Morton laboured to compose things, and at last a truce was agreed on, July 24. 1559.

---

* Spotiswood, lib. 3, fol. 126. Buchanan takes no notice of this part, and I do not take so much care to trace J. Knox; because it is questioned whether that History be genuine or spurious, and Spotiswood says positively the latter.
† Spotiswood, lib. 3, fol. 126, 127. The particulars of these letters, proclamations, and declarations are set down.

By this truce the Protestants, on the one hand, were to be free in the exercise of the reformed religion, and the Papists were likewise to be unmolested; their religious houses not insulted, nor their tithes obstructed; the Congregation was to quit Edinburgh, but no injury was to be done the citizens, nor any garrison put upon them; and all things were to be referred to a Parliament, to meet on the 10th January next.

Though the Queen Regent kept this truce better than any before, yet it was not long; for a thousand French foot arriving to her assistance, she began her usual deviations, first with fortifying Leith for a Port, by which she might secure her supplies, and secondly, sending for more troops from France, by both which she visibly prepared for war.

This occasioned that famous meeting at Hamilton, where the Lords of the Congregation agreed to write a common letter to the Queen Regent, which was dated September 29. 1559, and subscribed by the Duke of Chattelerault, the Earls of Arran, Argyle, Glencairn, and Menteith, and abundance of Lords and gentlemen.*

The Congregation were so alarmed at the fortifying of Leith, and the French troops the Queen had fixed there (for she had now 2000 foot more arrived, with money, arms, and ammunition), that they gave notice by letters into all parts of the kingdom; and long messages, proclamations, charges, and recriminations, past between the Queen Regent and them, in which they insisted upon the dismissing the foreign troops, and demolishing Leith; but all to no purpose.†

Upon this the Lords armed again, and advanced

---

* Spotiswood, lib. 3, fol. 131.
† Ibid. 132, 133.   See there the Queen's Proclamation, the Lord's Declaration, the Lord's Letter to the Queen at Leith, the Queen's Message by Lyon, King at Arms, to the Lords, &c.

to Edinburgh, the Queen retreats to her new fortifications at Leith, and, with her French forces
and friends to the number of 6000, shutting herself up there, sends messages to the Duke and the
Lords, by the herald at arms, charging them with
rebellion, &c.

The Lords convened a great assembly, little less
than a general Convention, wherein the Lord Ruthven
was president; and having there considered how they
had made all the peaceable applications to the Queen
Regent for their liberties, both civil and religious,
for the dismissing strangers, and demolishing the
fortifications raised there, and having not been able
to obtain redress by reason of the obstinacy of the
Regent, they began to deliberate how, reserving their
loyalty and obedience to their Sovereign, and her lawful authority, they might yet depose the exorbitant
power of the Queen Regent, or at least restrain
it, as being exercised in breach of the laws, and
injurious to the authority and royal dignity of their
Sovereign.

It was a bold offer at that time of day, and startled
the assembly at first; some were for it, some against
it, and they resolved to ask the opinion of the ministers about it. I have not room here to insert the
messages, declarations, proclamations, &c., they are
to be found at large, as noted below; for Buchanan
meddles not with them. But the ministers' opinion I
cannot omit. *

The ministers who were called were two, Mr
John Willock and Mr John Knox, whose opinions are
faithfully enough related by Mr Spotiswood, and agree
with the accounts in Knox's History, and are as follows.

Mr Willock first gave his opinion: "That albeit
magistracy be God's ordinance, and that they who

---

* Spotiswood, lib. 3, fol. 136, 137. Knox's History, lib. 2, fol. 202.

bear rule, have their authority from him, yet their power is not so largely extended but that the same is bounded and limited by God in his Word : and albeit God had appointed magistrates his lieutenants on earth, honouring them with his own title, calling them God's; yet never did he so establish any, but for just causes they might be deprived : for even as subjects, said he, are commanded to obey their magistrates, so magistrates have directions given them for their behaviour towards those they rule ; and God, in his Word, hath defined the duty both of one and the other. In deposing princes, and those that have born authority, God did not always use his immediate power, but sometimes he used other means, such as in his wisdom he thought good ; as by Asa, he removed Maacha, his own mother; by Jehu, he destroyed Joram ; and by divers others he deposed from the government those whom he had established before by his own Word. From which he inferred, that since the Queen Regent had denied her chief duty to the subjects of the realm, which was to minister justice indifferently, to preserve them from the invasion of strangers, and to suffer the Word of God to be freely preached ; seeing also she was a maintainer of superstition, and despised the counsel of the nobility, he did think they might justly deprive her from all regiment and authority over them."

Mr Knox coming to speak after, approved all that his brother had said, adding this more, " That the iniquity of the Queen Regent ought not to withdraw their hearts from the obedience due to their sovereign ; nor did he wish any such sentence to be pronounced against her, but that when she should change her course, and submit herself to good council, there should be place left to her of regress to the same honours from which, for just causes she ought now to be deprived."

Mr Spotiswood is very angry with the ministers for

two things here,* in which, though he is a good historian, he shows himself of a party against them in
behalf of the doctrine of passive obedience, a thing not
much talked of in those days.

First, he says, the ministers should have refused to
have meddled in this matter, or to have given their
opinion.

Secondly, he says, the examples they brought were
not to the case : and then he subjoins his own opinion,
in which he takes upon him to condemn the practice
of nations in deposing tyrants,† and rescuing themselves by force from bondage and slavery, when all
other means have been found to no purpose, which
was exactly the case here. But we all know when
this good old man wrote ; I mean, in an age when
these nations lulled asleep by the wheedling arts of
tyranny, under the gay-painted visor of loyalty and
subjection, became agents to their own bondage ; but
they have grown wiser since, which, if Mr Spotiswood
had lived to see, I dare say he had so much good sense
and good meaning in him, he must have altered his
opinions.

As to his first objection, which strikes at the discretion of the ministers only, and charges their pru-
dentials, it may be briefly answered, that their case
differed. This was a case begun in, and carried on
for, the matters of religion. The nobility and the
ministers had all along gone hand in hand, aiding,
assisting, and advising one another, and it would have

* Spotiswood, lib. 3 fol. 137. It had been a better and a wiser part in
these preachers to have excused themselves from giving any opinion
in these matters ; for they might be sure to have it cast in their teeth,
to the scandal of their profession.
† Spotiswood, Hist. fol. 187. lib. 3. Neither was the opinion they gave
sound in itself, nor had it any warrant in the Word of God; for howbeit, the power of the magistrates be limited, and their office prescribed by God, and that they may likewise fall into great offences :
yet it is no where permitted to subjects to call their princes in question, or to make insurrections against them, God having reserved the
punishment of princes to himself. [It were to be wished the author
had proved this last affirmation.]

been very unkind if the ministers, in a case of conscience too, should have declined their opinion to those gentlemen who, at that time, by their instigation, very much, at least with their full concurrence, had ventured their lives, families, and estates in the public affair of religious liberty; it had been abandoning their friends, and, which was worse, their cause too.

Nor was this all, but the case required it; for if it was against their opinions that authority might be resisted in cases of invasion of right, what did they there? And if it was their opinion, silence had only signified that it was their judgment, but that they feared the chief priests (John xii. 42), that is, were cowards, and durst not own their principles.

Again, it was a general convention of the Estates of Scotland, that on such an emergency demanded their opinion; and this was to them the lawful authority at that time, and they ought not to have disobeyed them in any lawful thing, if they esteemed them a lawful authority.

His doctrine about deposing rulers is on so many occasions answered, both in print, as also in the practice of nations, that I shall not take up any of these sheets in it; but this I thought necessary to say in defence of the ministers of the First Reformation, I hope none of the clergy of the Church of England will blame them, seeing they owe now the settlement and deliverance of their own Church from Popish invasions to the same deposing doctrine at the Revolution.

But to return to the story: The Assembly, or Estates of the kingdom, call them which we will, for some historians call them one, some another, after the ministers had given their opinion, unanimously voted the Regent out of her office, renounced their obedience to her, and bid her and her Frenchmen depart.

They exhibited to her a long charge, wherein they

c

did not spare her; but setting out her false and treacherous dealings with them, they concluded thus: Wherefore we, in the name of our King and Queen, suspend and inhibit that public administration which you usurp under their names.

I have been the longer upon this part of the story, and shall atone for it in my brevity in other cases; because, as the reason of these memoirs is to set the matter of the past and present state of the Church of Scotland in a true light, cleared from those mists and darkness which the partial glosses of some late patrons of tyranny have spread over her history; so these being some of the most capital parts of her progression to the present happy settlement which we see her now in, it is essential to my work to leave this part as clear and explicit as I can.

And it may be particularly pleasant to the friends of her establishment, to observe how wonderfully Divine Providence has wrought for her, not barely in rescuing her by violence out of the jaws of superstition and its handmaid tyranny; but the same Providence has given a sanction to the very method, by obliging those very people who upbraid her with the manner of her establishment as being popular and tumultuary, and built on the foundation of rebellion against lawful authority, to be beholding to the very same lawful means for the establishment they now are built upon.

Nor is there any case that I meet with so parallel to the late Revolution in England as this Revolution in Scotland, and yet we are not of the opinion that the Revolution in England was tumultuary at all.

They both began, and both were carried on by the same methods, and no other, by which nations oppressed have, in all ages, recovered their liberty, and snatched themselves out of the jaws of tyranny and oppression,—ways honourable and justifiable by the laws of God, of nature, and of nations.

I shall keep my word as to brevity in the following part of the story :—The nobility having thus renounced the Regent, they sent to summon the town of Leith; but the French had made it too strong to part with it so easily.

They were, indeed, formidable to the Congregation; for they had command of the sea, and being at least 8000 men, well officered and disciplined, they transported themselves over into Fife, and ravaged the country from Stirling Bridge to St Andrews.

The Congregation had no proportioned forces for this work, nor wherewith to supply them. They sent to England and borrowed 4000 crowns for present occasion; but the Queen, who had her spies upon them, got intelligence of it, and surprised both the man and the money.

Their affairs thus running backward, they came to the last and only expedient, which was to put themselves under the protection of the Queen of England, and seek assistance; and here it is to be noted, that the Presbyterians did not fly to foreign help to invade their sovereign, as some will have it to be; the establishing the Reformation did not seek foreign help; for the nation having so universally embraced the Protestant religion, there was not one in ten to stand against them.

But the case turned just the other way. The Lords of the Congregation had, as has been related, engaged in the Reformation; the Queen Regent had by several treaties assented to it, part at one time, part at another; but keeping no faith with them, resolving, if possible, to root them out—she flies to foreign aid. Mark it; she brings in an army of strangers, takes possession of their towns, and fortifies them, in order to support her in the tyrannical measure she had taken.

To root out this mischief the war began, and not merely for religion. Had the nation been cleared of foreigners, on either side, the work had soon been done ; but being invaded by France, they flew to England for help, and soon obtained it.

The Queen of England, upon a treaty signed in her name by the Duke of Norfolk, and in the name of the Duke of Chattelerault by commission appointed, sent the Lord Gray with 2000 horse, and 6000 foot, and after that a reinforcement of 2000 foot more.

By these, after a long siege, and an obstinate resistance, the town was at last surrendered, and the French soldiers, by capitulation, conveyed home to France.

During these things, the Queen Regent had retired to the Castle of Edinburgh, where she fell sick and soon after died. Some say, she broke her heart for grief that she was thus reduced. Bishop Spotiswood says, that she sent for the Duke and the confederate Lords, before she died, and exhorted them to end this war, and send home both French and English; that she asked pardon of all she had injured, and died very christianly.* But he quotes no authority for it, neither do any historians that I have met with say any such thing.

Her death finished this first war, as I may call it, and hastened the surrender of Leith, which held out but a little while ; not but that it might have held longer, and no doubt it would, the garrison being resolute, well provided, and relief expected ; but the Queen of England and the King of France having brought matters to a treaty abroad, a treaty at home followed of course, so ambassadors from either met at Edinburgh, and a truce being at first agreed on, the capitulation and general peace followed; and the 16th of July 1560, the English army marched for Berwick, the French set sail for France, and a general peace was made ; in which, among other articles, this glorious stipulation

---

* Spotiswood, lib. 3. fol. 146. She sent for John Willock, the preacher (Bishop Spotiswood would not call him minister), and conferring with him a reasonable space, declared openly that she trusted to be saved only by the death and merits of Jesus Christ, and thus ended her life most christianly.

was one, viz.—that the Reformation was acknowledged ; and considering the infancy of the Church,
and the difficulties her first champions had waded
through, it was a very great step to her future establishment.

The death of the Queen mother was followed by
another event, which had no less influence upon the
affairs of Scotland, and this was, that the Queen became a widow, Francis II. the King of France, dying
the same year, a few months after his mother-in-law.

This gave a new turn to the affairs of Scotland, and
the Popish party was, and not without cause, exceedingly surprised at it ; for they had before the whole
kingdom of France concerned to support them ; and
their Queen being then married to the King of France,
they had them jointly concerned in the affairs ;
whereas now, another King succeeding to the Crown
of France, the Queen became but a Dowager, an ally,
and her interest and power would be the less to support her friends in Scotland.

The Congregation had now the Government of the
whole kingdom in their hands, and the Queen was, as
we may say, at their mercy ; and this was a special
Providence to them, as for settling the Reformation,
so to clear up the reputation of the Reformers, and
purge them from the charge the late Queen Regent
had laid upon them, of aiming at the subversion of the
Government, and dethroning their Sovereign, to set
up either Lord James, or the Duke of Chattelerault
in her place.

But this still tended to their reputation, and to ex-
onerate them as to the charge ; for when the Regent
was dead, the Queen a desolate widow, and they had
all the power in their hands, their upright design
could never better appear ; for they had no one to
hinder their project, if they had had it in their view ;
but being sincerely bent for the Reformation of religion, and the establishment of their civil liberties,

and aiming at nothing else, they applied themselves wholly to that work, and no other, as will appear in the pursuit of this story.

In order to this, having dismissed the English army, and shipped off the French, the first thing that was done was, that in the great Church at Edinburgh, the Lords of the Congregation, and all the gentlemen, their adherents, who were there, met to give solemn thanks to God for their deliverance from the tyranny of foreigners, and establishing the true religion, and their civil liberties.

Then, says Bishop Spotiswood,* for I must be particular here as to the authors, they distributed ministers among the burghs, and appointed superintendents for the direction of the Church affairs.

I note this the rather here, because some gentlemen, who are angry with the Church of Scotland for the present Establishment, would call this superintendency an infant Prelacy ; and from thence argue, that the First Reformation was Episcopal, which difficulty we shall see cleared up as we go on.

In the meantime, it will receive its full answer in these two observations.

1. They had no power : What they were to do, or what power they had for the planting or displacing ministers in the kingdom, had these two things attending it, which quite enervates the Bishop's allegation, viz.

(1.) That it was all subservient to the assembly of ministers ; nay, these superintendents were subjected to the respective Presbyteries : They might be dis-

---

* Spotiswood, lib. 3. fol. 149. Then were the ministers, by common advice, distributed among the burghs :—John Knox for Edinburgh, Christopher Goodman for St Andrews, Adam Herriot at Aberdeen, &c. Besides these they did nominate (but he does not say who) for the direction of Church affairs, some to be superintendents, viz. Mr John Spotiswood for Lothian and Merse, Mr John Winram for Fife, John Erskine of Dun for Angus and Mearns, Mr John Willock for Glasgow, and Mr John Kerswell for Argyle and Isles. With this small number of Bishops (he would have called them) was the plantation of the Church at first undertaken.

placed by them, and supplied by them; and the Assembly does still, on extraordinary occasions, depute or commission ministers, in like manner, for the planting or displacing their ministers, visiting of churches, and the like.

(2.) They had neither superiority of dignity, or enlargement of stipend, or any other thing which might invade that parity which is professed by the Presbyterian Church.

2. The case was extraordinary, and it is what is never practised in the Church but on extraordinary occasions, of which this is allowed to be one: and there is no question but on the like extraordinary occasions, the like offices would be made use of again, which, in short, were only delegations, or substitutions by and from the General Assembly. The men had neither personal dignity nor personal power; their commission was temporary, and the limitation of their authority was such, as whenever the Bishops of the Church of England please to reduce themselves to, there is no Presbyterian Church in the world but would receive them.

The debate therefore of this supposed Episcopacy must fall to the ground, unless the gentlemen that are for it, are content to subject Episcopacy to Presbytery; for the assembly of ministers, either general, synodical, or presbyterial, had a power over those superintendents, and the remark would be very well worth note what kind of a Bishop it is these gentlemen plead for.

The superintendents were, in short, a temporary expedient for the necessity of the first planting the Church, and the ministers who appointed them were the most antiepiscopal in principle that could be found, as we shall see presently. But I return to the story.

The Lords having thus settled the Church's affairs for the present, all things rested till the meeting of a

Convention or Parliament, which was appointed to be in August following.

Here another dispute happened, which the Popish party have still insisted on, viz.——how this could be called a Parliament, since it was not called by the Queen, neither had her Majesty any body there commissioned to represent her person.

But the treaty of peace solved this; which being stipulated in the name and by the ambassador of the King and Queen, authorized the council of twelve to call a Convention or Parliament, and this fully legitimated it, though there was no person to represent the Sovereign.

In this Parliament all that had been done before was ratified; and having a sufficient warrant, as before, for the holding this Parliament, they esteemed what acts passed authentic, though the Queen afterwards refused to ratify them, as we shall hear presently.

Four acts passed in this Parliament, though they had not the royal assent till several years afterwards.

1. The Confession of Faith. Note, it passed in Parliament August 17. 1560.

2. An act for abolishing the jurisdiction and authority of the bishops.

3. Repealing or annulling all former acts made for the maintaining of idolatry.

4. For punishing the sayers and hearers of Mass.

A messenger was sent over to the Queen with these acts, to desire her Majesty to sign them; but the Queen would not so much as give an answer to him, but treated him with the utmost contempt. However, the acts being past, the Assembly was dissolved, and this was the first settlement of the Reformation.

It is to be observed here, that the articles of the Confession of Faith contain all the doctrinal part of the reformer's profession, but have not one word of the discipline or government of the Church, nor was the form of worship settled here; and to this it is needful to say something, because great pains are taken here to make the First Reformation look as if it had been Episcopal.

That they had a form of discipline and worship before this, is allowed by all historians, which was the order of Geneva;* the new one Spotiswood calls the Form of Church policy.†

It is necessary to digress a little here to the story of Mr John Knox. He had long been at Geneva, and was minister of the English Church there. He had also been at Frankfort, where the English who fled from Queen Mary's persecution had a church, and Mr Knox preaching there. A difference arose about the English Service Book, which drove him back to Geneva.

Here he drew the model of Church government which he after presented to the Reformers in Scotland for the scheme of theirs; and by this was that book of polity or discipline formed which we are now to treat of. Some historians have called it John Knox's work; others say it was done by a committee.‡

They that would call it John Knox's strive to do it because the article of superintendents being mentioned in this Book of Discipline, they would have John Knox to be acknowledged to be of Episcopal principles.

But I conceive that all this dispute about the superintendents would be at an end if it were examined

---

* Calderwood's History, fol. 14. Before the Confession of Faith was formed, and the Book of Discipline contrived, the reformed Kirk had that book which is before the Psalms in meter for their direction in discipline and external worship; which book is called in the Book of Discipline, the Book of Common Order, or the Order of the Church at Geneva.

† Spotiswood, lib. 2, fol. 152. In the Convention kept at Edinburgh in January preceding a form of Church policy was presented, and delivered to be ratified.

‡ Commission was given to Mr John Winram, John Spotiswood, the Bishop's father, John Willock, John Douglas, John Rew, and John Knox, to draw up a Book of Policy and Discipline of the Church, as they had done of the Doctrine.

whether these superintendents were not really bishops, and whether the true Episcopacy is not plainly to be reduced to the ministerial function.   So that this is so far from justifying the authority, dignity, and superiority of bishops, as now practised, that it rather brings down the bishops to the station of those superintendents, the utmost of whose authority is by Dr Rule plainly proved to be very consistent with Presbyterian parity, a thing which, if well considered, would soon put an end to this debate.*

This Book of Discipline, however, could not obtain with the Lords to a general assent.   Whether Mr Knox formed it or not, it is plain he exceedingly pressed to have it passed in the Convention.   Bishop Spotiswood says, the Estates at that time did not think it meet to enter into the examination of the polity. By this he would insinuate, that the Reformation was settled in general as to doctrine, and that all agreed in the suppression of Popery; but that the manner, order, polity, or discipline of the Church was left uncertain and undetermined.   But neither will this answer; for though, as an assembly or convention, they did not sign it, yet, as private men, the whole body of the first Reformers, who had been called the Congregation, and who had done all the work, signed it.   These were the Duke of Chattelerault, the Earls of Arran, Argyle, Glencairn, Marshall, Menteith, Morton, and Rothes; Lords James Hamilton, Yester, Boyd, Ochiltree, Sanquhar, Lindsay; and abundance of the gentry, barons, and burgesses, with one bishop—viz., of Galloway, and the Dean of Murray.

But to go on with our history.

Thus far the Convention had acted in behalf of the Church :   1. They pulled down, and by an act abolished, Popery for ever.   2. They declared the Con-

---

* Spotiswood, lib. 3, fol. 174.   It had been framed by John Knox, partly in imitation of the reformed Churches in Germany, and partly of that he had seen at Geneva.

fession of the Protestant Faith, and passed articles of it into an act.   And thus they set the Church upon her own legs, and then left her to settle and fix herself upon such foundations of discipline and government as she should determine.

In order to this, the first General Assembly of the Church of Scotland sat down at Edinburgh, the 20th December 1560.

Their chief work was appointing and receiving ministers, and that alone determined that the very office of superintendent was subjected to the Assembly; but if that did not, we shall see in a few years they take upon them to limit, approve, and disapprove of their actions.

Even in this first Assembly, the other party made some struggle about the authority of assembling without the Queen's command; and as this has been a point frequently pushed at since, and once not very long ago, and may, in time, come to be pushed at again, it cannot be amiss to set down the argument then used, which, in short, was this principally.

They had then a Popish Queen, who unwillingly stooped to necessity in the Reformation. Their words are these—viz., If the liberty of the Kirk should depend upon the allowance and disallowance of the Sovereign, we may be deprived, not only of assemblies, but of the public preaching of the gospel. Take from the Church the freedom of assemblies, and you take from us the Reformation; for how shall the government of the Church be supported, order and unity in doctrine be maintained, but by the liberty of holding assemblies, and keeping up the judicial authority of the Church entire? This way of arguing was never yet answered, and, I presume, will not easily be answered.

It was then moved in the Assembly that the Queen might be desired to ratify the Book of Discipline; but it was deferred for that time.

The Queen was now returned to Scotland (1561), and began to take cognizance of her affairs, in which she very early discovered her dislike of what was doing, and her general aversion to the Reformation.

It seemed, however, that the Queen inclined to stoop to the necessity of the times, and to acquiesce in the new Church settlement, with allowing her the liberty of her own opinion, and to have Mass said in private in her own chapel. But this gave great offence, and the ministers particularly insisted upon it, that it was against their engagements for the abolishing idolatry ; and, inculcating this on the people, the Queen found she lost very much of their affection by it, and not only so, but met with some afronts in it also. However, resolved to support, not only her authority, but her party, she proceeded warmly.

She put the Provost of Edinburgh into the Castle, and obliged the citizens to choose another. This was done for their forbidding the Popish priests to be received into the town. She then commanded the Town Council of Edinburgh to choose a new Provost, which they, for fear, at that time complied with. Next by proclamation, she made the city of Edinburgh free, as she termed it, for all her subjects to repair to on their lawful occasions. This restored the Papists. And here she not only had the better of the city, but really seemed to have some right on her side, and therefore the Lords did not stand by the citizens in it, as was expected.

Indeed, the Court being now formed, and the Queen acting with great candour in other things, the nobility began to be drawn in by offices, salaries, and preferments, together with the emulation and ambition usual in such cases ; so that the Lords, who were before the most zealous for the Reformation, though they retained their sincere profession of the Protestant religion, yet they remitted much of their former zeal, and seemed to be drawn off from their strictness in the prosecution of, and their warm application to, the great work of all. And this our historians of both parties very much complain of, as if they had abandoned the Reformation. However, they soon gave good evidence to the contrary.*

Little passed now for some time in the affairs of the Reformation; the Assembly had their constant diets, and peaceably proceeded in Church affairs, as matters presented. The Queen suffered them to go on, but at the same time she shewed, on all occasions, that she secretly resolved to cut them short, as opportunity should present.

In this interval, one thing happened which might have shewn her that the Protestants, their religion being but secured to them, were very loyal to her person, and to her Government also; for in the insurrection which about that time was raised by Huntly and the Gordons, she saw the Papists in arms against her; and the Lord James Stuart, who was now Earl of Murray, and was the most zealous Reformer, fighting for her with a band of Protestants at the battle of Corriche, where Huntly was routed and killed, and all his Popish party scattered.

The long accounts now intervene in our histories of the Queen's proposed interview with the Queen of England, and how the Papists disappointed it, from the very same principles which they did the interview of King James V. and Henry VII. of England long before. Also the history of the Queen's amours with the Lord Darnley, and that wretched marriage from whence so many mischiefs ensued; how the exor-

---

* Spotswood, lib. 4. fol. 183. Some of the noblemen who had, in former times, showed themselves most zealous against the toleration of idolatry, were grown a little more cold by the flatteries of the Court; and all of them emulous of each other's greatness, were striving who should be in most favour with the Queen.

Calderwood, Hist. fol. 84. The Courtiers and Lords depending upon the Court came not to the Assembly; but the day following, to avoid suspicion. they came. These he names.—viz. the Duke, the Earls of Argyle, Murray, Glencairn, Morton, Rothes, &c., the very authors and beginners of the Congregation.

bitance of David Rizzio brought not only his own ruin upon his head, but the exasperated King running into the unhappy excess of jealousy and murder, so alienated the Queen from him, as to run her into the same extremes of murder and revenge ; and this upon the very person of her husband. These are sad stories, and as they have no concern in this work, so I am not delighting enough in such tragical relations as to make a digression here to introduce them ; neither do they relate at all to the affairs of the Church, to which I return.

Soon after the defeat of the Gordons, the Queen called a Parliament ; when she made so many concessions to the Protestants that some blind sort of people began to fancy the Queen would come over to the reformed religion, but she soon undeceived them. For the match between the Queen and the Lord Darnley now coming forward, the Protestant nobility took umbrage at the consequences, the Lord Darnley professing himself Popish.

The Queen summoned the Estates of the kingdom to Stirling, to give their assent to her marriage.

There was little opposition made in that Parliament either to that or any thing else ; the nobility, in compliance to the Queen, complying more readily than was expected, only one Lord opposing it.*   But the Papists shewed themselves so much exalted, and behaved with so little caution in their hopes, that it occasioned great jealousy among the nobility, and was partly the occasion of what followed ; for no sooner was this assent of the Estates to the marriage made public, but the people fell into a rage, saying, that the Lords of the Estates had broken in upon their

---

* Spotiswood, lib 4, fol. 189. Lord Ochiltree only opposed it openly, professing that he would never consent to admit a king of the Popish religion.
  Ibid. lib. 4, fol. 190.   The Earls of Murray, Argyle, Glencairn, and Rothes, assisted by the Duke of Chattelerault, meeting together at Stirling, after the Queen was gone, resolved to oppose the marriage.

engagements, and would overthrow the Reformation. Several tumults also happened, particularly in Edinburgh, which the Queen prosecuted with great severity.

But now the Lords, of whom I noted before that they were suspected to be yielding too much to the Court, began to open their eyes and come to themselves, joining themselves together to oppose this marriage, and to maintain the Reformation.

The General Assembly of the Church was sitting at the same time, and as all people began to entertain jealousies of the Queen's designs, and strong apprehensions filled the heads of those that were most concerned for religion, seeing the Queen resolved to support Popery, and that she was now going to strengthen that interest with a Popish match; so they formed a petition to her Majesty, containing eight heads. The 2d article of which was, that the Protestant religion should be openly professed by all persons, and by the Queen herself. The Queen's answer, very sharp and satirical, is, with the articles of the petition, set down at large in Spotiswood's history,* wherein she rejects their petition, and tells them plainly she will not change her religion, nor put the patronage of benefices out of her hands.

Though they could expect no other answer, yet this inflamed matters, and served to fix the confederation, and restore the zeal of the nobility, who had now begun to oppose her, and in which she afterwards found her ruin.

The match was now fixed, and the Queen married to the Lord Darnley, in July 1564, disregarding the representation of the discontented Lords, who openly professed it to be against the liberties of the kingdom, and began to arm.

The Queen prepared to oppose them, and marched

---

* Spotiswood's History, lib. 4, fol. 190, 191.

towards Stirling, and the King with her ; but the
Lords, not prepared for resistance, fled to Paisley,
near Glasgow ; from thence, being followed by the
Queen's forces, they fled to Hamilton, thence to Edinburgh, then separated, some fled to England, and some
reconciled themselves to the Queen ; thus the first
beginnings of this fire were quenched for a while, and
the people quieted, who nevertheless were zealous in
the cause, though discouraged by these unhappy beginnings.   The nobility being thus dispersed for
some time, the Protestant cause seemed to lie bleeding.   The Lords who fled to England, obtained the
Queen of England to intercede for them by her ambassador ; but she was, as it were, bid to mind her
own business, and not to concern herself in these
matters.*

The Duke of Chattelerault, seeing the Queen both
resolute and powerful, made his peace, and was well
received.

The Assembly met as usual, and solicited the
Queen still to increase and settle the stipends of their
ministers, in which they did at length obtain some
supply ; but in the affair of religion itself they received
no satisfaction at all.

The broils of the Court and the murder of David
Rizzio began the year 1565.   Spotiswood, in his History, fol. 195, makes very good remarks on this,
viz. :—That it had been much better to have brought
him to public justice, and executed him by the hand
of the hangman ;† for it brought on all the miseries
which followed, one on the neck of another, almost
to the ruin of the nation, and effectually to the ruin
of the King, and, in the end, of the Queen also.

---

* Spotiswood, fol. 192.   The messenger had his answer in writing,
viz. that Queen Elizabeth would do well to have no meddling with the
affairs of Scotland, but leave them to the discretion of their princes,
seeing neither she nor her husband did offer to trouble themselves
with her subjects.
† Buchanan says, they de-igned to hang him publicly, but that Morton and his men had not patience enough with him.

The Queen resolved to ruin the Lords who had fled, and called a Parliament to forefault or attaint them. In this Parliament, say some, she designed to make Rizzio Chancellor,* and this occasioned Morton's falling upon him. Others say, he had plotted the destruction of the nobility, and had proposed to the Queen the cutting them off by way of massacre. Again, he is charged with a scandalous familiarity with the Queen, which, whether it were true, or that it was suggested to the King to irritate him, and bring him to be concerned in the fact, is not material, farther than this—that, by it, the enmity between the Queen and him, which was before begun, was made so irreconcileable, that, as he never rested till he had caused the Italian to be murdered, the Queen never rested till she had caused her husband to be murdered, and divine justice, after all, never rested till it had caused her to be murdered; so that blood followed blood, till that whole knot was destroyed. And thus the enemies of the Reformation made way, by their own destruction, for the more legal and more peaceable completing of this great work of the Reformation, to the glory of God, and the honour of true religion, as shall presently appear.

The murder of this obscure fellow, however, had this influence, that, upon this prospect of the Lords of the Court engaging with the King against David Rizzio, the banished Lords took courage to come home, and the Parliament being sitting, offered themselves to trial, and no body appearing against them, the Lords being all banded into parties on the other occasion, they were acquitted. Again, the Queen, terrified with the strength of her husband's party, and the resolution which they appeared to have taken, faced about to the Lords that had fled, received them

---

* Spotiswood, lib. 4. fol. 195. The Queen designing he should act as Chancellor in this Parliament, Morton, who, after Huntly's death, had supplied that place, took it as an affront to him.

D

into favour, and bent her fury at the murderers of her favourite.

In this juncture she was brought to bed of a son, who was afterwards King James VI., who was born in Edinburgh Castle on the 19th of June, in a little room facing the Castle Hill, which is still remembered as the birth-place of that king. It is reported she was so irritated at the King for the murder of Rizzio, that she had determined to destroy the child, as not bearing to nourish anything of his begetting. I do not say this was any more than a report; but it gives us a hint of the spirit that then reigned, and she having, as there is reason to believe, at the same time resolved to murder the father, it might not be improbable she had as barbarous thoughts towards the child. But God had other designs to bring to pass in this birth, whether for the good or ill of the Church of Scotland, the consequence will make appear.

Another note is made here upon this Prince, how justly I will not determine—viz., that the fright and terror his mother was in at the drawn swords which were in the hands of the persons employed in this attempt (for Rizzio was fallen upon in her presence), so far influenced the child in her womb, that his retentives generally failed him at the sight of weapons ever after. But this by the way. It is no scandal to say of him, he was no man of war.

The Assembly being then sitting, they sent some of their number to congratulate the Queen on the birth of a son, and humbly to desire the Prince might be baptized into the Protestant Church. The Queen gave no answer to it at that time, but very effectually made a reply to it afterwards, causing him to be baptised after the Popish manner, at Stirling Castle, by the Archbishop of St Andrews.

The Church now began to see which way things were going; for the Queen not only honoured the

Archbishop of St Andrews with the baptizing the Prince, but gave him also a commission, whereby he was restored to his ancient jurisdiction in several things, which clashed with their authority; such as confirming testaments, collation to benefices, &c., both which being directly contrary to the acts of Parliament, which established the Reformation, and to the true interest of the Protestant settlement, the Assembly was exceedingly alarmed at it; but finding it in vain to address the Queen any more, they formed a paper in manner of an appeal; but called it a supplication, directed, as appears in the title, to the nobility and Lords of the secret council, who had professed Jesus Christ, and who had renounced the Roman Antichrist. These proceedings on both sides ripened things for the sudden change which soon after followed.

The murder of the King was the next tragedy that come on the stage of this unhappy Court. The Queen, after her being delivered of a son, and, if she had the wicked design of murdering it, being prevented the execution of that murder, retired to Alloway, a house of the Earl of Mar near Stirling; the King followed her, but was refused admittance (she resolving to have no more of his race, as she openly declared), and was treated with great contempt. Upon this the King (say some, with grief, others say, by poison) fell sick, and was carried to Glasgow.* The Queen after some time, whether she relented at her usage of him, or whether in the plot for his ruin, or whether Bothwell formed his destruction upon an apprehension of the Queen's being reconciled to him at that time, is uncertain to this hour; but she went to visit him, and after some words they were openly reconciled again, and the King was, at the Queen's ap-

---

* Buchanan, Hist. Eng. says, he fell sick, the Queen having given him poison, which, working before its time, broke out all over his body, and so nature expelled the poison.

pointment, carried to Edinburgh, where he had not
been many days but he was most barbarously murdered in his bed, and the house blown up with gun-
powder, as by the histories of those times more largely
is to be seen.

It is not to the case to inquire here into the manner and circumstances of this barbarity, and who
did it, of all which authors also differ.*   All agree
that it was vilely contrived between the Queen and
Bothwell, and more vilely executed by Bothwell,
either in person or by his agents.

But I am, by the course of things, hastening to the
great revolution which now happened, and which all
these horrid things were but as so many preparatory
steps to bring to pass.

First, the abominable marriage between Bothwell
and the Queen, which was brought to pass soon after,
which made the matter so black that nothing could
be worse, next to owning the fact—viz., that a
woman should link herself in marriage to the murderer of her husband.

Secondly, her behaviour at the Parliament which
then approached, where she positively refused all that
was desired of her in behalf of the Reformation, and
behaved with a quite different air from all she had
done formerly.

Thirdly, manifest designs and secret attempts of
the Queen to get the custody of her son out of the
hands of the Lord Mar, who claimed it by birth as
hereditary keeper of the King's children.

The first step to what followed was by the Earl of
Athol, who, fully satisfied of the guilt of Bothwell in
the murder of the King, and meditating how he
might with most ease bring him to justice, begins to

---

* Spotiswood, lib 4, fol. 200, says, Bothwell came upon him in the
night, as he lay asleep, and strangled him.   Buchanan says it was the
conspirators, but seems not to be positive that Bothwell did it with
his own hands, though he owns him in the conspiracy.

start among the nobility his just suspicions that the same villany might be practised upon the infant as had been upon the father.

Upon this the Protestant Lords appoint a meeting at Stirling, in order to protect and secure the person of the Prince; and in this meeting the destruction of Popery, treason, and murder took its rise. They all met with their fate together, and this abominable generation, with their short lived joy, vanished in stink and smoke, being grown noisome to the whole world by the most horrid actions that were ever read of.

The Queen, hearing of this meeting, and that the Lords had entered into bond one to another for mutual assistance, pretended a journey to visit the borders, and thereby, according to custom, summoned the subjects to attend her with arms and provisions for fifteen days. Upon this, a rumour being spread that the Queen designed to seize on the young Prince, and take him from the Earl of Mar, the Lords aforesaid took arms; the Queen published a declaration that she did not design to remove the Prince; but this not satisfying the Lords, they surrounded her in Brothwick Castle, but not being able entirely to invest the place, Bothwell and the Queen made their escape to Dunbar, and then, though too late, she raised forces.

The Lords advanced to Edinburgh, and the Queen to Musselburgh, but when the armies faced one another, the Queen's men did not care to fight,—Bothwell's guilt was too great, his heart failed him, and he ran away. The Queen, who had both more courage and more presence of mind, staid, but was obliged to put herself into the hands of the Lords, who carried her to Edinburgh, and from thence, shewing her indeed but very little respect, sent her prisoner to the Castle of Lochleven. Thus ended the reign of Popery in Scotland, I mean barefaced, professed, downright Popery; as for Popery in masquerade, eventual

Popery, disguised Popery, it is but a very few years since that went off the stage also; and we shall, in the course of these memoirs, see many a farce of its acting, and some bloody tragedies also, till at length it vanished with as much contempt as the other.

Buchanan tells us that when the Queen had surrendered herself to the Lords, the second battalia, or line of the men, when she came among them, used her very barbarously, and cried out for putting her to death, painting a standard with the murdered King and his little son lying by him, and displaying it before her.

It was, without doubt, a very great revolution, and in it the justice of heaven visibly pursued the murder of the King, the barbarity of which hath hardly had its parallel in any age; and, as this is one of the reasons why I enter into that part of the story, so, though I cannot go through all the particulars, yet I cannot but remind the reader of one nice reflection— viz., that though Queen Elizabeth is blamed, and perhaps justly, for putting her to death afterwards, yet it is plain it was the work of a superior power, and that vengeance which followed them all, suffered her not to live.

Bothwell, who had been the chief contriver and actor of the whole tragedy, never saw her more.   He fled to Shetland, an island of the north, where, for a while, he turned pirate; but, being beaten from thence, he fled to Denmark, where he was taken up, by the King's order, and kept in a loathsome prison, and, being reduced to extreme poverty, lived about ten years in a jail, and at last died raving mad.

The Archbishop of St Andrews, who, as Buchanan relates, had been one of those that voluntarily undertook the murder, was hanged by the Regent, the Earl of Murray,—being taken in the surprise of Dumbarton Castle.

John Hamilton, who was one of the actors, died of

grief, after he confessed the murder to a priest, the schoolmaster at Paisley.

Even Morton himself, who had the least concern in it, and at most was no otherwise guilty than that he knew of it, and concealed it after it was done, was beheaded for that concealment many years after, at the cross of Edinburgh.

The Queen's guilt was particularly demonstrated by her own letters, taken in Bothwell's silver cabinet, where, under her hand, she transacted the whole affair with him, and among which was a contract of marriage, signed by her own hand, to him, in her husband's life, to be consummated after he should be dispatched.

These things made her guilt so plain, that her name became odious to all the world; and the Regent afterwards made them all so plain to everybody's understanding, when he was at London, and when the Queen of England inquired of the reasons why they deposed their Sovereign, that, the same author says, Queen Elizabeth declared she was not worthy to be assisted.

And yet, after all this aversion manifested to her person, and detestation of her crime, she formed such parties among the people, who, after the first heat, began to relent and commiserate her, that she found means to escape out of Lochleven Castle, and raise new commotions.

In the meantime, the nobility considered of settling the government, and of entirely deposing the Queen. The first step to this was, by procuring her to demit or resign the crown. She at first resolutely opposed it, but afterwards signed anything they brought her,* as it is said, without so much as reading it, upon this

---

* Spotiswood, lib. 4, fol. 211. She was persuaded to it by Robert Melvill, who was sent from the Earls of Athol and Lethington, to advise her as she loved her life not to refuse them anything they should require. He likewise brought a letter from Sir Nicholas Throckmorton, the ambassador from England, to the same effect, declaring

foundation, that, being under confinement, nothing she did now could be binding upon her for the future.

Thus she signed several instruments, one for the surrender of the crown, renouncing and demitting the government in favour of her son, commissioning the Lords for his solemn investiture. One other was a power to some noblemen to make the solemn resignation, in her name, in the public meeting of the States. One other was for nominating the Earl of Murray, who was then in France, Regent of the kingdom in the minority of her son; and the other for naming governors to her son. But afterwards, when she made her escape out of Lochleven, she revoked all those writings as done by her under the restraint of a prison, and under terror of her life, which, they say, the Lord Lindsay threatened when he came to her with the instruments. However, the Lords took her at her first word, and, in the meantime, proceeded upon the authority of these demissions; and, having put all other things in order, they proclaimed her son King of Scotland, and crowned him July 29. 1567, and made James, Earl of Murray, Regent, though then absent in France. This is the same I have always called Lord James, being the Queen's half-brother, who was after called the good Regent, and who was, under God, the blessed instrument of the establishing the Reformation in Scotland.

The Queen, as I noted, having made her escape, raised an army about Hamilton. The Regent, though inferior in number, marched to Glasgow, and at Langside, a village not far from Glasgow, gave her battle, and her forces being overthrown, she fled into England.

There she past a long imprisonment, by order of Queen Elizabeth, during which, for carrying on innu-

that no resignation made in the time of her captivity would be of any force, and in law was null, because done out of a just fear.

merable plots and contrivances against the said Queen
and her subjects, she was at last brought to the block,
on pretence of conspiring against the English. Whether their pretence against her was just or not, I do
not determine ; but that justice pursued her, as is
said before, for the most abominable fact above—I
mean the murder of her husband—I think is plain
from all histories of those times.

The realm was now under the conduct of the Regent, the King an infant, and they had brought the
Queen to make a kind of assent to the crowning her
son, and to appoint him governors. The Regent
managed with a prudence not to be described ;—in
diligence unwearied, in action undaunted, in government sagacious, in religion zealous and exceeding pious,
in life sedate, and in his violent death patient and
resigned. He was barbarously murdered by James
Hamilton, set to work by the Queen's party. He
shot him through the body in the street at Linlithgow, as he was riding out of the palace amidst a great
throng of the people crowding to see him. The murderer made his escape out of a back-door, and could
not be apprehended.

Upon this disaster great contention followed among
the several parties. The nobility came several times
together in order to choose a new Regent, and parted
without bringing it to a conclusion ; and the Queen's
party grew very strong, particularly the city of Edinburgh sided with her. At last Matthew, Earl of
Lennox, father to the late murdered King, was
chosen Regent.

He carried on the war against the Queen's party,
and taking possession of Leith, had several skirmishes
with her troops, as at Leith, Dalkeith, and other
places ; but at last he was surprised at Stirling, with a
great many of the nobility and gentry, by a party of
the Queen's men, who took the town by surprise, and
took the Regent, the Earl of Morton, and sundry

other prisoners; but the Queen's men being beat out of the town again, and forced to quit their prisoners, the Regent was shot through by him that had him prisoner, because he could not carry him off; for which deed he was afterwards hanged, as he well deserved.

The Lord Erskine, Earl of Mar, was then chosen Regent; but the Queen's interest was so strong at that time, and the King's so weak, that there was great danger of a new turn in affairs, and Popery began to hold up its head; but they had the pleasure of being disappointed in that particular also, by the turn of affairs in England with the Queen, who, on a discovery of her plot there with the Duke of Norfolk, was closer confined, and afterwards tried for her life, and beheaded. With her fell all the hopes of Popery in Scotland. But the Church found other enemies to struggle with, in some respects as fatal to her prosperity as the Papists, of which we shall find cause to speak more particularly in the second part of this work.

But to return to the affairs in hand. As this revolution was against the interest of the Queen and her party, so it was a farther, and I think I may call it a complete, establishment of the Church; for whatever factions and parties were formed in the State, the nobility frequently changing parties as their interests and fortunes guided them, yet they all joined in the matter of the Reformation, and the confederated Lords were entirely in the interest of religion: but to look into this we must go back again to the first seizing of the Queen.

The Earl of Murray being declared Regent, as above, was, while he lived, a very great furtherance to the establishment of the Church; that great man being not only a vigorous and constant friend to the Reformation, but a most pious, religious, and sincere professor of it himself.

Things being in so good a posture for the Church

when the Queen was taken prisoner, the first Parliament was holden at Edinburgh, December 15. 1567, in the name of the King, though but an infant; and the first thing they went about was to recognise the whole proceedings of the Reformation in the following acts :—

1*st*, An act abolishing the jurisdiction and usurped authority of the Pope, which was still no more than confirming the act made before for that purpose; but it was done because the Papists raised some objections against the validity of that Parliament, the Queen having not given her assent to their meeting, nor confirmed the articles at Leith.

2*d*, Another act passed for repealing former laws for establishing Popery.

3*d*, The Confession of Faith was ratified.

4*th*, An act appointing that all kings and magistrates should, at the time of entering upon their offices, swear to maintain the Church, expressed in these words : " *To maintain the true religion as now received.*"

The polity and jurisdiction of the Church was, says Spotiswood, referred to delegates, and the thirds of benefices were, for the present, granted to the Church. The necessity of the times made it impossible to obtain the rest; for the public affairs requiring the assistance of all its interest, the remaining revenues of the Church were retained to the service of the nation.

In this Parliament the King's authority being acknowledged, the Queen, his mother, was condemned to *perpetual imprisonment*, which was then thought very severe, and brought a great many to espouse her quarrel, in mere compassion to her circumstances; and this facilitating her escape, as before, filled the nation with a long series of blood, tumult, and disorder.

Yet, under all these turmoils, the Church was supported in her jurisdiction as well as doctrine, and, therefore, here I fix the period of what I call her infant state : and I think my opinion is backed very much by that famous letter of the General Assembly of the Kirk, *anno* 1567, being the same year I am now upon.

The letter was to Mr Willock, one of their ministers, and one who was particularly famous for his share in the Reformation, but was fled into England from the troubles of the first years of the Queen's return. This man the Assembly writes to, to invite him to come back again : and their reasons to move hime to return were, " That they had a religious and zealous magistrate constituted, meaning the Earl of Murray, commonly called the *gude Regent ;* sufficient provision appointed for ministers, the Church established, and religion flourishing throughout the realm." And they conclude their letter, " *Now you shall see the copestone of that work whereof you laid the foundation.*"

It is true that the Book of Polity or Discipline was not to this day established by Parliament, and therefore the Church had not all the authority that they wished in the matters of jurisdiction, government, and discipline. But the gentlemen that would dispute here the priority of Episcopal government in the Church to Presbyterial, will get nothing by that ; for all this while the Church exercised a complete Presbyterial jurisdiction, and no other,—had their exact regular meetings of kirk or parochial sessions, presbyteries, synods, and general assemblies.

The nobility, upon all occasions, signed the Book of Discipline, and the Book of Polity was frequently revised, and in this Parliament it was ordered to be revised again.

The bishops that remained had nothing left them but a ministerial authority, and were equally subjected to presbytery, synod, and assembly ; and the superintendency, of which so much is alleged to prove it another equivalent to Episcopacy, was under all the essential articles of a parity, a famous instance of which was the Bishop of Orkney, who was, as a private minister, censured in the first Assembly of the King, for solemnizing the adulterous marriage of the Queen with Bothwell, and was deprived by them, by virtue of an act of Assembly, against marrying a divorced adulterer,—for such, it appeared, Bothwell was,* having been divorced from his wife to come into that horrid marriage.

Again, the next General Assembly, *anno* 1568, the said bishop was restored,† upon his humiliation and satisfying the Assembly.

At the same Assembly‡ the Superintendent of Fife was censured for his negligence in visitation, and that he was careless in punishing adulterers.

These are such plain acts of presbyterial jurisdiction over the superintendents, that nothing can be needful to add to it. In the same Assembly was the form of excommunication approved, and ordered to be printed, and is affixed just before the psalms in metre.

One other thing is very essential to this debate, which will be also found at large in Calderwood's history, folio 45.

The principal and some of the regents at the College of Aberdeen were deprived, by order of the Assembly, for refusing to acknowledge the several laws of establishing the Church, and other things objected ; but they were deprived not by the superintendent, but by the superintendent together with the ministers and commissioners, and the superintendent

---

* Calderwood, Hist. fol. 44. He was deprived till the Assembly was satisfied for the scandal.

† Ibid. He is restored to his ministry, but they ordained that he publicly make a Confession of his Faith in the Kirk of Holyrood House, on the Lord's Day, at the end of sermon.

‡ Ibid. And the Superintendents of Angus and Lothian were to report their diligence to the next Assembly.

acted only as commissioner from the Assembly, as is to this day to be seen in the register.

As to discipline, the practice of it was, though not established, yet every day regulated and directed by the Assembly ; and if there were any difficult things in matters of order and discipline, it was only owing to this, that the polity of the Church was not perfected and settled.

PART II.

OF THE CHURCH IN HER GROWING STATE.

~~~~~~~~~~

I have fixed the period of the Church's infancy at the dethroning Queen Mary, when the glorious topstone of the Reformation seemed to be laid in Scotland, and the Church arrived to a condition to stand upon her own feet.

Her doctrinal articles were assented to, and her worship established, and both confirmed by sundry acts of Parliament, under the administration of the first Regents, the Earl of Murray and the Earl of Lennox. Likewise her judicatories took place, her churches were planted, and her discipline was agreed to ; so that, as in the letter of the Assembly to Mr Willock it is noted, the Church was fully planted. As to her intestine troubles, they seemed indeed to be but begun ; for the polity of the Kirk, it was not yet established, nor could they ever bring the Book of Discipline to be passed into an act in the Convention or Parliament of that day. At this door crept in all the mischiefs that for above 120 years after continually harrassed this Church, and brought her several times under the yoke, both of temporal and ecclesiastic tyranny, several times into cruel and bloody persecutions, and more than once to the very gates of destruction, as shall be seen in its order.

The Church had been now fourteen years in her first struggles with Popery, had enjoyed her General

Assemblies twelve years ; and though the government of the Church was not passed into a law by the civil sanction of a Parliament, as is observed above, yet the greatest part of the nobility and gentry had signed it ; and all that part which was needful to the true discipline of the Church was fully practised by the ministers in their particular churches, and frequently regulated in their General Assemblies.

But as in all the ages of the Church the prosperity of their affairs has led them into mutual jarrings, divisions, and jealousies, which consequently ushered in multitudes of innovations, so it was here. The ambition and emulation of the clergy and nobility ushered in a model of Episcopal government, which, as it was at first a motley scheme of Church government, composed neither of Presbytery nor Prelacy, so it laid the foundation of its own corruptions, and in them of all the confusions which followed in the Church, as will appear hereafter.

The first step to this was in the year 1572, when, upon the old foot of settling and perfecting the polity of the Church, that fatal commission was granted to settle the Kirk, of which in its place. The Regent was now the Earl of Mar, who, though a Protestant, was, it seems, particularly inclined to the new scheme of Church government which had been proposed in an Assembly or Convention of the Church at Leith, viz., to restore the government of Bishops as it was in the time before the Reformation ; and as there was a strong party even among the ministers who fell in with the Court, and no doubt the hopes of Church preferment had moved some, they soon were prevailed with to join with the party that pretended to settle the Church according to that scheme.

In order to this, a commission was granted to a certain number of gentlemen to treat with a like number of ministers to be commissioned by the General Assembly, and to consider of, settle, and conclude anent all things tending to the establishing the polity of the Kirk.

And this was that famous, or rather fatal commission which first brought Episcopacy into the Church of Scotland, and their act was expressed in these words—

" They think good, in consideration of the present estate, that the names and titles of archbishops and bishops be not innovated, nor the bounds of the dioceses confounded, but stand and continue in time coming, as they did before the Reformation, at least till the King's majority, or till consent of Parliament."[*]

Episcopacy being thus brought in, as we call it, by head and shoulders into the Church, did not, however, answer their end who brought it in; for at first it came in so fettered and shackled with limitation of power and castration of stipends, that there was little in it more than was before in the ministers who were called superintendents, the name and dignities excepted. And here it is worth observing, that the true reason appeared both why the Church could never obtain a Parliamentary establishment of their Book of Discipline, as also why the nobility and gentry fell in so suddenly with this new model. The case is very plain. Under this model the gentlemen retained to themselves the revenues of the Church, either in temporalities feued to themselves, as they call it in Scotland, or pensions and payments which they obtained from the churchmen,[†] which they could never before obtain under the ministers; for the ministers would not so far betray the Church as to alienate her revenues to the courtiers and gentry. But now it was done effectually, and the gentlemen hold many of these things to this day, to the great impoverishment, as

---

* Calderwood, Hist. fol. 50.
† Ibid. Hist. fol. 51. Hence they were called Tulchan Bishops. A tulchan is a calf-skin stuffed with straw, placed to make the cow give milk; for now the bishop had the title, which was but the straw, but the lord got the milk of the benefice.

E

well as discouragement of the Church, and hindrance of the planting ministers in many parts of the country.

However, the clergy found ways to help themselves as to the revenue in after times. This was the first condition they came into the Church in, and this simoniacal project, for it was no less, viz. giving part of the Church's revenues to the nobility, that they might have their vote to possess the rest—this simoniacal project, I say, was the first reason of the introduction of bishops into the Church of Scotland.

We shall now see how this matter relished with the Reformers, and whether, as some allege, it was a general act of the Reformation, yea or no. In February 1572, a new bishop was inaugurated at St Andrews. Mr Knox protested against it, and pronounced his anathema, or great curse, against both giver and receiver.

But the case was much altered in Scotland at this time among the gentry and nobility. (1.) Abundance of the first Reformers, debauched by the luxury of the Court, and touched upon by the niceties of allegiance, adhered to the Queen, who was Popish, though they themselves were Protestants; such was the Duke of Chatellerault, the Earls of Argyle, Rothes, Laird of Grange, and others. (2.) Of the rest, the interest of the nobility in the Church's revenues, made them all slack in the matter of the Church polity, shy of the extraordinary authority of the Assembly, and averse to the severity of discipline.

The two first Regents, the Earls of Murray and Lennox, adhered honestly and faithfully to the Church, and were the constant patrons of her settlement. The Earl of Mar, the third Regent, was both zealous for the Reformation, and religious in his person; but gave way a little too early to the above-mentioned Court principle,—I mean as to their retaining the Church's revenues. But the Earl of Morton, who succeeded him, openly invaded the authority of the

Assembly, and, throwing off the mask, protected the bishops in usurping an authority independent of the Assembly ; and, by the same consequence, placing an authority in the prince to appoint the bishop. And thus he did the drudgery of the party, for which they ill rewarded him afterward, as will appear in the course of this story.

The first introduction of bishops, as above, left them fettered and shackled, as I noted, under the power of the Assembly ; and though even the name gave offence, yet they were so reduced, as that the name began not to be questioned, and such the Church will not dispute to this day : for though they were allowed to be called bishops, yet they were really only superintendents ; and not that neither very long, for the Assembly, *anno* 1574, voted the bishops to be only pastors of one parish, and delated several of them afterward for not preaching, and for not attending at their charge.* The Bishop of Dunkeld† was actually deposed by the Assembly. The Bishop of Glasgow was delated for not preaching—the Superintendent of Lothian was censured for inaugurating the Bishop of Ross when he was admonished by the Assembly not to do it.

Innumerable instances are to be found in the history of those times, as well of superintendents as of bishops, who were tried and censured by the Assembly. On the other hand, Bishop Spotiswood affirms positively, that the superintendent's power was Episcopal, but gives not one instance to prove it.

At last the grand affair came before the Assembly, and was decisively asserted ; for the Assembly, be-

* Spotiswood, lib. 5 fol. 226. The question was proposed to the Assembly, whether bishops, as they were then in Scotland, had their function warranted by the Word of God. The Assembly, without giving a direct answer, approved the opinion of the last Assembly, with this addition, " That bishops should betake themselves to the service of some one Church within their diocese, and name the particular flock of which they would accept the charge."
† Ibid. The Bishop of Dunkeld was deposed by the Assembly for dilapidations.

ginning to see themselves encroached upon, came immediately to the root of the question, Whether the function of a bishop be warranted by the Word of God? The name of a bishop no body disputed, but the extent of the title and office was the thing.

In the sixth session of the Assembly 1575, the brethren did not conclude finally, but came to this resolution, that they asserted their own superiority,* and their power to turn the bishop out, after which they stated the thing in general thus :—

"That the name of bishop is common to every one that hath a particular flock, over which he hath a peculiar charge, as well to preach the Word, and to minister sacraments, as to execute ecclesiastical discipline, with consent of his elders. And this is his chief function by the Word of God.

"Out of the number of bishops some may be chosen to have power to oversee and visit such reasonable bounds, besides his own flock, as the General Assembly shall appoint ; and in these bounds to appoint ministers, with the consent of the ministers of that province, and with the consent of the flock (mark that) to whom they shall be appointed ; as also to appoint elders and deacons in every particular congregation where there is none, with consent of the people thereof (mark that also), and to suspend ministers for reasonable causes, with consent of the ministers aforesaid."

This is, in short, the Church of Scotland's first opinion of the office of a bishop. They did not declare directly against the very word bishop, for the court run high for the new project, and they were not forward to fly in the face of the Regent, yet they were resolute in the substance of the thing.†

---

* Calderwood, fol. 69. If any bishop be chosen who hath no such qualities as the Word of God requireth, let him be tried by the General Assembly, de novo. and let him be deposed if there be cause.

† Calderwood, fol. 69. They answered not directly to the question at this time, by reason of the Regent's authority, who was bent upon the course whereof he was the chief instrument, yet they agreed upon such points as overthrow the authority and power of a Bishop.

It is very remarkable, that when these resolutions were past in the Assembly, there were present the Archbishop of Glasgow, the Bishops of Dunkeld, Galloway, Brechin, Dunblane, and Isles : and all these, by their silence, acknowledged they understood themselves to be bishops in such a sense ; and Spotiswood complains upon them for it.*

Thus the Church asserted her authority, and the project of the Court was very much disappointed.

Hitherto, intrigue, subtilty, and management had been the method in all the steps which had been taken to have introduced this novelty into the Church ; but these were all defeated by this proceeding ; for the Assembly took away the power, and left them the name, which, it is plain, did not answer the end.

There remained no other way, then, but to open violence ; and here we find the Regent making the first invasion upon the Kirk, and leading the way to all the assaults which have been made upon her ever since.

The Bishop of St Andrews dying, the Regent recommended, or rather appointed, the chapter to choose one Mr Adamson, his chaplain, to succeed the bishop.

The chapter deferred the election till the General Assembly, and acquainted them with it. Mr Adamson, who was present in the Assembly, was hereupon asked if he would submit to trials, and accept the office with those injunctions which the Church would prescribe. He answered, the Regent had forbid him to accept of the office otherwise than as appointed by Church and State.

---

* Spotiswood, lib. 1. fol. 276. It doth not appear by the register of these proceedings that the bishops who were present did so much as open their mouths in defence of their office and calling. What it was that made them so quiet ; whether, as I have heard, that they expected that these motions should have been dashed by the Regent, or otherwise, that they affected the praise of humility, is unknown ; which was no wisdom in them to have given way to such novelties, and have suffered the lawfulness of their vocation to be thus called in question. The persons present he names—Archbishop of Glasgow, Superintendent of Lothian and Angus ; Bishop of Dunkeld, Bishop of Galloway, Bishop of Brechin, Bishop of Dunblane, and Bishop of Isles.

I give this *verbatim* out of Bishop Spotiswood ; because his authority is least questioned by the advocates of this cause.*

Upon this answer, which showed a direct invasion of their authority, the Assembly could do no less than assert their right, and therefore rejected him ;† but the Regent commanded the chapter to elect him,‡ and they did so in defiance of the General Assembly.

The Assembly, justly provoked at this, gave a commission to the Superintendent of Lothian§ and two other ministers to call him before them, and prohibit him to exercise any jurisdiction till he should be authorized thereto by the General Assembly.

Here we see a bishop suspended, the royal mandate disputed, and a superintendent who, Spotiswood in another place, says, had Episcopal power, yet a commission from the Assembly, together with other ministers, to suspend only ; which, had he been a bishop, he might have exercised without a commission, if it had been in his own bounds, and could not if he had been a bishop, out of his diocese, by any commission.

Upon this attack of the Church, the Assembly resolving to act with as much temper and moderation as possible, consisting with their right and dignity, and the just authority they possessed, and in order to prevent any more disputes of this kind, resolved, if possible, to fix upon a form of Church polity, and accordingly it was drawn up and offered,‖ in their names, to the Regent ; but the troubles which quickly followed upon this in the State, put a stop to the

---

* Spotiswood, lib. 5, fol. 227. Imparted to them the warrant they had received. The Bishop owns it was a command to the chapter to choose him.
† Ibid. Inhibited the chapter to proceed.
‡ Ibid. Upon a new charge given them, they convened and made choice of him.
§ Calderwood says it was the Superintendent of Fife, which is most likely, St Andrews being in that province.
‖ Spotiswood, lib. 5, fol. 277. The form of Church polity was presented to the Regent by Mr Robert Pont, Mr David Lindsay, and Mr James Lawson.

settling it at this time also, as it had done several times before.* Mr Calderwood gives a long account of the conference of the ministers in the west, with those appointed by the Assembly, in order to fix this ecclesiastical polity, to which I refer; the thing not being obtained, it is not my purpose to enter into particulars other than this, that the Presbyterial authority was clearly established in it, and the very name, as well as office and power, of a bishop left out.

The Regent, who opposed them in all things, did so underhand in this; for it was evident he pushed not at the introducing the bishops only, but even at the dissolution of the Assembly, whose authority was too great for him, and made him uneasy. However, the form was presented, as above, and he did not openly reject it; but started objections, and appointed questions to be answered, and named a Committee of the Council to confer with them about it.

But now a new revolution of affairs happened; for factions rising among the nobility against the Regent, and, as it was thought, he being sensible of his being too weak for them, was advised to stoop to the juncture of affairs, quietly to concede his authority, and demit that power which, it was manifest, he could not keep.

The King was now almost twelve years old, and though he was under governors, yet the faction of Lords not agreeing who to repose the trust in, it was resolved to declare the King major, and put the government into his own hands. This also seemed the more honourable for the Regent; for to have named another after him, had been plainly to have told the world he was turned out; but to resign his government into the King's own hand, had a much greater appearance of honour.

---

* Calderwood, fol. 73, 74, 75, 77, 80. The Regent ever resisted the work of the polity, which was then in hand, and pressed his own injunctions and conformity with England.

He did so; but as great men's fall seldom stop with the loss of their preferments, so it was with him; he past through various troubles, till at last the persecution of his enemies brought him to the block.

The King was young, but began to be informed of things, and as well from Morton at first, as the rest of the courtiers about him afterwards, he received too early prejudices against the constitution of the Church, and in particular he took all occasions to intrench upon the power of the Assembly.

The debate was now wholly about bishops; the Assembly was for reducing their power, which was effectually done as before; they were now for reducing the name too, as a thing which they furnished matter of continual disturbance. So, in the third session of the Assembly 1577, it was ordained, that all bishops and others bearing ecclesiastical function, be called by their own names, or brethren only.*

In the seventh session of the same Assembly they put a stop to the number, and ordered that no bishop be elected or admitted before the next General Assembly; forbidding ministers and chapers to elect, or any way proceed to the election of any bishop, on pain of deprivation.

In the Assembly at Stirling, in June 1578, they made the said law perpetual, and that all bishops already elected be required to submit themselves to the General Assembly; and thus that infant mongrel Episcopacy, so it was then called, was voted out of the Church as a nuisance.

In the same Assembly they appointed a Committee to wait upon the King with the book of polity and a supplication, which was done; and they were received well enough by the king with good words and promises of kindness and countenance, and a certain

---

* Calderwood's Hist. fol. 82.   That the said Act shall be extended to all times to come, and till the corruption of the state of bishops be utterly removed out of the Church.

number named by the council to confer with them;
though the King himself secretly hated both their
persons and measures, for which reason nothing could
be obtained by that conference.

The 16th of July after, the Parliament met; and
the Commissioners appointed by the Assembly to
wait upon the Parliament solicited to have the book of
polity brought in there and confirmed; but the nobility always put it off, having, as afterwards appeared, no kindness for the strictness and severity of
Presbyterian discipline.

Morton's fall was not yet; for he still guided the
King, and instilled early thoughts into him in prejudice of the Kirk, and in favour of the bishops.

However, the Church went on against them, and
the Assembly fell particularly upon two by name—
viz., Mr Patrick Adamson, whom Morton, by his letter, had made Bishop of St Andrews, and Mr John
Boyd, Bishop of Glasgow.

But now a second attempt was made upon the
Church, and that was by the King himself, or at least
in his name. The Assembly, as has been noted, having long struggled to obtain their book of polity, they
had been always, though not absolutely, denied to have
it passed, yet so delayed and postponed, that it was easy
to see the Court was against them, and that it was not
designed to be passed at all; nevertheless, they went on
upon the foot of the scheme formed, as what was their
just right to demand, though they had not influence
enough upon the Government to obtain the grant.

Being thus, as I have noted, proceeding upon the
footing of the polity as their right, they received a letter
from the King, dated at Stirling the 6th of July
1579, inhibiting them to proceed, and commanding
them to refer all the matters undecided in the polity
of the Kirk to the decision of the next Parliament. *

* Calderwood, fol. 86. The words in the letter are—forbearing any
proceedings at this time that touch matters heretofore not concluded

The Assembly, notwithstanding this letter, went on; but with all the caution and respect possible.

They examined the articles referred, and presented an address to the King, desiring a farther conference upon the affair of the polity, and following this with a long supplication, to move the King to farther this book of polity.

While this was in consideration, and two or three years spent in the pressing the polity on the one hand, and putting it off on the other, in the year 1580, the General Assembly, finding, as they apprehended, that all they had yielded to before as to the word bishop, was improved to enlarge the office and extend the power of a bishop, resolved to pull it up by the roots, and remove the very name of it out of the Church; and in order to this they passed two acts, entirely abrogating the office as unscriptural, declaring it void and unlawful, as having no warrant or foundation in the Word of God—which acts, being very remarkable, are worth perusing, and therefore, as abridged, are in the notes underneath.*

---

by our laws, or received into practice; but whatsoever in the former Conferences, touching the polity of the Kirk, was remitted to be decided by our estates in Parliament, let it so rest without prejudging the same by any of your conclusions at this time.

* Forasmuch as the office of a bishop, as it is now used and commonly taken within this realm, hath no sure warrant, authority, nor good ground out of the Book of Scripture, but is brought in by the folly and corruption of men's invention, to the great overthrow of the true Kirk of God: The whole Assembly, in one voice, after liberty given to all men to reason in the matter, none opposing themselves in defence of the said pretended office, findeth and declareth the same pretended office, used and termed as abovesaid, unlawful in itself; as having neither fundament, ground, nor warrant in the Word of God; and ordaineth, that all such persons as brook, or hereafter shall brook the said office, be charged *simpliciter* to demit, quit, and leave off the same, as an office whereunto they are not called by God, and siclike to desist and cease from preaching, ministration of the sacraments. or using any way the office of pastor, while they receive *de novo* admission from the General Assembly, under the pain of excommunication, if they be found disobedient, to be pronounced and executed against them.

THE SECOND ACT.—For the better executing the former Act, it is ordained, that a Synodal Assembly, the 17th of August next to come, shall be holden in every province where any usurping bishops are. whereunto they shall be summoned by the visitors of the said country —viz., the Bishop of St Andrews to compear at St Andrews, the Bishop

Putting all these accounts together with as much impartiality as possible, it is manifest, and, I think out of dispute, that the Church of Scotland was in its original Presbyterian. I have nothing to do here with the differences or the disputes about which is the most Scriptural, Episcopacy or Presbytery,—that dispute is handled very strongly by itself; but the reason I have been so long on this part, is to clear up the question which has been the occasion of so much debate in the world, whether the First Reformation of Scotland was Episcopal or Presbyterian.

The Court had, indeed, from the latter end of the Earl of Mar's administration, struggled hard with the Assembly to reserve its own power, and to have some share in the matter independent of the Assembly; and at the Convention at Leith, they got ground as has been hinted; but the Assembly vigorously opposed it, and afterwards overthrew it all again, and by these acts entirely abolished the very name of a bishop in the Church.

I come now to enter into a sad series of strife between the Church and the Court upon this very subject; which continued with infinite struggles, ups and downs, intervals of liberty, storms of tyranny, some horrid scenes of ruin and destruction, and perhaps some extremes on both sides; all which harrassed this poor kingdom, till at last the restoration of King Charles II. brought the Church quite under foot; and there begins her persecuted state, of which by itself.

The Court were, no question, very ill pleased with this proceeding of the Assembly, but they went still

---

of Aberdeen in Aberdeen, the Bishop of Murray at Elgin, the Bishop of Glasgow in Glasgow, to give obedience to the said Act, which if they refuse to do, the said Synodal Assembly shall appoint them to receive admonition out of the pulpit, warning them to compear before the General Assembly in Edinburgh, the 20th of October next, to hear the sentence of excommunication pronounced against them for their disobedience.

NOTE.—The Bishop of Dunblane quietly conformed and submitted to this Act.

on with steadiness. Several of the bishops submitted to this order of the Assembly, and made their submission, the copies of which, by after times, their successors being ashamed so plain a testimony of fact should appear, have been erased out of the registers.*

At length the King being advanced by the death of the Queen of England to the united crown of Great Britain, the disputes rested for some time, the Court being taken up with the rejoicings of their new acquisition, and with the other incidents of the new government ; and by this means the Church of Scotland may be said to have got some ground, even at that time when the King, who was their avowed enemy, was so increased in power as to be formidable to them.

But the King was taken up with mirth, and the Court in revels, I had almost said in debauchery ; and not the King only, but the nobility also, who were always the hinderers of the Reformation, were now absent, and not so much concerned about what became of the Church, when they had their private fortunes to make by the favour of their Prince. This absence of the Court, I say, gave the Church great advantage, and the General Assembly continued to assert and maintain their Establishment as Presbyterian in opposition to Episcopacy, notwithstanding all the injunctions and interruptions which they met with from the Court; and, therefore, this may very well be called the growing state of the Kirk.

But to go back to what happened in the meantime. It was about the year 1582, that the King by the ill Government of the Duke of Lennox, Earl of Arran,

---

* Calderwood, fol. 92. There wanteth here in the register part of the third session, the whole fourth, fifth, sixth, and part of the seventh, riven out, as the rest of them were by the same sacrilegious hands in the year 1584, where the submission of the Bishops of Glasgow, St Andrews, and the Isles were set down, every one of whom accepted a particular kirk (and so from bishops, as now meant, became ministers only, or bishops in a Scripture sense).

&c , who had him, as it might be said, in tutelage, had not only imposed and intruded the so much abhorred Prelacy upon the Church, but had insulted the Church in their discipline and government, on many occasions too long to relate ; as particularly in the affair of Montgomery, and the tumult in Glasgow, where, in defence of a man excommunicated for notorious scandal, they mobbed the Presbytery, beat and very ill treated Mr John Howison the moderator, and wounded several of the students of the college ; nor was it far from setting fire to the college itself.   It was said, that some of the King's guards were employed upon this riot, to encourage a tumult; for that the common people could not otherwise be brought to injure the ministers after such a manner.

But the Kirk recovered all this, when a few weeks after happened that memorable attempt of the noblemen against Lennox and Arran, called the Raid of Ruthven, taking the King out of their hands by force, and carrying him to Stirling.   This, I say, was called the Raid of Ruthven, of which we shall hear a great deal more, and was put in execution, August 20. 1582, as the King came back from the great annual hunting in Athol.

It is not our purpose to enter into the history or causes of this attempt.   It is enough to say, that the power of these two noblemen, or at least their imprudent exercising of that power, was become intolerable to the nation ; and the rest of the nobility and gentry concerned, found no other way to deliver themselves from it but to set the King at liberty to act by better council.

They presented a declaration to the King of their reasons for this conduct, and, carrying his Majesty to Stirling, they gave him full liberty of his person, and a free exercise of his government, only taking care that the administration was entirely removed from the hated hands of Lennox and Arran.

The King, though he never forgave this action, and to his last resented it against the Kirk, as if they had been the only instruments, yet complied with the time, and the Earl of Arran being clapped up in Dupplin Castle, and the Duke of Lennox charged by proclamation to depart the country, his Majesty consented that a proclamation should be published, intimating that he was in the town of Perth, at full liberty ; that he staid there of his own choice for some time, and that he approved of all the Lords had done as for his interest and service.   At the same time a proclamation was also published for restoring the liberties of the Kirk, the freedom of their assemblies and judicatures, and for encouraging the ministers in discharge of their duty.

Thus the Church got the day of their adversaries, and all violences offered to their judicatures, the laws made to restrain their liberties or abridge their rights, were declared to be unjust and illegal, and were laid to the charge of the said Duke of Lennox and Earl of Arran ; such as the disposition of benefices *pleno jure*, without the examination of the persons, and admission by the Kirk, making the King and his council judges in matters merely ecclesiastical ; discharging or prohibiting the General Assembly to proceed to excommunication ; annulling the sentence of excommunication when past ; Prelacy obtruded upon them contrary to the principles of the Church of Scotland, who had declared in the General Assembly, that the same was unscriptural, devilish, and of human invention, and the like.

Upon this declaration a General Assembly was convened to meet at Edinburgh the 9th of October 1582, and this was perhaps the first Assembly, even from the Reformation, in which it might be said the Church had an uninterrupted liberty to exert her full power in her own establishment.

At this Assembly the Laird of Paisley, in the

name of the associated Lords, declared that the dangers of the ecclesiastical constitution, and of religion itself, as well as the danger of the King's person and of the civil government, were the principal causes of their late undertaking, and they desired the concurrence of the Assembly, as well in recognising the necessity of what had been done, as in concerting what was yet to be done, for the establishing and securing both the Church and State.

The Assembly unanimously voted (every member being severally asked) the reality of the dangers attending the Reformation and the Church. The King, upon the Assembly's sending some of their body to him, readily declared, that not only his own person, but religion itself was in peril, and that such measures had been entered into as must necessarily have overturned the Reformation ; that he esteemed his own safety and the safety of religion to be inseparble, and exhorted the Assembly to do their duty to remove the dangers that threatened both him and them.

This occasioned that famous act of the Assembly wherein the Reformation is recognised, and the pursuing it recommended earnestly as well to ministers as people ; all the ministers are exhorted to set forth the dangers of the Church, the King, and the commonwealth, to their flocks, in the most pressing manner, urging all who love and tender the glory of God, the prosperous state of the King and commonwealth, to concur with them in their endeavour to their full deliverance.

After this the Assembly proceeded with vigour to exert themselves. They erected Presbyteries and Church judicatures in such parts where there were none before, as in the northern provinces of Sutherland, Caithness, Ross, Murray, Aberdeen, &c.

Then they empowered the Presbyteries to summon before them the bishops, and to cause them to answer to the said Presbyteries for such offences as they should be accused of. The crimes the said bishops were thus accused of were such as these : Not preaching, and administering the sacraments, as is the duty of a gospel minister ; neglect in discipline ; error in doctrine ; associating themselves with excommunicated persons ; wasting of the patrimony of the Kirk ; letting leases of land against the prohibitions of the Kirk ; collating to benefices against the tenor of the acts of the Kirk ; scandal in life and conversation ; and many other things, not then articled, which were left to the examination of witnesses. And the Presbyteries were farther empowered to hear, try, acquaint, and condemn, as the matters of fact should appear to them.

The time was now come when the authority of the Church had its full establishment. The convention of estates, which was then called, and which met at Perth, gave room to the Assembly to lay all their grievances before them, which was done in twenty-two articles, and their demands of particular redress for wrong and wreck, as it was called, in eleven articles more.

The bishops were now deposed, and many of them submitted to become pastors of private parish churches.

The Laird of Minto, who, at the head of a mob, had insulted the Moderator of the Presbytery of Glasgow, submitted himself to the Assembly, and begged pardon.

Mr Robert Montgomery, whose case had raised such disputes between the King and the Church—the Church excommunicating him, and the King restoring him by proclamation—came in and submitted, offering to undergo the injunctions of the Presbytery of Glasgow, and desiring to be received into the bosom of the Church.

And thus stood the affairs of the Church at the beginning of the year 1583, but it continued but for a short while ; for the King, impatient of the good government of the Lords, and inwardly hating the Church, contrived to make his escape from Falkland, which, by the assistance of another faction among the nobility, he effected the 28th of August 1583, taking refuge in the castle of St Andrews. Thither repaired immediately all those among the nobility who were privy to the design ; and thus they laid the foundation of an entire change of measures and persons in his administration.

As in the State so in the Church, all things tended to change ; saving only that the Assembly, maintaining their principles, stood their ground against the Court with a constancy of zeal which could never be subdued.

However, the bishops immediately got footing by this turn of the Court, and the Bishop of St Andrews being in the castle there, immediately re-assumed his office and character, presuming on the King's protection as openly as if he had been placed in it by a legal authority, even the King himself not yet declaring his consent to his attempt.

During these transactions the General Assembly convened at Edinburgh, viz. the 20th of October ; nor did they slack their hands in their proceedings against the bishops, notwithstanding the King appeared now openly of the Prelatic party ; for they called for the report of their commissioners appointed by the former Assembly to proceed against four delinquent bishops, viz. the Archbishop of St Andrews, the Bishops of the Isles, Dunkeld, and Dunblane.

The Archbishop had been summoned by the Synod of Fife, *apud acta*, to appear at this Assembly, which, he now thinking himself too high to submit to, declined to do ; so they proceeded against him as in contempt ; and the process against his woman counsellor, Alison Pearson, as a witch, was also brought before the Assembly, and a committee was appointed to examine witnesses against them both.

F

They also resolved now to make a representation of their grievances, and of the state of the Church and kingdom, and lay the same before the King himself in discharge of themselves.   This some of the ministers pressed with the more earnestness, prophetically suggesting that a cloud of darkness and persecution was coming upon them, and would break over their heads in a violent and furious storm, as well from the prelates as from the King himself.   The heads of this representation are at large to be seen in the histories of those times.   Having drawn out their grievances,* some of which pointed directly to the King as a favourer of the enemies of God, as well Popish as Prelatic, they sent ten commissioners with it to the King, then at Stirling.   They were very coldly received, and told that the King advised the Assembly to keep within the bounds of their proper business.   The commissioners were sent back again to desire a more particular answer, but were told they had been fully answered already.

At this time, two of the most bold and zealous members of the Assembly died, viz. Mr Alexander Arbuthnott, Principal of the College at Aberdeen, and Mr Thomas Smeton, Principal of the College at Glasgow.   By the loss of these two great men, their hands were extremely weakened in the struggles they were quickly to meet with.

However, during the sitting of this Assembly, they abated nothing of what they thought their duty. They prosecuted the Archbishop to such a height, that he was obliged to feign an embassy into England upon public affairs, though others said he was worse employed ; and, fearing a sentence of deposition, he obtained from the King to be freed from censure during his absence.   It was said that, during this journey into England, he concerted with some of the

---

* Calderwood, Hist. fol. 142.

Episcopal clergy there those wicked measures by which he afterwards oppressed the Church of Scotland, and in the end overthrew it for a time.

That famous supporter of the Church's cause, Mr John Durie, was one of the first that felt the effects of the new change, being commanded by the King to depart from Edinburgh, and remain at Montrose, which he submitted to; but both the Town Council and the Kirk-session of Edinburgh gave him noble testimonials both of his life and doctrine; which was more to his honour than all the reproach his enemies laid upon him could overbalance.

The persecuting the ministers was the first work the new Establishment began with, before they fell upon the Church itself; and even in their dealing with the ministers they acted cautiously, and strove to begin with such things as they called legal prosecutions for pretended offences. Afterwards they grew bolder, and fell upon them in a grosser manner.

In these pretended legal prosecutions, Mr Andrew Melvin's case was the most famous example. He was summoned before the Council, where he was questioned for offensive words spoken in the pulpit on a fast day, reflecting on the King and his administration, saying that the King was unlawfully promoted to the crown, with other seditious words. The University, resolving to assert their privileges, sent two of their body with a testimonial in his behalf, signed by thirty of their principal men, masters as well as students, and demanded that he should be censured only by the University; the Presbyteries of the bounds sent commissioners to protest against the proceedings as against the liberties of the Church; and Mr Melvin himself declined the jurisdiction of the Council in his case, in a long declaration, which is to be seen at large in Mr Calderwood's history, fol. 144, 145. But all these were rejected by the Council. In this declaration, he both positively denied the words, solemnly and before

God protesting that he never spoke them, accused the informer of malice and declared prejudice, and justified what he had really said to be according to God's Word and his own duty. Upon giving in this declaration, he retired into England, having notice that he was to be confined in Blackness Castle. After his retreat, he was publicly praised, and prayed for in the pulpit by the ministers in Edinburgh, which, as the history of those times expresses it, pleased the people, and galled the Court.

In the meantime the land was full of troubles. The Lords of Angus and Mar surprised the Castle of Stirling; but their great friend Gowrie being taken, and others secured, and they being not strong enough to defend themselves against the young King, who came against them with a great army, they fled into England; the castle was surrendered, and the captain and three others who surrendered it were hanged. This attempt weakened the hands of the Church and their friends, making their enemies not only more strong but also more furious than they were before. The General Assembly was appointed to be held at St Andrews the 24th of April 1584, where the number of ministers who durst appear were but very few—the Commissioner whom the King sent to them, Graham of Halyards, at the time Justice-Depute, being their declared and enraged enemy.

This Graham used them after an unaccustomed manner, exerting a power which they allowed not to be the right even of the King himself. He treated them in a rude and imperious manner also, with all possible disrespect. First he demanded of them, on pain of rebellion and treason, to annul a former act of Assembly, approving the Raid of Ruthven, and by a new act to condemn it. At the same time he entered into a treaty with the Provost and Bailies of St Andrews to imprison those ministers that should not comply. But the ministers got notice of it, and being resolved not to comply, they silently declined the Assembly, and dropt out of town one by one, leaving the Commissioner to sit by himself. He had, it seems, private instructions to seize upon four of the leading ministers—viz., Mr James Lawson, David Lindsay, Patrick Galloway, and Andrew Hay. The three first appeared in the Assembly, but he being willing to snap them all at once, waited for the fourth, till those that were there got notice and escaped, and so he missed them all; for which he was very much laughed at. The few ministers that remained refused to act, giving for answer that they were too few to constitute an Assembly; so the Commissioner retired.*

The four ministers above named were sought after high and low to be apprehended, and would have been put to death, especially Mr Patrick Galloway; but they made their escape for that time, as did also many other ministers, such as Mr John Davidson, Mr James Carmichael, Mr Andrew Polwart, and many others.

Now was the Court resolved, in conjunction with the bishops, to ruin and overthrow the Church; and to this end, the negotiations of the Archbishop in England having succeeded so far as to have all possible concurrence from thence, to finish it the King called a Parliament. In this Parliament matters were managed so underhand by the Court, that it seemed rather a private council than a Parliament. The Lords of the Articles, which were a committee so called whose work it was to prepare business for the cognizance of the house, were sworn to secrecy, and when the house sat the doors were locked up.

---

* At this Assembly, the Court exercised great and undue authority: for the nobility, barons, and gentlemen, who, as ruling elders, were used to be sent up from the provinces, and were allowed to sit and vote with them, were forbid to come up and take their places in the Assembly.

However, the ministers got intelligence of what was doing. Calderwood, in his account of this part, says one of the Lords of the Articles betrayed them, fol. 155. Be that as it will, a letter was privately sent to the ministers in Edinburgh, from an unknown hand, assuring them that the whole business of that Parliament was to destroy the Church, and bid them take speedy care about it. The ministers knew not what to do, but they deputed Mr David Lindsay, minister of Leith, who was thought to be a man acceptable to the King, to represent their case, and to pray, in the humblest manner, that an Assembly might be called and heard in Parliament, before any thing was done to the prejudice of the Church; but instead of hearing this, the King caused Mr Lindsay to be apprehended as he was going into the palace, and carried away to Blackness Castle, without permitting him to deliver his message. They sent other messengers to make protest in open Parliament, but to no purpose; they could not get in. However, two ministers, viz. Mr Robert Pont, and Mr Balcanquell, by their private interest, did get in, and did make a protest against the proceedings.

Not content with this proceeding, the King and Council sent an order to the Magistrates of Edinburgh, that in case any minister did in the pulpit offer to speak any thing against the proceedings of the Parliament, they should instantly pull them down from the pulpit, and commit them to prison. So the acts were passed to destroy the Church, and to erect the Episcopal hierarchy in its room, and were proclaimed at the Market Cross of Edinburgh. The said Mr Pont and Mr Balcanquell took instruments of their protest against it in the name and on behalf of the Church; but the said ministers had no sooner done so but they were obliged to fly, as did also Mr James Lawson, and several others.

These acts of Parliament, for protesting against

which the ministers were thus used, amounted to neither more nor less than an acknowledgment of the King's supremacy, and the government of the Church by bishops, &c.

It has been an observation, which, I believe, will hold good throughout all ages of the Church since the Reformation, that no sooner was Episcopacy, upon any occasion, set up in the Church of Scotland, but it began always to persecute the Presbyterian Church. And this was the case here; for soon after this the Parliament sat again, viz. the 28th of August 1584, when an act was made, enjoining all ministers, masters of colleges, and other ecclesiastical persons, to appear within forty days, and subscribe the new constitution of the Church, as it was then called, and submit to their diocesan, on pain of loosing their stipends.

Some ministers refused this, and were sorely persecuted by the Council; but they continued to declare against it as illegal, and being questioned by the Council how they durst oppose or condemn an act of Parliament, they answered boldly, that they would condemn every thing that was repugnant to the Word of God. Mr Craig, one of these ministers, was greatly insulted by the Earl of Arran; but he answered him in a kind of prophetic rage, that God should, in a short time, cast him from his horse, meaning his pride and power, and humble him for mocking the servants of God. This came literally to pass in a few years after, the Earl being unhorsed by Douglas of Parkhead, and killed.

On this occasion Mr Craig was deprived, and forbid to preach in Edinburgh, and the Archbishop went up into his pulpit to preach, by order of the King and Council; but when the people saw him come up into the pulpit, instead of their own minister, they universally rose and went out of the church, the Court party only remaining in the place. The copy of the subscription required of the ministers was as follows:—

"We, the beneficed men, ministers, and masters of schools and colleges, testifie and promise, by these our hand-writes, our dutiful and humble submission to our Sovereign Lord the King's Majesty, and to obey, with all humility, his highness' act of his late Parliament, holden at Edinburgh the 22d day of May 1584. And that according to the same we shall shew our obedience to our ordinair bishop, or commissioner appointed by his Majesty to have the exercise of spiritual jurisdiction in our diocess. And in case of our disobedience in these premisses, to be content that our benefices, livings, and stipends vaik *ipso facto*, and that qualified and obedient persons be provided in our room, as if we were naturally dead. Witness," &c.

The ministers that refused to subscribe this paper went into voluntary banishment and remained in England, but mostly about Berwick, where the banished Lords also resided; but they had their preaching even there, but in private; for such was the correspondence between the Episcopal people in Scotland and the Church of England, that albeit the Queen of England permitted the banished Lords and ministers of Scotland to harbour in England, yet she would not admit them to have preaching in public, as not being consonant to the worship of the Church in England. Great instance was made to Queen Elizabeth to deliver up those noblemen and fugitive ministers, which nevertheless she would never do; but she yielded at last to oblige them to reside farther from the Borders.

During these oppressions, many ministers of the Kirk complied with and subscribed the form above, with some alterations. Mr Andrew Simson, minister of Dalkeith, subscribed thus :—

"I Master Andrew Simpson, minister of Dalkeith, swear by the name of the great God, that I shall not preach any heresy or seditious doctrine, nor shall privately or publicly stir up the King's Majesty's subjects to any rebellion, and shall obey all his laws and acts of Parliament, so far as they agree with the Word of God."

Others absolutely refused, and Mr Dalgliesh, minister of the West Kirk at Edinburgh, was one; insomuch that a scaffold was erected for his execution, which, however, could not bring him off, neither would he ever comply. At last the Court was fain to publish an explanation of it, softening the meaning; but though this explanation, which was penned by the Archbishop, was accepted with much applause in England, and the Scotch ministers were censured then for rejecting it, yet it gained but very little upon the ministers in Scotland, and served only to shew the weakness of those acts which they took so much pains to explain.

In this condition stood the Church for some years, struggling with daily innovations, the King their open and declared enemy, and only supported by the integrity of her ministers and people. The great subject upon which the ministers were persecuted was, the subscribing the obligation mentioned; all such as refused were displaced and turned out; and this continued to the year 1587, when it pleased God to give a new turn to the affairs of Scotland, of which the following brief account will inform us.

The banished Lords, who, as has been said, the Queen of England had been unkind to, were gone south: but an accident happened upon the Borders which brought them back; for, on the 26th of July 1585, at a meeting of the Wardens of the Borders on either side, to adjust some disputes, instead of an agreement, they fell to blows, and the young Lord Russell, eldest son to the Earl of Bedford, with some other Englishmen, were slain by the laird of Ferniburst. Queen Elizabeth resenting this as a high affront, showed her resolution to revenge it; and immediately, as a beginning, she smiled upon the refugee Lords, and encouraged them with money and promises of assistance to return into their country by a strong hand. The confusions which then happened at Court gave them a very good opportunity; and several discontented Lords, some under prosecutions for different causes, not religion, all joined with these to recover their liberty by force, and to lay hold of this occasion as offered by heaven for their return.

About the beginning of October, the banished Lords from abroad, and the discontented Lords at home, met at Jedburgh; and, mustering their forces, found they had between nine and ten thousand men well appointed. The King and the Earl of Arran lay at Stirling with few forces; the Lords advanced to Falkirk, and the next day to Stirling. The Earl of Arran, the Archbishop, and all the wicked crew passed quickly over the Forth, pursued faster by their own guilt than by their enemies. The castle surrendered the 4th of November, and the Lords presented themselves to the King.

And now the hypocritical face being put outermost, they were received with kindness and favour, though nothing less intended or desired; the Episcopal crew flew while none pursued; the King owned he had been abused, promised to be directed by their counsel, and pretended to acknowledge the good hand of God in bringing things to their due course again, and restoring them, who were his faithful friends, without bloodshed.

The scene being thus changed, Episcopacy vanished in a moment as a vapour before the sun, a Parliament was summoned, and the Church got its Assembly again, which had been suppressed for nearly three years.

This Assembly was appointed for the 23d of November 1587, and the place named was Dunfermline, the plague reigning both at Edinburgh and Stirling; but when the ministers came thither, they found the ports of the town shut against them, by order of the laird of Pitferren, so they adjourned to Linlithgow.

But the King, who mortally hated the Kirk, began now to work another way ; for, as he could not recover the party that was now banished and fled, he fell to flattering the returned Lords, and by smooth words, entreaties, promises, bribes, &c., to bring them off from their engagements with the ministers ; so that, when the Assembly applied to the King to abrogate the acts of Parliament which were their present grievance, the King flew out in the greatest rage imaginable, giving them vile and scurrilous language, and railing them out of his sight.

Having met with this repulse, they applied to the Lords, but were sorely abashed when they found them cold and backward ; some proposing delays, others declining to meddle with it at all, others promising fair, but doing nothing, and all of them willing to put it off to another occasion.   But the ministers besieging the King with continually insisting upon redress, he commanded them to exhibit what they alleged against the acts of Parliament in writing.   This they did at large, with a supplication to the King to do them right ; all which are at large in Calderwood's history, fol. 192, 193.

The King made a declaration, in answer to this, explaining the acts of Parliament, and justifying them in all points.   And thus it seemed to be a dispute between the Kirk and the King ; for this declaration is said to be penned by the King himself.   The King would grant no more than this declaration allowed, so the Kirk returned a supplication to the King, and thus it stood for that year.   This declaration and supplication are curious pieces for those to read who desire to be fully masters of this dispute, and much has been said of the extraordinary nicety and subtilty of the composition.   They are to be found at large in the history of those times.*

---

* Calderwood, Hist. fol. 193 to 193.

As the Assembly was now revived, so were the Provincial Synods ; and as that of Fife especially had been discontinued because of their having fallen upon the Archbishop of St Andrews, upon their being now revived, they renewed their accusation, and it came in its order before the Synod assembled at St Andrews, who, after very mature debates, the Archbishop himself being at first present, excommunicated him. The sentence was very particular, and merits a place in these memoirs, as follows, viz.——

" The Assembly anent the process deduced against Mr Patrick Adamson, having considered and tried the same with mature deliberation, and after conference held, hath found, that the said Mr Patrick Adamson hath no ways amended his contumacy and disobedience to the voice of the Church of God, and of the said Assembly, convened in the name of our Lord Jesus ; but rather continuing therein, contemptuously travelleth to usurp and exercise his tyrannical ambition and supremacy over the Church of God, his brethren, and this Assembly, with sundry slanderous untruths, as well against the word as against some of the brethren; and being desired by diverse admonitions, given him in the name of the Assembly, to hear the voice of the Church, he not only contemptuously and disdainfully refuseth the censure and judgment, and to be tried by the said Assembly, but, claiming supremacy and judgment above them, heapeth up contempt upon the ordinance of Jesus Christ ; adding thereunto the notoriety of the former accusation against him before the General Assembly, wherein he was thought worthy, for weighty causes and great crimes, to be suspended from all function of the ministry, as by the said act of suspension appears; contrair to the tenor whereof he hath not only usurped again the said function, &c. against the ordinance of the Church, but also hath displayed a banner against the whole good order and government of the Church: Therefore, and for divers other notorious slanders, whereof he stands accused, and refuses to undergo lawful trial, the Assembly, in the fear of God, and in the name of Jesus Christ, moved by zeal to the glory of God, and for purging of his Church, excommunicates him the said Patrick Adamson, and ordains the said sentence of excommunication instantly to be put in execution in the face of the Assembly, and by the mouth of Mr Andrew Hunter, minister of Carnbee, declaring him to be one of those whom Christ commandeth to be holden as an heathen or publican—ordaining the said sentence to be intimated in all the kirks, that none pretend ignorance thereof."

The Archbishop appealed, and excommunicated several of the ministers; but he was answered by Mr James Melvin at large, and this is the sentence which the Bishop begged at his death to be absolved from. These things held the world in suspense till the next Assembly met, which was in May 1585. This was that famous Assembly, called the Assembly of Conference; wherein a conference was managed by commissioners on both sides, and an accommodation was proposed. The King insisted upon the name of Bishop, the Assembly upon the power and office. The Assembly granted the name, and the King gave up the power; and thus the matter seemed to be compromised between them. And it is from this Assembly, that, to this day, the Episcopal party say, that the Presbyterians did acknowledge Episcopacy; but if they look into the particulars of the Bishop which they allowed, they will find that he was to be a pastor of a congregation, and that he was to be subject to the Assembly, and that he came under several other circumstances, which will very ill support that assertion.

In this Assembly, at the King's request, and upon the Archbishop's submission, they took off the excommunication, pronounced at the Synod of Fife against the Archbishop of St Andrews, and absolved him.

But against this absolution one of the ministers, viz. Mr Andrew Hunter by name, gave in that memorable protestation, which stands upon record in the book of the Assembly, and to which afterwards most of the rest of the ministers adhered, which I have added at the end of this part, No. I.

It was observed that the King wrought with this Assembly by much policy and cunning. He had, by experience, found that rigid methods, persecutions, and prosecutions, would not answer, and that the ministers became rather the more constant, or obstinate, as he called it, by such methods; wherefore he went other ways to work, and seeking by all secret and underhand dealings to divide and draw off, to please, wheedle, persuade, entreat, and deceive; by these methods he got many of the brethren to act a different part from what they would otherwise have done. This was evident in the case of the Archbishop, where he formally submitted, but secretly abhorred them; the Church formally absolved him, and yet secretly believed him to be unreformed.

However it was the Church, in all this time kept upon its feet, though in continual broils with the King upon the subject of Episcopacy, and as well about the authority as the name of a bishop. There were two Assemblies in the year 1587, but the latter was convened extraordinary, because of the growing danger of Popery; the island being under great apprehensions at that time from the threatened invasion of the Spanish Armada, and during which the disputes at home were somewhat abated; and it was on this occasion that the agreement, called the General Band, was subscribed by the King, Council, and several persons of divers estates through the whole kingdom, which, in short, was neither more or less than what we now call an association, and was done against the Papists, in which are these words—" And for our farther hearty union in this service, we are content, and consent that all and whatsoever our feuds and variances, fallen, or that may fall out between us, be within forty days hereafter amicably referred and submitted to seven or five indifferent friends, chosen by his Majesty, of our whole number ; and by their moderation and arbitriment taken away and componed.   And finally, that we will neither directly or indirectly separate or withdraw us from the union or fellowship of one another ; and as we shall answer to God upon our consciences ; and to the world, upon our truth and honour, and under pain to be esteemed traitors to God and his Majesty, and to have lost all honour, credit, and estimation in time coming."

They were at this time under apprehensions, as is said, of the Spanish invasion, and the next Assembly being on the 6th of August in Edinburgh, appointed a solemn Fast upon that occasion.*

Things now remained in tolerable quiet ; the fears of Popish powers were over by defeat of the Spaniards ; and the King, intent upon his marriage with the daughter of the King of Denmark, went over sea to Copenhagen.   The next General Assembly was at Edinburgh, August 4. 1590, and now the King and the Church seemed perfectly reconciled, and, which is more, united.   Of this Assembly I must record something, the truth of which is not to be doubted ; but the more it is certain, the greater brand of infamy and reproach will it leave behind upon the person, who, after this, acted so contrary, in his station, to what he appeared that day.

---

* The Assembly, not the King, appointed this Fast. And at the end of October the same year, a solemn Fast was kept three Sabbaths successively, a Communion celebrated, and the whole concluded with giving thanks for the defeat of the Spanish Armada by the English. All this was without the King.

The eighth session of this Assembly the King came in person into the place where the ministers held their meeting, and being seated in a chair of state, the Moderator, Mr Patrick Galloway, proposed three things to him, viz. the ratification of their liberties, the purging the land of Jesuits, Popish seminaries, &c., and the provision of salaries or stipends in every parish for the ministers. For the first, the King answered, that in every Parliament their liberties were ratified, and should still be so. That he would, with heart and good will, join to do the second ; and for stipends, he referred them to the Council, and ordered them to name Commissioners to treat with the Council about it. After some other debates, the King stood up, and taking off his bonnet, with his hands and eyes lifted up to Heaven, but hypocritically, say the writers of these times, he broke out, as it were, in an ecstacy of praises and thanksgiving to God. " 1. That he was born into the world at a time when the light of God's word shone clearly forth, eclipsed neither with the mists of ignorance, or the false lights of superstition. 2. He blessed God that had honoured him to be a King over such a Kirk, the sincerest Kirk in the world," repeating it three times. To strengthen this he flew out upon other Protestants, " The Church of Geneva, what are they ? they keep Pasche and Yule, what authority have they in God's word, and where is their institution ? As for our neighbour Church in England," said this most sincere and wise King, whom our English Churchmen after this compared to Solomon for wisdom, " their service is an evil mass said in English, they want nothing of the mass, but the liftings. I charge you my good people," turning himself to every side of the kirk, ministers, doctors, elders, nobles, barons, and gentlemen, " to stand to your purity, and to exhort my people to do the same, and I, forsooth, so long as life and crown be left to me, shall maintain the same against all deadly."

Had he been sincere in this, these words were to be recorded to his honour, but we shall soon see his Majesty acting quite another part. However, for the present, the words, and above all, the affectionate manner with which they were spoken, and their coming from the mouth of their King, unthought of, unexpected by the auditory, so affected the ministers that many burst out into tears for joy ; and Mr Calderwood, relating this passage, says, there was nothing heard for a quarter of an hour in the Assembly, but praising God, and praying for the King.*

While the King continued in this mood the Church got ground, and went on in a truly growing condition ; her judicatories were acknowledged, her authority established, and her Episcopal enemies truckled. And I cannot give a better instance to confirm this last than the submission and recantation of the Archbishop of St Andrews, the most implacable and inveterate enemy of the Church, who had mortgaged faith and conscience for the cause of Episcopacy, and had made shipwreck of both, as will appear under his hand. This recantation being so eminent, and the character of the man so well known, it is necessary to record it with the history of the times, because it is a standing monument of the subjection of the Episcopal hierarchy to the Presbyterial institution.

Nor can the friends of the Church of Scotland desire two greater testimonies to her divine institution than these from the mouths of her two greatest opposers, viz. the King and the Archbishop. The acknowledgment of enemies has a double force in it. It is a confession that comes generally extorted by the force of truth, and the influence of conscience, as Julian the apostate acknowledged Christ, when the

---

* Calderwood's History of the Church of Scotland, fol. 256.

G

poisoned dart stuck in his flesh.   If we may believe
the history of that time, the Church of Scotland had
not two more such powerful, and perhaps implacable
enemies in that age, nay, scarcely before or since, as
the King and the Archbishop, and both of them are
now brought to acknowledge the purity of her doctrine
and the exactness of her discipline ; the one to thank
God for being born under such a sincere and heavenly
institution ; the other to cry God and the Church's
mercy for his apostatizing from it, and desiring to die
in the arms of that Church of which before he had
been so cruel a persecutor.

But to go on with the Bishop's story.   He had been
excommunicated by the Synod of Fife, as has been
said ; one of his crimes was marrying the Marquis
of Huntly, without requiring him to subscribe the
Confession of Faith, and after the Presbytery of Edinburgh had inhibited any minister to do it.   For this
he was pursued at law, and stood out to a horning,
as it is there called, viz. to a contempt or execution ;
and the King beginning to be weary of the contest,
and willing, perhaps, at that time to please the Assembly, abandoned him and deprived him of the
revenue of the bishoprick ; whether these misfortunes,
or the reproaches of his own conscience, brought him
down, I will not determine, charity bids us judge the
best.   But he fell into a languishing and grievous
sickness.   In this condition he acknowledged his offence against God and against the ministers, and sent
to them to let them know it, and to offer himself to
make public confession in the pulpit, to give satisfaction to all who had been offended at his behaviour.
He sent also to the Presbytery of St Andrews, desiring they would give him absolution, and receive him
again into communion, and into the fellowship with
the saints.

The ministers were doubtful of him for a long time,
they knew not the just reasons, however were loath to

resist the work of repentance, if begun in sincerity, and were inclined to receive him, upon his giving satisfaction by a public acknowledgment, as he proposed : but it soon appeared there was no room for it, his sickness being violent and dangerous ; so they directed two of their body to go to him, and inquire of his circumstances, and make their report. These were Mr James Melvin and Mr Andrew Moncrieff. As soon as the Bishop saw them enter his room, he pulled off his cap, and raising himself he said, calling them by their names, " Forgive me, forgive me, for God's sake ; for I have grievously offended you in particular." They replied that they forgave him with all their heart, and gave him their hands thereupon ; but began to talk with him about his public sins, and to exhort him to an unfeigned repentance and amendment. This he received with great affection. Then they proceeded to ask him if he acknowledged the validity of the Church's censure, and of the excommunication he was under. He told them yes, he acknowledged it ; and cried out, I pray ye loose me, loose me, for Christ's sake ; and this he spoke with such earnestness, and with so many tears, that they could no longer doubt of his sincerity, and having comforted him as well as they could, they left him, and making their report to the rest of the ministers, they met thereupon, and in a solemn manner absolved him, giving thanks to God who had been pleased to restore him by conviction and repentance.

In April following, the Synod of Fife meeting at St Andrews, the Bishop (I call him so for distinction, they called him only Mr Patrick Adamson) sent his recantation in Latin ; but the Synod desired him to cause it to be drawn again in English, and that he would make it as full and clear as he could, and set his hand to it, which he did, and which is so worthy to be read with the rest of the story, that I could not omit placing it in the appendix to this part, No. II. There needs no more to be added of the bishop, save that about February, the year following, he died.

At this time, if ever in this King's reign, the Church may be said to have been in its full grown strength, though it lasted not long ; for the King having, as was said, smiled upon them, carressed and complimented them, though it soon appeared that it was no more, and their arch-enemy having, as above, been reduced, they enjoyed a great measure of liberty and authority. Some few things indeed were wanting, which they set forth in their petitions to the King and Council in nine articles, which, though the King did not immediately grant, yet they had kind answers, and so much was done as to make them something easy. These articles were—

1. That all laws that have been made for the weal of the true Kirk be ratified in Parliament, and a new act passed, establishing the jurisdiction of the Kirk, and all contrary laws be abolished.

2. That the Kirk and country be forthwith purged from Popish priests and excommunicates.

3. That a law be made for repressing and punishing the abusers of the sacraments.

4. That ministers be maintained in the possession of their glebes, manses, &c.

5. That order be taken with the author of the tumult at the Bridge of Dee.

6. That laws be made against violating the Sabbath, and disturbing of ministers in, or going about the execution of their office.

7. Ibid. for repressing of rapine and murder, that the land may be purged of blood.

8. That all churches be forthwith planted with ministers, &c., and sufficient stipends allotted them.

9. That the lands mortified to the Church, i. e. given by deceased persons in their will, with the

residue of the tithes, which are not employed for ministers' stipends, be bestowed on the schools, colleges, &c. As also for provision for the poor, and repairing the kirks.

All these things the King had promised in general terms formerly to perform, but it seems the ministers found not the effect of those promises as they desired, and therefore to the said articles they added one, which the King took not well at their hands, viz., That in respect many things had been promised, but few performed, that now the manner and time of performing should be expressed, and the execution of every part agreed to. This clause seemed to reproach the King with evil treating the Church, which he laid up in his heart.

And now the ministers thought the time was come, and an opportunity presented, when the polity of the Church might be confirmed, and the Book of Discipline be recognised; and though they foresaw that they would find it very difficult to bring the King and his great men to it so as to get it enacted in Parliament, they resolved, however, to give it all the sanction they could. The Commission of the General Assembly therefore published an act to " Order and appoint (these are the very words) that whosoever hath borne office in the ministry within this Kirk, or presently bear, or hereafter shall bear office therein, do, and shall subscribe the heads of the discipline of the Kirk within this realm, at length set down and allowed by act of the whole Assembly, in the book of polity, registered in the register of the Kirk, and namely in the heads controverted by the enemies of the discipline of the reformed Kirk in this realm, and that they be charged to do so by every particular presbytery where they be resident ; and this, under pain of excommunication, to be executed against the non-subscribers, and the presbyteries which shall be negligent shall receive public rebuke before the whole Assembly."

It is observed, however, in history,* that several ministers in the Church shunned to subscribe, and others that did subscribe fell off and accepted bishopricks in the innovations which soon after were made by the King upon the Church.

Nor was this all. But farther to prove what I have observed of the Church's being arrived to its full grown state, it is to be observed that the Parliament being now summoned to the 29th of May 1692, the Church obtained, in that meeting, a complete ratification of their privileges and government, and particularly of their General Assemblies, Synods, and Presbyteries, which they had for many years before struggled with their princes and governors for, but to no purpose. The tenor of this valuable, and indeed unexpected act of Parliament, is too long to insert at large; but the principal enacting clause is as follows. The whole is to be found among the Scots Acts of Parliament.†

" Our sovereign Lord and estates of Parliament, following the loveable and gued example of their predecessors, have ratified and approved, and by the tenor of this present act, ratifies and approves all liberties, privileges, immunities, and freedoms whatsoever, given and granted by his Highness and his Regents, in his name, or any of his predecessors to the true and holy Kirk, presently established within this realm, and declared in the first act of his Highness' Parliament, the 20th of October 1579, and all and whatsoever acts of Parliament and statutes made before by his Highness and his Regents, anent the liberty and freedom of the said Kirk, and especially the first act of the Parliament of 1581, with the whole particulars there mentioned, which shall be also sufficient as if the samine were here expressed, and all the other

---

* Calderwood's History, fol. 257.
† Scots Acts of Parliament, Part I. p. 607.

acts of Parliament made sensine in favour of the
true Kirk, and sicklike ratifies and approves the
General Assemblies, appointed by the said Kirk, and
declareth it shall be lawful to the Kirk and ministers,
every year at the least, and oftener *pro re nata*, as
occasion and necessity shall require, to hold and keep
General Assemblies, providing that the King's Majesty, or his Commissioner with them, to be appointed
by his Highness, be present at ilk General Assembly, before the dissolving thereof, nominate and
appoint time and place, when and where the next
General Assembly shall be holden; and in case neither
his Majesty nor his said Commissioner be present for
the time in that Town where the said General Assembly shall be holden, then and in that case, it
shall be leesome to the said General Assembly, by
themselves, to nominate and appoint time and place
where the next General Assembly of the Kirk shall
be keeped and holden, as they have been in use to do
thir times by past. And also ratifies and approves
the Synodal, or Provincial Assemblies, to be holden
by the said Kirk and Ministers twice ilk year, as they
have been within every province of this realm, and
also the presbyteries and particular sessions appointed
by the said Kirk, with the whole jurisdiction and discipline of the same Kirk."

Agreed upon by his Majesty in conference had by
his Highness with certain of the Ministers convened
to that effect.

It was at this time that the Assembly took that
freedom which they have been so often reproached
with since, and which, they said, King James never
forgave them, viz., to admonish the King. I shall
give it impartially in the words of their own historians: "The Assembly directed their brethren who
were appointed to present the articles (that is, those
above mentioned) to go immediately to his Majesty,
and to admonish him gravely, in the name of the

eternal God, to have respect in time to the estate of
true religion, to the many murders and oppressions,
daily multiplied, through impunity and lack of justice,
and to discharge the kingly office in both, as he will
eschew the fearful challenge of God, and avert his
wrath off himself and the whole land, and that he
might be the better informed, to lay down the particulars to him, and crave answer."

It is true, it was a freedom which kings have not
been much acquainted with in this age; but the ministers of that age thought it their duty, and perhaps
if ministers had since done their duty with the same
care and conscience, though their kings had been ill
pleased, they had done better for the public, and for
religion also.

However this was done with dutiful respect, and
when the King complained of the freedom, they, for
vindication of their own behaviour to their Prince,
caused the Assembly to pass an act, ordaining that
" no minister within this realm utter from the pulpit
any rash or irreverent speeches against his Majesty,
or his council, or their proceedings; but that all their
public admonitions proceed upon just and necessary
causes, and sufficient warrant, in all fear, love, and
reverence, under pain of deposing the offenders." And
this most effectually clears them from the charge of
being mutinous and rebellious, and of refusing to submit to lawful authority.

It is worth noting, for the observation of the curious, that this happy Parliament, wherein the Church of
Scotland was thus established, and her rights of every
kind recognised, met on that particular day from which
her overthrow was, seventy-two years after, dated.
I mean at the Restoration, viz. the 29th of May.

The authority of the Church being in this flourishing estate, it is necessary to record, to their eternal
praise, as no doubt it is in heaven to their eternal
comfort, how the ministers made use of their time,

and how they applied themselves to discharge the duty which lay upon them as a national Church. I shall single out one or two examples.

1. They appointed a visitation of all the Presbyteries in the kingdom ; and that the Church of Scotland may be a standing example to all the Protestant Churches in the world, I shall give the very words of the act of the Assembly, of the meaning and design of this visitation, as follows :—" Forasmuch as the visiters of Presbyteries, universally throughout the whole realm, are thought a thing very necessary, and from diverse Assemblies commission hath been given for that effect, a necessity yet remaining, which craveth the continuing of the said commission, the Assembly hath given commission to certain brethren, to visit, and try the doctrine, life, conversation, diligence, and fidelity of the pastors, within the said Presbyteries ; and sicklike to try, if their be any of the beneficed number within the samine, not making residence, having no reasonable excuse. If there be any that have dilapidated their benefices, set tacks, and made other dispositions of the same, without the consent of the General Assembly ; any slanderous person, unmeet to serve in the Kirk of God, unable and unqualified to teach and edifie ; and with advice of the Presbytery, within the which the said persons remain, to proceed against them, according to the quality of the offence, according to the acts of the Kirk."

2. The Synod of Fife being met at St Andrews, September 25. 1593, and being informed of the threatenings, the insolence, and the growing power of Papists and other enemies of the truth, and how the impunity in suffering these things to go unpunished was a great and a national sin, moved with this and other signs of imminent danger, made the following conclusion.

" That the pastors of every congregation, being first prepared themselves, by abstinence, prayer, and diligent study, and attendance upon their charge, travel carefully by their doctrine and good example to move and dispose the hearts of their flock to unfeigned repentance, calling for mercy and preservation at the hands of God, that thus both pastor and people may be prepared against that general and solemn fast which the Synod thinketh most needful to be published throughout the realm. The causes whereof, beside the general reasons for humiliation in time past, are as follows."

The causes which are here referred to were summed up in many particulars, referring chiefly to the growth of Popery, idolatry, profaneness, and immorality.*

To this the said Assembly added the directing some of their members to the King. "To tell plainly to his Majesty (these be also their own words) that which all his true subjects think, touching his too much bearing with, favouring and countenancing Papists and traytors, his negligence in repressing idolatry, and establishing the Kingdom of Christ within his realm, and to declare freely to his Majesty the resolution of all his godly and faithful subjects, viz. that they are ready to give their lives, rather than to suffer the same."

This was plain dealing, and this was what the courtiers afterwards called disciplining of the King. But the Synod stopt not here; for they went on to excommunicate the Popish and Spanishly affected nobility, so they then called them, as persons " who, by their idolatry, heresy, blasphemy, apostacy, perjury, and professed enmity to the Kirk and true religion, had, *ipso facto*, cut themslves off from Christ and his Church." This excommunication by the Synod is registered at large in the Acts of the Church, having been afterwards approved by the Assembly. But the King took great distaste at it, and from hencefor-

---

* Calderwood, fol. 289.

ward began to withdraw his countenance and assistance, and favour from the Church, as soon appeared in the consequences : for the Church pursued the excommunicated Lords, the King protected them ; the Church desired the King to give them no access to his person, and the King openly received them at Jedburgh, and the like.

Upon this a meeting, or Convention of ministers, commissioners of boroughs, and barons, met at Edinburgh, and deputed some of their members to wait upon the King. The King refused to admit them, and sent them word he did not acknowledge their Convention, it being without his advice. They insisted upon the legality of their meeting. At last the King yielded, and gave such answers as he thought fit to their advices, but with little satisfaction and perhaps as little sincerity. However, the excommunicated Lords offered themselves to trial, and the King agreed to it, giving a commission for that purpose to a certain number of the Peers and gentlemen to try them. Their names were as follows, viz., the Earls of Huntly, Angus, Errol, laird of Auchindown, and Sir James Chisholme. But the King abolished the whole process afterwards, and by his own royal declaration absolved them all, and that upon conditions not at all acceptable to the General Assembly, who, being met at Edinburgh, May 7. 1594, ratified the excommunication against the Lords, ordered it to be pronounced in every Church in Scotland, and deputed a committee of their ministers to lay a representation of the DANGERS OF THE CHURCH (mark it is an old phrase) before the King, and report his answer. The representation was very long, and the King's answer particular ; but in short, the King promised to forefault the excommunicated Lords ; that is, to outlaw them, and that the Parliament should meet according to the time appointed,—all which was made good, and the excommunicated Lords were declared guilty of high

treason, their coats of arms torn by the herald, and
their estates forfeited ; upon which they broke out into
open rebellion, and thereupon followed the battle of
Balrinness between the Earl of Argyle and the Earls
of Huntly and Errol, wherein the excommunicated
Lords were defeated ; but that is not to our purpose.

Having often quoted Mr Calderwood's history to
the matters of fact here related, I shall now give the
words of that ancient and grave historian to the subject I am upon, confirming what I have said of the
full grown state of the Church ; and I do it here, because that state seemed now to be at its height, and
that this was the time from whence it began sensibly
to decline ; for now the Church fell into difficulties
and strife which eclipsed her glory for many years,
from whence, however, we shall see her quickly rising
again with a double splendour.   Mr Calderwood's observation is this :—

"This year is a remarkable year to the Kirk of
Scotland, both for the beginning and for the end of it.
This Kirk was now come to the greatest purity that
ever it attained unto, so that her beauty was admirable to foreign kirks ; but the devil envying the happiness and laudable proceedings of the ministry, and
assemblies of the Kirk, stirred up both Papists and
politicians to disturb her peace.   The Papists perceived there was no rest for them in Scotland, if the
authority of the Kirk continued ; the politicians feared
that their craft and trade, which is to use indifferently
all men and means to attain to their own ends, and to
set themselves up as it were in the throne of Christ,
should be undone.   Whereas at her earnest desire, the
apostate Earls, Angus, Huntly, and Errol, were fore-
faulted for an unnatural and treasonable conspiracy
with the Spaniard, and were expelled out of the
country ; and she was now setting herself to reform
whatsoever abuses and corruptions were perceived in
her members, and against the re-entry and restora-

tion of the said Earls, but was forced by craft and
policy of politicians and dissembled Papists to take
herself to the defence of her own liberties, and of that
holy discipline which was her bulwark, and to desist
from farther opposition to the re-entry of the excommunicated Earls; for some thorny questions in points
of discipline were devised, whereby her authority was
in many points called in doubt. Ministers were called
before the council to give account of their rebukes in
sermons, and to underly their censure. The ministers of the Kirk of Edinburgh were forced to lurk,
and that Kirk, which was a watch-tower, and shined
as a lamp to the rest, was darkened, and no less danger appeared to threaten the rest. In a word, in the
end of this year began a fearful decay and declining
of this Kirk."

To confirm this, we shall give a summary, and that
a very brief one, of the transactions for the few years
next following, in which the ministers struggled with
the defections of the times, the refractory disposition
of their prince, and the growing insolence of courtiers
and enemies, till they were crushed, and forced to
submit to the pleasure of him who thought fit, at
that time, to bring them under the feet of their enemies for a season.

The next Assembly met the 25th of March 1596;
the King himself came thither. It seems it was to
desire the ministers to forward a loan of money, which
he had designed to propose to the whole kingdom, on
the extraordinary occasions which were then before
him. The ministers declined it, alleging, that the
forfeited estates of the rebels were to have been applied to that use, it being just that those who had
been the occasion of his extraordinary expense should
contribute to defray the charge of it.

The ministers fell to complaining of his conduct,
his personal sins, and the sins of those in his family,
which it was his duty to restrain. The King ans-

wered, if there were any gross faults in him, or his
house, he would not decline the judgment of the
Assembly, provided it was done privately.   Old
Andrew Melvin answered bluntly, they could not
justify private rebuke for open offences ; and, speaking
to the Moderator, charged him, as he would answer
to God, that he should now do his duty, and speak
to the King plainly and freely, as was his place to
do.   The King stood silent a while, and then withdrew.

This Assembly was famous for three things. First,
for their search into and regulation of their own corruptions as ministers, extending to all the ministers
of the Church ; which regulation consists of eight
heads, and are to be seen in the registers of the
Church.   And secondly, for that famous humiliation
and solemn renewing of the Covenant, which was
begun in the Assembly the 30th of March 1596, and
was carried on through all the ministers of Scotland.
And thirdly, for their humble, but faithful representation to the King of the sins, as well of his person
and family, as of his Council and nobility, and the
remedies thereof, which were exhibited in five articles,
and it must be owned this was the last time he had
the blessing of a faithful ministry to advise and exhort
him ; and this Assembly being over, it was observed
by many, that the Church never had another like it
during that King's reign, and it is at this period that
Mr Calderwood places in capital letters these words,
" Here end the sincere General Assemblies of the
Kirk of Scotland."

The ministers of this Assembly went on with renewing the Covenant in all the Presbyteries, and at
last in parishes ; but when it came to particular
persons, and especially to the Court, or to those who
lived near the Court, viz. in Edinburgh in particular,
they declined it, and it began gradually to drop and
be omitted.   What followed we shall soon see.

The excommunicated Lords were not without their friends at Court. The King had been prevailed with to consent to their return, but was not willing to take it upon himself for fear of embroiling himself with the Church, whom he feared as well as hated. It was concerted therefore to summon a Parliament, or Convention of Estates, to meet at Falkland, and to get such especially to this Convention as were in the secret. At the opening of the session a motion was made by Alexander Seaton, brother to the Lord Seaton, to recal the Lords. It was seconded by several others, using some threatenings, as it would be best to do so, least they should join with the enemies of their country.

To carry on the point, several ministers had notice given them to be there, but it was only such as they thought might be easiest brought to comply. But Mr Andrew Melvin, a famous and most faithful champion of the reformation, went unsent for. It seems he was appointed or commissioned by the last Assembly to watch against the imminent dangers that might threaten the Church, and this was his authority.

When the ministers were called in, he appeared at the head of them. The King taking notice of it, asked who sent for him. He answered, " Sir, I have a call to come here from Christ and his Church, who have a special concern in what you are doing here, and in direct opposition to whom you are all here assembled ; but be ye assured that no Council taken against him shall prosper. And I charge you, Sir, in his name, that you or your Estates, here convened, favour not God's enemies whom he hateth." After he had said this, and more to the like purpose to the King, he turned his speech to the members of the Convention, and "challenged them with being assembled there with a traitorous design against Christ and his Church, and their native country ;" and was

going on, when the King interrupted him, and commanded him to withdraw, which he did, but soon
let the King hear of him again upon the following
occasion.

The Commission of the last Assembly was sitting
at that time, and, finding which way things were
going, they resolved to send some of their members
to the King, to expostulate this matter with him.
Of these the same Mr Andrew Melvin was one.
When they came to the King, who received them
in his closet, Mr James Melvin, being first in the
Commission, spoke as the mouth of the rest, and told
the King their errand from the Commission.   The
King took him up roundly, and charged the Commission with sedition, and the ministers with being
spreaders of seditious reports, alarming the people
with imaginary dangers, and creating needless and
unjust fears.   Mr James being a courteous, fair-
spoken man, began to answer the King with respect
and with great reverence, when Mr Andrew, taking
the words out of his mouth, said, " Man, this is not a
time to flatter, but to speak plainly ; for," said he,
" our commission is from the mighty God, to whom
the King is but a silly vassal."   Then, taking the
King by the sleeve, he told him, " Sir, we will
humbly reverence your Majesty always, namely in
public ; but we have this occasion to be with your
Majesty in private, and you are brought in extreme
danger, both of your life and of your crown, and with
you the country and Kirk of God is like to be wrecked,
for not telling the truth, and giving you a faithful
counsel.   We must discharge our duty, or else be
enemies to Christ and you.   Therefore, Sir, as diverse times before, so now I must tell you, that
there are two kings and two kingdoms.   There is
Christ and his kingdom the Kirk, whose subject
King James the Sixth is, and of whose kingdom he
is not a king, nor a head, nor a lord, but a member ;

and they, whom Christ hath called, and commanded to watch over his kirk, and govern his spiritual kingdom, have sufficient authority and power from him so to do ; which no Christian king nor prince should control nor discharge, but fortify and assist ; otherwise they are not faithful subjects to Christ.   Sir, when you were in your swaddling clouts, Christ reigned freely in this land in spite of all his enemies.   His officers and ministers convened and assembled for ruling of his kirk, which was ever for your welfare also, when the same enemies were seeking your destruction ; and have been, by their assemblies and meetings since, terrible to these enemies, and most steedable for you ; will you now, when there is more than necessity, challenge Christ's servants, your best and most faithful subjects, for their convening, and for the care they have of their duty to Christ and you ; whenas you should rather commend and countenance them as the godly kings and emperors did. The wisdom of your counsel, which is devilish and pernicious, is this, that you may be served with all sorts of men to come to your purpose and grandeur, Jew and Gentile, Papist and Protestant.   Because the ministers and Protestants in Scotland are too strong, and control the King, they must be weakened and brought low, by stirring up a party against them, and the King being equal and indifferent, both shall be fain to flee to him.   So shall he be well settled.   But, sir, let God's wisdom be the only true wisdom ; this will prove meer and mad folly ; for his curse cannot but light upon it : so that, in seeking both, you shall lose both ; whereas in cleaving uprightly to God, his true servants shall be your true friends, and he shall compel the rest counterfeitly and lyingly to serve you, as he did to David."

It is easy to guess how well this pleased the King. However, though the King was at first very warm and angry, yet he grew calm and pleasant, protested

H

that he had no knowledge of the return of the Lords, and that, offer what they would, they should have no favour from him, till they had fully satisfied the Church.   This discourse of Mr Melvin to the King, Mr Calderwood says, was taken out of his own memoirs, left behind him, written with his own hand.

The King kept ill his promises in this 'case also ; for now dissatisfactions grew high between the King and the ministers ; the King encroaching daily upon their liberties, which they by no means would give up, they deputed four of their body to the King, to represent · that there was a most dangerous jealousy begun between him and the Church, which could not but be fatal to both, and to desire his Majesty to declare plainly what offended him, that, if possible, they might give him satisfaction.

The King answered in few words, " That there could be no agreement between him and them till the marches of their jurisdiction were ridden."   This is a Scoticism in speech, alluding to the people who used to ride annually over the marches or borders of both kingdoms of England and Scotland, to settle and ascertain the bounds, as our parish-officers do annually in England for the parishes.   This intimated plainly that the King resolved to put limits to the Church's power, and to restrain them in some of those liberties and privileges which they claimed as their due.   When the King had given them this hint, he gave also four heads of complaint against them, in which, he said, he expected redress.

1. That in their preaching, they should have nothing to do to speak of the King's affairs, or of matters of State.

2. That the General Assembly should not meet but by the King's authority and special command.

3. That he have a negative voice in the Assembly.

4. That the Church judicatories meddle not with civil matters, or with any matter of law.

The ministers now began to see plainly that the platform was laid for the overthrow of the ecclesiastic constitution. They thought it was a good providence to the Church that the King spoke so directly to his own designs, and they acted with the greatest prudence and caution possible to take from him all occasion of advantage over them. They ordered therefore, (1.) That all the acts of Parliament, acts of Council, declarations of the King, or other documents in favour of the liberties and discipline of the Church, should be searched out and collected. (2.) That the Presbyteries should be advertised not to enter into any debates or disputes upon the King's proposal, that they might not be supposed to call in question the undoubted liberties and authority of the Church. But he that has a nail to drive will not want a hammer. The King had an ill turn ready for the Church, and he let them know it on the following occasion.

One Mr David Black, a minister in St Andrews, had used some distasteful speeches in a sermon some months before, which having given offence to the King and Council, they resolved to begin there, and summoned him to appear before the Council to answer the same.

Thus the King began with them, and they, on the contrary, found him work enough; for, in the 1st place, they went on in their judicial process against the two great women, whose cause the King had openly espoused, viz. the Lady Huntly, and the Lady Levingstone. To the first they directed a libel or summons to answer their charge: this was, if possible, to prevent her being received at Court, as she could not well be, while under the process of the Church, before she had given satisfaction. 2d, They ordered the Presbytery of Stirling to proceed to excommunication against the Lady Levingstone. And as to Mr David Black, they ordered that he should decline the judicatory of the King and Council, or, as we call it in England, plead to their jurisdiction, and refuse to answer before them.   Then they came to a resolution in the Assembly, *nemine contradicente*, that all judgment of doctrine appertaineth to the pastors of the Church *in prima instantia ;* and they appointed a committee, and farther ordered all the ministers to search all the warrants of Scripture, or precedents in the laws of the realm, to support that position.

It would swell these memoirs too much to give a particular of all the disputes which passed between the King and the Assembly of ministers on this occasion.   They waited on him with their other demands, and got tolerable answers, though the King was highly affronted with Mr Patrick Galloway, one of those that was sent to him, who told him that their enemies got grants and performance, but the Church got fair words and promises only.   However, the King, upon a new application, promised them positively, that all they desired should be granted with respect to the Popish Lords and the two ladies above named.   But there was yet a sting in the tail, about Mr David Black, of whom the King said, he must appear and answer for himself, to satisfy the English Ambassador, who, it seems, had complained against him ; and take heed, said the King, that you decline not my judicatory, for, if you do, it will be worse than you imagine.

Hereupon the Assembly went upon it openly, resolving not to give up their rights, and directed Mr Black to give in a writing of declinature under his hand, which, as it is a very curious piece, and of great consequence in the question, and being penned with much art as well as maintained with much vigour, I cannot omit publishing it, as follows :—

*The Declinature of the King and Council's judica-
ture, in matters spiritual, namely in preaching
of the Word, given in to the same at Holyroodhouse, by Mr David Black, minister at St Andrews, in his own name, and in name of his whole
brethren of the ministry, the 18th day of November 1596.*

" Unto your Majesty and Lords of Secret Council,
with all reverence in Christ humbly meaneth, I Mr
David Black, minister of the Evangel at St Andrews ;
that where I am charged by your Highness' letters
to compear and answer for certain unreverend, un-
famous, and undecent speeches, alledged uttered by
me in some of my sermons made in public, in the kirk
of St Andrews, in the month of October last bypast
1596, as at more length is contained in the said letters :
Wherein albeit the conscience of my innocency up-
holdeth me sufficiently against whatsoever calumnies
of men ; and that I am ready, by the assistance of the
grace of my God, to give a confession, and stand to
the defence of every point of the truth of my God,
uttered by me in the said sermons, either in opening up
of his word, or application thereof, before your Majesty or Council, or whatsomever person or persons that
upon any lawful cause will crave an account of that
hope which is in me, in whatsomever place or manner,
so far as shall be requisite for clearing and maintenance
of the truth, and of my ministry, and may be done
without the prejudice of that liberty, which the Lord
Jesus hath given and established in the spiritual office-
bearers of his kingdom ; yet, seeing I am at this time
brought to stand before his Majesty and Council, as a
judge set to cognosce and descern upon my doctrine,
where through my answering to the said pretended
accusation might import, with the manifest prejudice
of the liberties of the Kirk, an acknowledgment of
your Majesty's jurisdiction, in matters that are mere

spiritual, which might move your Majesty to attempt farther in the spiritual government of the House of God, to the provocation of his hot displeasure against your Majesty, and in end either a plain subverting of the spiritual judicature, or at least a confounding thereof with the civil, if at any time profane and ambitious Magistrates might by such dangerous beginnings find the hedge broken down to make a violent irruption upon the Lord's inheritance, which the Lord forbid ; therefore I am constrained, in all humility and submission of mind, to use a declinature of this judgment, at least *in prima instantia ;* which I beseech your Majesty to consider earnestly, and accept of, according to justice, for the reasons following :—

" The Lord Jesus, the God of order, and not of confusion, as appeareth evidently in all the Churches of the saints, of whom only I have the grace of my calling, as his ambassador, albeit most unworthy of that honour, to bear his name among his saints, hath given me his word, and no law or tradition of man, as the only instructions whereby I should rule the whole actions of my calling, in preaching of the word, administration of the seals thereof, and exercise of discipline : And in the discharge of this commission I cannot fall in reverence of any civil law of man, but in so far as I shall be found to have passed the compass of my instructions, which cannot be judged, according to the order established by that God of order, but by the prophets, whose lips he hath appointed to be keepers of his heavenly wisdom, and to whom he has subjected the spirits of the prophets : And now, seeing it is the preaching of the word whereupon I am accused, which is a principal point of my calling, of necessity the prophets must first declare whether I have keeped the bounds of my directions, before I come to be judged of your Majesty's laws for my offence.

" Because the liberty of the Kirk, and whole discipline thereof, according as the same has been and is presently exercised within your Majesty's realm, has been confirmed by diverse acts of Parliament, and approved by the Confession of Faith, by the subscription and oath of your Majesty and Majesty's estates, and whole body of the country, and peaceably enjoyed by the office-bearers of the Kirk in all points; and namely, in the foresaid point, touching the judgment of the preaching of the word *in prima instantia*, as the practice of diverse late examples evidently will shew : Therefore the question touching my preaching ought first, according to the grounds and practice foresaid, be judged by the ecclesiastical senate, as the competent judge thereof, in the first instance.

" In respect whereof, and for diverse other weighty causes and considerations, namely of eschewing the great and dangerous inconveniences that might fall both to religion and to your Majesty's own estate, by the appearance of distraction of your Majesty's affection from the ministry, and good cause of God in their hands, to the grief of your Majesty's best subjects, and to the encouragement of the adversaries, both of your Majesty's estate and religion : Therefore I most humbly beseech your Majesty, and in the name of my brethren the Commissioners of the General Assembly, and the remnant of the brethren of the ministry, who, for testifying their earnest affection and allowance of the premises, have subscribed these presents with their hands, that your Majesty in this action would manifest your earnest care to maintain that liberty which the Church of Christ within the country, for the comfort of the saints, hath with so great blessing enjoyed since the gospel was first revealed in this land, wherethrough the godly may be comforted, the adversaries frustrated of their expectation, and your Majesty truly honoured in honouring the Lord Jesus."

The foundation of discontent being thus laid on both sides, all things tended to an open rupture between the parties ; the King at the head of the civil power, and the Assembly at the head of the ecclesiastic, pushed at one another without any appearance of a reconciliation.   It is without doubt that the King was aggressor ; he found the severity of the ministers a burthen that he could by no means bear. They said the same of his invasions upon their liberties.   Several proposals of accommodation were made, and sometimes they came very near to one another ; nay, at one time the King was brought to agree to the mediums they proposed, but the next morning they found his mind quite altered again ; and if it be true, which one of the writers of those times affirms, viz. that the King was resolved upon setting up Episcopacy, and had named the bishops to every diocese,* before Mr Black's declinature above, it is no more to be wondered at, that, though his Majesty might sometimes seem to comply with them for delay, or for other private reasons, yet that they always found he changed his mind when it came to the point to be concluded.

It would be endless to set down here the many particulars of this breach.   Take the sum of them thus :   Upon the failing of the many attempts to accommodate matters, the ministers preached openly and vehemently against the King's proceedings, defended the jurisdiction of the Church, and daily drew the people to them.   This nettled and alarmed the King.   He attempted to persuade the Commissioners of the Assembly, by fair means, to direct the ministers not to meddle.   They answered, they could not be silent, while he went on to sap the foundations of their liberties, and overthrow the discipline ; that it was their duty to speak freely and plainly.   When persuasions availed not, he used force ; he charged the Commissioners of the Assembly to depart from the

---

* Calderwood, fol. 358.

City of Edinburgh, and published this charge at the
cross of Edinburgh.   He ordered the council to proceed against Mr David Black, notwithstanding his
declinature, and to condemn him of contumacy, sen-
tencing him to enter into ward, upon pain of rebellion and horning.   His crime was said to be for
treasonable, uncivil, slanderous, and seditious words,
calumnies, and speeches uttered by him against the
Queen, the Queen of England, the nobility, council,
and session.

Besides this, the King refused to grant the stipends
to the northern ministers, for whom the Commissioners of the Assembly had petitioned ; the King's answer was, that such as would acknowledge his authority should have their salaries ; but he would give no
fee to such as would disclaim their obedience.

Upon the Commissioners being warned to depart,
they published an exhortation to the Presbytery of
Edinburgh, as they should answer it to God and his
Church, to discharge their duty in so necessary and
dangerous a juncture, and to call before them the
open and malicious enemies of the Church, of whatsoever rank, and proceed against them, even to excommunication, if they relaxed not : likewise to the ministers of Edinburgh, to stand to their calling, and
not to be slack in their duty ; with caution, however,
that, if violence was used, for there was a report that
they should be pulled out of their pulpits by armed
men, they should give place to the fury, and make
no resistance ; and then, publishing a long declaration, for vindication of their proceedings, and protesting against the injustice that was used towards them,
they departed.   This was in December 1596.

The same month the King fell upon the ministers
of Edinburgh, and without any particular accusation
or crime alleged, charged four of them, viz. Robert
Bruce, James Balfour, Walter Bacanquell, and William Watson, to enter into ward ; that is to say, to

go to prison, within six hours after the proclamation, upon pain of horning ; they not doing it, orders were sent to the magistrates of Edinburgh to apprehend them ; but they fled to the Borders.   There were also several of the inhabitants of Edinburgh in the same condition, being all such as were eminent for their zeal to the true religion.   But this was not all ; for the King, resolving now to carry his game on to the uttermost, contrived a writing of recognition, which was called there the Band, which all the ministers were required to sign, on pain of losing their stipends.   The copy of which band or engagement is as follows, viz.——

Copy of the Band, ordained by his Majesty and Estates, to be subscribed by every one of the Ministry under the pain of losing their stipends.

" We, the pastors and ministers of Scotland underscribing, humbly acknowledging our duty to God, and obedience to the King our Sovereign, whom for conscience sake we ought to obey, confess, that he is our Sovereign Judge, to us, and every one of us, in all causes of sedition and treason, and other civil and criminal matters ; and to all our speeches, which may import the said crimes, albeit uttered by any of us publicly in pulpit (which God forbid) or in any other place :   And that the said pulpits, nor no other place whatsoever, have that privilege or immunity, to be occasion or pretence to any of us of declining his Majesty's judgment, in any of the said civil or criminal causes intended, or to be intended against any of us, in time coming ; but rather that our offence is the greater, in case any of us commit such crimes in the said pulpits (which God forbid) where the Word of God, his truth and salvation, should be preached by us unto our flocks.   In witness whereof, and of our humble acknowledging of our duty in the premisses, we have subscribed these presents with our hands, and are content the same be registrat in the books of our Sovereign's secret Council, *in futuram rei memoriam*."

After this, for now the mask was thrown off, a proclamation was published, by sound of trumpet, at the cross of Edinburgh, empowering and requiring all magistrates, barons, and gentlemen of power, to interrupt any of the ministers if they should utter any speeches tending to sedition from their pulpits; or any speeches, in reproach, contempt, or disdain of the King, his progenitors, or his council, and any of their proceedings; and to imprison and detain them till notice should be given to the council, and orders from thence received about them.

To this pass things were come, in the space of one year. The ministers, generally speaking, refused the band with abhorrence; and published their reasons for it, with their apologies and defences in abundance; and some public meetings did the like, as the Synod of Fife, in particular.

We are now come to a meeting, called by the King a General Assembly; but not owned to be such by the Church. The King having, as is said, claimed the right of calling the General Assembly, though the Church had by no means yielded up that point, his Majesty thought fit to act upon that right, and summoned a convention of ministers at Perth, to meet the 28th of February 1597. The ministers who came thither met at the King's appointment, so there was a violation of the liberties of the Church in the very entrance; for, by the constitution, the Church has the right of calling, as well as of constituting their Assemblies. But this was not all; for, as the Assembly was called by the King, so were the members nominated chiefly by him, and especially the northern ministers, who appeared in an unusual number; and yet, as it was, they were for some time doubtful whether to have it called an Assembly or not. Old James

Melvin denied it to be an Assembly ; but the northern men out-voted them, the King also joining his authority.   However, eight Presbyteries entirely opposed it ; eleven, on the other hand, approving it.   The commissioners of the Presbytery of Fife made a protestation against it, and against all that should be done in it.

Two things the King attempted here upon them, yet neither succeeded thoroughly.   First, the King, on pretence of conferring with them on some affairs of moment, appointed them to meet, in the same place, with the King and his estates.   This was a wyle, to bring them to have sitten as it were in Parliament ; but the sound ministers saw it, and protested against it.   Next, the King would have entered into discourse of the point in controversy, but the same ministers refused to put any of the heads of their discipline in question ; neither would they reason or speak upon them at all.   The King pressed it, but to no purpose.   The King tried them again, and they came to the place, but would enter upon no business there, but made a long protestation against whatever should be done in that meeting, as not being lawfully constituted.

Having thus denied the legality of this Assembly, and refused to act, the King was left to go on as he liked ; nor are the things done, said to be lightly recorded, or any dependence to be had upon them. But in a word, the King went on his own way, and brought his ends about by such arbitrary methods, and yet by a specious pretence of legal steps, as may easily be imagined.   He exhibited thirteen articles to them, every one of which was a violation of their former discipline ; the consequence of this was bringing in the excommunicated Lords, and at length setting up Episcopacy in the Church.

In the meantime the legal Assembly had been appointed to meet at Aberdeen, on the 27th of April

1597, and the Moderator of the former Assembly went thither accordingly; and though the number was not great, yet they met in form, constituted themselves regularly, and having begun the Assembly with prayer as usual, and appointed a fast for confession of sins, they made protestations for the liberty of the Church, and referred all other business to the next meeting. This is the Assembly which the King disowned.

The King in the meantime went on the other way, and appointed another Assembly of his new model to meet at Dundee, in the month of May after. Thus the Church was miserably divided, and her discipline trodden under foot. At this Assembly, the King, as it is said, aimed at two things—viz., 1st, bringing in the excommunicated Lords; and 2d, acknowledging the meeting at Perth for a legal Assembly of the Church; both which the King, who had by this time wheedled off, or brought off many of the poorer of the ministry to his party, easily obtained; some complying for preferment, some for the honour, and some the profits of the Court; for it was an easy matter, says the historian of that time, Mr Calderwood, to draw such as thirsted for gain and glory, to farther the intention of the Court. Thus a dreadful schism was made in the Church, which also became wider every day. The Assembly of Dundee absolved the Popish Lords; gave up the liberty of rebuking the crimes of the great ones; committed matters of the greatest import to a few, and those such as appeared devoted to the Court; quitted summary excommunication, though for notorious crimes; abolished all meetings of ministers not warranted by the King, or forbidden; and all ecclesiastic matters to be treated of in the Assembly were, by this model, to be first prepared and determined of by the King. So, says the same writer, the Assembly was now no more than the King's led horse; and all this was brought to pass by a subtle dividing the ministers, and awing or enticing some from the rest ; who, backed and supported by the King, and joined with the creatures of the Court, carried on his designs to the ruin of all true religion.

And now came on the grand design ; for the King having gained a number of false brethren (a remarkable word), he had everything done to his hand. The Parliament being sitting, the Commissioners of the General Assembly petitioned, in the name of the Church, though falsely, for the main body of the Church abhored the thought of such a thing, for ministers to be allowed to sit and vote in Parliament. This was granted, and passed into an act, and the very words of the act openly declared the meaning of the thing, viz., that those ministers who should vote in Parliament should be bishops or prelates. The words are these : That such pastors and ministers as his Majesty shall, at any time, please to provide to the office, place, title, and dignity of bishop, abbot, or other prelate, shall at any time hereafter have vote in Parliament, as by the act may be seen at large.* This was in December 1597.

On the 7th of March 1598, another royal Assembly, for such it was, not an Assembly of the Church, met at Dundee, of which I need say no more than this, that by the same art and management that the rest was carried on, the act of Parliament for ministers to vote in Parliament was approved in the said Assembly, with all the formality and pretence of good to the Church imaginable.

The glory of the purest Church in the world (I use the King's own words) being thus under an almost total eclipse, was strangely represented that same year in the firmament, the most glorious lamp of heaven, the sun, suffering at this time a most fearful eclipse, so the historians of that day call it, the whole

* Acts of Parliament for Scotland, Part I. page 177.

face of the sun being covered and darkened; but it pleased God to put them in mind by it, that although it was of a long duration, viz. nearly two hours before it went quite off, yet the sun recovered again its full lustre.   And thus the Church of Scotland likewise has since done after many dreadful eclipses and hours of darkness.

The next year finished the work.   The giving the ministers a vote in Parliament had been already past ; the King summoned a number of ministers to a conference at Holyroodhouse, where he thought fit to have some of the best sort called ; but took care to secure a majority of his own party.   Here, for formality sake, those things were debated and resolved which the King before had resolved without debating. The questions were not, if the giving the ministers votes should be confirmed ; that was past and over before ; but how many their number should be, who should choose them, and what title they should have ? —where, finally, their number, and the choice of them, was left to the King ; and it was ordered that they should have the title of Bishop.   And thus this long contrived design obtained its finishing stroke, and Episcopacy was established in, or rather upon the ruins of, the Church of Scotland.

I have been more particular in this part, as it relates to the manner how Episcopacy got its first footing in the Church of Scotland ; that the fraud, the artifice, and hypocritical fawnings, the arbitrary and outrageous dealings, which were practised with the ministers, might appear ; as also the strugglings and opposition it met with for so many years.   The next succeeding years will require little to be said : the King had gained his point ; the gradations by which Episcopacy proceeded, as it ever did in Scotland, from power to persecution, and at length to its own ruin and downfall, as they were public, so our account shall be more concise and general.

The time drew near now that the King was to receive an addition of glory, and be called to a kingdom infinitely more opulent, populous, and powerful than his own; and withal, wrapt up in that ecclesiastic hierarchy which he so much desired.   In the mean time, he spent the hours in daily contests with the Presbyterian ministers, for the other are not now to be called so, oppressing, imprisoning, removing, banishing; so that no sooner was he become a King of an Episcopal Church, but, as was always natural to the spirit of Episcopacy in Scotland, he became a persecutor; nay, a persecutor of that very Church, which, as before is observed, he had, in the face of the Assembly, with eyes and hands lifted up to heaven, solemnly praised and blessed God for being born in, and made King of; calling it, alas! with what hypocrisy! the purest, the sincerest Church on earth.

This was the time when the King wrote that flattering letter to the Pope, styling him, in the beginning, *Beatissime Pater Pontificem maximum*, and the like; which, to escape the censure of, he caused, many years afterwards, the reproach of to be laid upon another person, who, it was pretended, deceived the King; and having privately penned the letter, got the King to sign it in a crowd of other writings which were to pass the sign-manual, and which the King signed of course, without reading; but if other authors may be believed, the King, who, was not so hurried with business, while King of Scotland, but that, in other cases, he was quick sighted enough, and used not to let the smallest matter pass unobserved, was not to be thus deceived.

This was the time when Mr John Spotiswood, who was prosecuted even by the King's friends in the Church, for having been at mass openly in France, was protected by the King from their censure, and afterwards made Archbishop of St Andrews; the same who writ the history afterwards of these times, and is so often quoted in these memoirs.

On the 31st of March 1603, an express arrived from England, bringing news of the death of Queen Elizabeth, with letters of recognition from the Privy Council there, who had proclaimed his Majesty King of England and Ireland.   As the King read the letters, his countenance changed; the Lords near hand feared he had been taken ill, when, on a sudden, he left off reading, and lift up his hands and eyes to heaven, as though he had prayed; and, giving the letter to one of the Lords that stood next him, said, " The Queen's dead : read that letter, man."

Immediately the Lords congratulated him, and the Court rung with joy ; the guns at the castle were fired, and the King was proclaimed at the market cross of Edinburgh, King of England, France, and Ireland, &c.

The next Sabbath, being the 3d of April, the King made the following speech to the people in the great Church, which, I observe, because he scarce ever performed one word of it at all.

" As God hath promoted me to a greater power than I had, so I must endeavour to establish religion, and to take away corruption in both the countries.   Ye need not doubt, but as I have a body as able as any king in Europe, whereby I am able to travel; so I shall visit you every three years at least, or oftener as I shall have occasion (for so have I written in my book directed to my son, and it were a shame to me not to perform that which I have written), that I may with my own mouth take account of the execution of justice of them that are under me, and that ye yourselves may see and hear me, and from the meanest to the greatest have access to my person, and pour out your complaints in my bosom.   This shall ever be my course."

The triumphs of this new accession of power to the King, his passage into England, his reception there,

I

his coronation and other ceremonies, are no part of this work ; I shall say only this of them, that they, together with the English business, almost took the King wholly off Scotch affairs for the first two or three years of his reign, and he did little but confirm and establish his new fabric in the Church.

In this condition things stood with the Church almost all the rest of the reign of King James ; the authority of the Church judicatories was wholly lost, their discipline destroyed, and the Government dissolved into a Prelatic hierarchy.

It is true, the King being absent, and embarrassed with the English affairs, they did not push on the designed persecutions so far or so fast as it is very likely they would otherwise have done ; but still the Council continued daily to invade the privileges of the Church, and by encroachments of one kind or other, went on to oppress them ; and upon every step the ministers took to assert their right, or defend their privileges, they were proceeded against by the Council as criminals ; and once no less than six of the ministers were tried for high treason, and condemned to death, for declining the judicature of the Council, and continuing to assemble at Aberdeen, without the King's authority.   But the King would not suffer them to be executed.   What he did with them we shall see presently.   First, a proclamation was published, forbidding all people, either in public or private, to call in question his Majesty's proceedings against the said ministers.   Then the cause slept a while, the Parliament being to meet.   This was the year 1606, when the Parliament met at Edinburgh, but was adjourned to Perth ; in which the act was passed, entituled, The Act for Restitution of Bishops, by which the temporalities of the old bishopricks were likewise restored to the Church, having before been given to the Crown by a law called the Act of Annexation.*

---

* Act of Scots Parliament, part i. p. 759.

The first thing of note which happened after the King's accession to the crown of England, and the last thing of this nature which we shall bring into these memoirs, was that memorable conference at Hampton Court, between the eight ministers of the Presbyterian Church and the King, upon the matters then in dispute.   The case, in short, was this :   The Presbyterian ministers had met in an Assembly, as was already noted, at Aberdeen, without the King's authority, as they insisted they might legally do ; the King discharged or dissolved their meeting as illegal : but they continued to meet for all that ; and when some of them were delated, or indicted, as we call it, before the court of justice for that contempt, they declined the authority of the King—that is to say, his authority to take cognisance of those affairs ; for they never disputed his authority in civil matters.   For this they were again indicted, brought to trial, found guilty of high treason, and received sentence of death, as above.

But the King, finding that this pushing things to extremity would not fully answer his end, and willing rather to proceed by other methods, concluded at length to have the cause brought to London, where it should be publicly heard before himself and the Council, not doubting but it should be so managed there, as that he should either really have the victory, or at least seem to have it ; hereupon, making show to desire an agreement, he (the King) caused a certain number of the Scotch ministers, on both sides, to be summoned to appear before him at London.   Their names were as follow, viz. :—Of the Episcopal party —the Archbishop of St Andrews ; the Bishop of Glasgow, Orkney, Galloway, Dunkeld.   Of the Presbyterian party—Mr Andrew Melvil, Mr James Melvil, Mr James Balfour, Mr William Watson, Mr John Carmichael, Mr Adam Coult, Mr William Scot.

And as this was a most eminent transaction, by

which the craft, drift, and weakness in argument, in the Scotch Episcopal party, and the capacity, fidelity, and courage of the ministers, were more than ordinarily conspicuous ; and that it is necessary the reader should have it faithfully and fully stated ; I say, for this reason, I shall impartially relate the fact, as it is set down in the histories of those times, taking one historian on one side, and one of the other, that the impartial reader may judge for himself, without any gloss or comment on our side, and the conduct of both sides may be clearly seen. And because some may think the reciting this story, however memorable and worth their reading, too long an interruption to the thread of story, and yet that those whose curiosity is worth obliging may not be disappointed ; and above all, that the truth of fact may impartially be handed down to posterity, that they may have a true notion, and be able to make a right judgment, of so remarkable an event, I have placed it at large, among other things, by way of *addenda* to, and at the end of, this second part of the work, where it may be read by itself, No. III. IV.

After that conference, as it was called, was over, and the King had found that neither by persuasion nor threatening anything was to be done with them, so as to get the power he had assumed confirmed by them, or the proceedings against their brethren approved, he dismissed them, and went to work with the ministers who were under sentence. He found it not for his purpose to put them to death ; he knew too well what a flame it would kindle in Scotland. However, to put as great a show of resentment upon it as he thought might answer his end, he appointed a court of justice to sit at Linlithgow, where the six condemned ministers were brought to receive their sentence, which the King was pleased to change from that of death into that of banishment, never to return, on pain of death. Their names were as follow :—Mr John Forbes, minister of Awford; Mr John Welch, minister of Ayr; Mr Robert Dury, minister of Anster; Mr Andrew Duncan, minister of Crail; Mr Alex. Straughan, minister of Creich; Mr John Sharp, minister of Kilmeny.

Besides these, by a letter from the King, directed to the Council, eight ministers more were confined for their lives, or during the King's pleasure, in the most distant, and most remote and barbarous places of his kingdom, viz.:—Mr Charles Farum, in the Isle of Bute; Mr John Monroe, in Cantyre; Mr Robert Youngson, in the Isle of Arran; Mr James Irwyn, in the Isle of Orkney; Mr William Forbes, in the Isle of Shetland; Mr John Ross, in the Isle of Lewis; Mr James Gray, in Caithness; Mr Nath. Inglis, in Sutherland.

These ministers thus sent into banishment were also commanded not to come out of the bounds of their confinement upon pain of death; and, by another proclamation, all other ministers were forbidden to recommend, in their prayers or sermons, any of those so sentenced. This was esteemed a greater cruelty than the rest. Likewise, the ministers at Court were forbidden to go back to Scotland; and one of them, viz. Mr Andrew Melvil, was taken up, on pretence of words spoken in London, and some Latin verses made by him, reflecting on the cathedral worship in England, and was sent to the Tower, and kept there three years, after which he was banished into France, where he ended his days.

But things ended not here; for the King, being not able to get his will of the ministers by the violences above, continued notwithstanding to make innovations in their discipline and government; and, therefore, in the Assembly held at Linlithgow, December 10. 1606, he brought in the overture of constant moderators in the Presbyteries; and the ministers of the Assembly being always a majority of the wrong side, after a few had opposed it, agreed to admit them upon some conditions, though they could never bring the Presbyteries to accept of them.

But now came on a blow which even the ministers themselves did not foresee, I mean the five articles concerning worship, called afterwards the Articles of Perth. The constitution of the church consists, as it is politically understood, of four principal heads, viz. 1st, her Doctrine ; 2d, her Worship ; 3d, her Discipline ; and 4th, her Government. The two last were effectually reduced, and the King had his will of them, as you have heard ; her doctrine and worship seemed still to remain. But now the King began to attack their worship, being resolved to bring the Church's neck under the feet of her enemies.

It was the year 1617 when the King took his journey into Scotland, and where it was expected, by his presence, he should carry every point ; but he failed in several. And first, at the meeting of the Parliament he proposed an article, importing, " That whatever was resolved or concluded by his Majesty, with advice of the archbishops and bishops, in matters of external polity in the church, should have the force of an ecclesiastical law." This was a bold stroke ; even the bishops themselves startled at it at first, and the ministers signed a general protestation against it, which the King coming to the knowledge of, the article was dropped, and so the protestation was not delivered in ; but the King resolved to exercise the power without the ceremony of an act, as we shall see presently.

The King summoned the bishops to meet him at St Andrews, where, in a set speech to them, he proposed what he after obtained ; the bishops referred him to an assembly ; but the King, who owned that he resolved never to have any more assemblies, was very averse to an assembly, and it was now evident that the reason why the King had proposed formerly the article above-named was, that the power of making ecclesiastical laws being vested in himself, he might have no more occasion for assemblies, which, even though episcopal, were very much his aversion.

However, in short, upon the entreaty of the bishops, and promises of compliance in some time-serving ministers, the King called an assembly to meet at Perth, the 25th of August 1617. There had been one held at St Andrews the November before, which disgusted the King very much in not complying with his demands.

In this assembly, the worship as well as the discipline was innovated, and the conclusions were passed in the following heads, afterwards called, as above, the Five Articles of Perth. The articles at large are to be found in the histories* of those times† ; but, in short, they contained—1st, the kneeling at the communion ; 2d, private communion at sick people's request ; 3d, private baptism ; 4th, confirmation of children ; 5th, observation of festivals. All which was now to be imposed upon the Church of Scotland.

When the articles were past, orders were sent to all the ministers to intimate them in their churches, to exhort the people to conform to them, and to preach upon the lawfulness of it. But this it was never in their power to do, nor, where ministers did conform, was it in their power to make the people comply with, or hear them ; but a dreadful rent being thus made in the church, the people divided from the ministers, and the dissenting ministers set up private communions, and were almost universally followed, as will appear presently.

But, to return to the affair of the ministers in England : the Scotch ministers behaved with such courage and such steadiness, that the court could get no ground of them, but was forced to have recourse to coercion

---

* Spotiswood. Hist. of the Church of Scotland, fol. 539.
† Calderwood, fol. 611.

and persecution in Scotland, and in England also :
the six ministers, instead of being disputed with,
were imprisoned, and long harrassed from place to
place ; so that some of them never saw Scotland more.
If I enter not far into the particulars of those times,
it is because I would not record some things practised
upon them by some of the clergy in England, which
it may not be grateful to posterity to hear ; for it is
not the conduct in England, but the conduct in Scotland, that these memoirs are written about.

The sum of the matter is this, in few words—the
King having missed of his triumph, and of reducing
the ministers to a necessity of submitting, resolved
however not to miss of his design in Scotland, and to
this end he established a high commission-court there,
to enforce the articles of Perth, and, in a word, to
abolish the constitution of the Church of Scotland.

First, instead of the General Assembly, the King
by his special warrant summoned a convention, not
of the estates, but of ministers, to meet at Linlithgow,
the 10th of December 1606 ; instead of the Presbyteries electing the ministers, as was usual, to represent
them, the King's letter was sent, directed to the
Presbyteries, ordering them to send such men, by
name, as the King had directed. Let any Englishman
conceive of this, as if the King of England were to
summon a Parliament to meet at Westminster, and
instead of issuing out writs, for elections of members,
should name the members whom they should send up.
This was the method in Scotland, and with the same
justice ; and because this is a novelty that never was
practised before or since, I have given the copy of the
warrant, for thus sending up of ministers, at the end
of this part, No. I V.

In this meeting the project of constant moderators
in the Presbyteries was proposed—it is called the King's
advice to the Assembly ; but any one may guess what
the meaning of such a phrase must be, when kings

advise, especially to their own subjects, they will not take it ill if their people take it for a command, and so it proved; for the Act passed without opposition.

Great arts were used, and some violence, to bring the Presbyteries to accept these constant moderators, nor could all the threatenings and violence that was practised bring them to it. The Presbytery of Edinburgh was told plainly, that if the Presbyteries refused them, the King would overthrow the Presbyteries themselves, and there should be no more in Scotland; but all would not do. They named a moderator *pro interim*, to continue to the next General Assembly, and would do no otherwise: and the like did other Presbyteries also.

At length the Presbyteries were charged, in the King's name, and on pain of rebellion, and putting them to the horn, to accept them. This prevailed with some, but many stood out, and some of the moderators themselves refused to accept. Not one of the Synods in Scotland would accept them except Angus; no threats, no cunning, for neither were wanting, could bring them to it.

By this time the Court found that all the arts hitherto used for subverting the Church, however they might establish a new constitution, would never bring the ministers to comply, till they came to downright persecution; and, therefore, it was resolved to take that course by a high Commission Court, in the pursuit of whose powers the ministers were to be brought by violence, by persecution, horning, that is to say, banishment and confiscation of goods, to abandon their flocks, and lay down the office of ministers.

It was in the year 1616 that the Commission Courts were first erected, viz., one in each archbishoprick. This Commission was the highest exercise of tyranny that was ever practised by any king in Great Britain since laws and constitutions were allowed to be the rule of the government; for it actually put

the King in possession of the bodies and goods of all
his subjects, and empowered him to use them as he
pleased, without the ordinary forms of justice, and
merely by the agency of the clergy, making the bishops the instruments of absolute power, not only to
ruin and destroy the liberties of the Church, but even
of the whole country, clergy or laity.   The copy of
this famous Commission is among the addenda, at the
end of this Part, No. V.

How they exercised this unlimited authority, the
histories of those times are witnesses, in which, whoever pleases to look, will find the Episcopal clergy
were not backward to merit the general reproach cast
upon priests of all religions.

There is scarce any kind of cruelty, injustice, and
oppression to be named in the world which was not
practised in consequence of this Commission upon
the ministers of the Church—present death, racks,
and tortures excepted.

The ministers were beset with spies, to observe
their words, gestures, and their expressions in their
prayers and sermons, in order to observe if they offered to speak against the new constitutions.   They
were delated or prosecuted before this Court upon so
many accounts, that it was scarce possible to avoid it ;
such as speaking against the bishops, disliking the
canon reproving wickedness, vices, and immoralities,
alledging they pointed at the dignified clergy.

They were delated in general upon the Five Articles
of Perth, upon points of doctrine, the supremacy of
the King over the Church, owning or disowning the
General Assemblies, and the like.

In their appearing at their courts, they were insulted, brow-beaten, and maltreated by the bishops,
neither treated as gentlemen, as scholars, or as ministers of the gospel.   The Bishop of St Andrews, in
particular, told them at one of his meetings that he
should proceed to sentence as he was directed, where-

in he should have no regard to wives, children, or estate, which he effectually made good; and indeed the King's order or letter gave them express encouragement to such cruelty. It seems the Court thought them too relax and slow in their proceedings, which, if our histories are true, there was little reason for. But after the first commission had tyrannized about three years, and the business seemed a little to rest, it was on a sudden renewed again, anno 1619; and, in November after, the Bishop of St Andrews, sitting in judgment upon some of the ministers, pulled out the King's letter, written from England, dated the 23d of November 1619, animating them to all possible severity against the ministers that would not comply. This most merciful letter being under the King's own hand, and upon such an extraordinary style, cannot be omitted, without leaving this account imperfect. The words, so far as relate to the present case, are as follows, viz.

" I command you, as you will be answerable to me, that you depose all those that refuse to conform, without respect of persons, no ways regarding the multitude of the rebellious; for that, if there be wanting numbers to fill their places, I will send you ministers out of England; and I charge you to certify us of your proceedings betwixt this and the 3d of March next to come."

As the bishops wanted no spurring to a work they so much delighted in, so they failed not to proceed, in consequence of this letter, with the utmost rigour; the ministers were everywhere cited, and upon their refusing to conform, were deprived, imprisoned, put to the horn; their goods plundered, many of them banished to the islands, and the like. In their examinations, they were used with all possible indignity and contempt; and in their imprisonments, with rigour and cruelty.

The laity were also fallen upon for not kneeling at

the communion, according to the articles of Perth, and at one time six of the citizens of Edinburgh were ordered to banishment from their houses, trades, and families, without trial, citation, or form of process, on pretence that they had countenanced the ministers in their disobedience.

I might fill this volume with the history of these violences, and enlarge, with great advantage on the unprecedented proceedings of this tyrannical court of bishops. It would also be very diverting, as well as profitable, to record here the conduct of the suffering ministers and people—how stoutly they stood in defence of their principles—how boldly they disputed, and often baffled and put to shame the bishops, especially of St Andrews and of Glasgow, in the arguments they used with them; as particularly Mr Thomas Hog, minister of Dysart, to the Bishop of Glasgow and Dr Lindsay, about the differences between capping and kneeling at the sacrament. The bishop, it seems, would have proved that capping, or pulling off the hat, and kneeling, were synonimous; that they were not *diversæ species gestus*, but that they who did the first, could not refuse the last; in which Mr Hog silenced them both, and brought the bishop to say, "It is long since I learnt my logics, &c." Mr Hog answered, "There is no difficulty here to any that are desirous to learn the sacred truths of the gospel. Capping in religious exercises is an outward act of veneration or reverence only, and this we do at the sacrament; because none can deny but that reverence is due to the celebration of that solemn ordinance. But kneeling in religious exercises is an act of adoration or worship, which is proper to God only, and therefore exception is taken at it in the sacrament, lest we seem to worship the elements which we receive."

This was so plain that the bishop could make no reply, and so broke off the discourse. Many such accounts, I say, might be given, both profitable and diverting, but the short compass of these memoirs admits not to enter into those things. It may suffice to note, that they got as little ground by their violence as they did by their disputations; and, after all they could do in this one article of kneeling, though the King sent down his letter also, strictly commanding all to kneel, yet, at the communion published in Edinburgh, for trial of the effect of this command, out of sixteen hundred communicants in the College Church there, they could make but twenty receive kneeling, and the next day but seven, and these few were either of the families of the complying Episcopal clergy, who administered, or the poor alms-people, who durst not refuse; yet they published in England that the people generally complied with the King's command, and that only a few obstinate Presbyterian ministers stood out. This practice we see revived even lately; for while we were told mighty stories of the willingness of the people in Scotland in Queen Anne's time to receive the English Liturgy, and how desirous they were to have it set up there, it since appears that it has not been received anywhere, except where the tyranny of their lairds and superiors imposed it, and that, as soon as that imposing ceased, by the subduing the rebellion under the reign of his present Majesty, we hear no more of it.

The last public step to the confirming all this wreck of the Church, was the getting the Five Articles of Perth established by the sanction of an act of Parliament, and so giving them the force of a law; for, till then, they acted merely upon the mandate and personal authority of the King.

The solemnity of this transaction was extraordinary. The Parliament met the 25th day of July 1621—the ministers were carefully fenced against, that none should get into the House to protest against it; for they knew they had a protestation ready to deliver. Mr David Barclay, one of the ministers, who resolved to present the protestation, got into the House to the second bar, but was discovered and put out again, and at last contented himself to read it at the door, and stick it up against the wall.

However, there was great opposition to this act, even in the Parliament itself; but the King, by management of the members, and by the assistance of the bishops, got a majority to vote it; yet a great many, both Lords and Commons, opposed it. Among the first, the Lords Rothes, Menteith, Eglinton, Linlithgow, Kintail, Gray, Ross, Yester, Cathcart, Coupar, Burly, Balmerino, Elphingston, Torphichen, and Forbes, all publicly voted against it. The Earls of Morton, Buchan, and the Marquis of Lauderdale, staid without the door, because they would not vote for it; and of the Commissioners for shires and burghs, forty-four voted against it, besides nine Lords and six-and-twenty Commissioners that cared not to appear on one side or other, and came not near the Parliament.

However, notwithstanding all that could be done, the articles were voted; the act passed, and was published with sound of trumpet at the Cross of Edinburgh, the 20th of August 1621.

It is recorded by several historians of those times, that when this act for confirming the articles of Perth had been voted and passed, and was presented for the royal assent, which is signified there by touching it with the sceptre, the moment the High Commissioner, the Lord Scone, stood up to touch this act, heaven declared its royal dissent in a most remarkable manner; for three flashes of lightning, one immediately after the other, darted in at the great window, and struck directly in the Commissioner's face. He confessed afterwards he felt the warmth of the fire on his face. The last flash was more

frightful than the two first, and they were rendered
the more visible by an exceeding dark cloud, which
for some minutes before hung directly over the city.
The thunder which followed, and broke upon the
city, and as it were more immediately on the Par-
liament-House, was very terrible, especially the third
clap of thunder, immediately after the lightning.
The darkness occasioned by the said cloud increased
to such a degree that it became frightful, and the
whole was followed by so violent and so heavy a rain
that the like had not been known in the memory of
man ; and the Lords and members of Parliament,
although their business was finished and the House
broke up, were kept prisoners by the fury of the rain
for above an hour, and so long it continued that when
they did go away every one shifted home as they
could ; so that this act could not have the honour of
a procession, and to have the regalia carried before
it, as was usual on like occasions.

The day got the name of Black Saturday upon
this account, as well as on the occasion of the black
work they had been about.

Nothing but a dark prospect of persecution, and a
cloud-threatening desolation to the Church, now appeared. The prisons were filled with deprived ministers, and the remote parts with the banished, and
the King's letters came every post pressing to more
and more severities ; nay, the magistrates of Edinburgh were threatened in express terms by the King
with being deposed, and the city of Edinburgh was
threatened with having the session or term for sitting
of the courts of justice removed from them to Linlithgow, because they were not careful to do their duty
in pursuing the ministers and preventing private conventicles ; for the deprived ministers preached in their
own houses, and multitudes left the churches and
flocked to hear them.

But the hand of heaven interposed in the very extremity, and by a surprising event put an end for the present to the fury of those people ; for just as the prosecution of Mr William Rigg, John Hamilton, John Meen, and several other suffering ministers was come to the extremity, and they were at the point of being sent into banishment, an express from London brought the news that the King was dead.

By this one blow the high Commission was dissolved of course, all proceedings depending before them dropped, and abundance of good men were, for the present, delivered from the oppressions of the bishops.

But the King being succeeded by his son, King Charles I., who was no less zealous than his father in the Episcopal part of church affairs, the Church of Scotland got no other advantage by the change than the stop above-mentioned, which, by that extraordinary incident of the death of King James, was put to the persecution of the ministers, as above.

On the contrary, the Episcopal model received all possible encouragement, as may be guessed by Archbishop Spotiswood being made Lord Chancellor of Scotland, till the unexpected folly and madness of the Court-party unravelled all their own work, and the Church rose again upon the ruin of her enemies.

Nay, such was the signal working of Divine Providence, as has been seen more than once in the case of the Church of Scotland, that the oppressions and persecutions of this Church were made the means of overturning, not the bishops only, who were the more immediate persecutors, but even the King himself, and all his family, as will eminently appear in the process of the story.

The King died March 27. 1625 : the first year of his son's reign appeared entangled so many ways, that he became less intent, for some time, upon the affairs of Scotland, than his father had been. He was left entangled in a war with Spain, and entered

afterwards rashly and inconsiderately into another
with France; in both which his people were uneasy,
and his generals unfortunate.

The mismanagement of the war, the indirect methods taken by the Court for raising money, and the
ill usage of those, who, upon principles of the people's
liberties, opposed it, made the Parliament fall upon
his favourite, the Duke of Buckingham, refuse sub-
sidies, and insist warmly on redress of grievances.
These put the King so out of love with Parliaments
in England, that no Parliament was afterwards called
in fourteen years; during which, so many illegal and
arbitrary things were done, that when the King was
afterwards driven, by necessity, to call a Parliament,
they carried their resentment at these illegal practices
to such a height, as drove both parties to arms, and
ended in the overthrow, first of the Episcopal people
in Scotland, where the flame first broke out; secondly, of the whole Establishment of the Church of
England in England; and, lastly, in the ruin of the
King, and of the Royal Family.

This short digression to the English affairs should
not have been made, for I have carefully avoided
suffering these memoirs to pass the Tweed, except
on extraordinary occasions, had it not been to reconcile
the history of facts, and explain what is said above,
viz., that the flame of the war in England began
first in Scotland.

During the long interval of Parliament in England,
the King had leisure to apply himself to the affairs
in Scotland, and being resolved to play Rehoboam's
part, he met with Rehoboam's fate. His father had,
as is said above, imposed Episcopacy upon Scotland,
and a long series of time had accustomed too many of
the people to it, or an indifferency about it; so that
it was thought, had the King sat still, he might, in
time, have reduced the nation at last to have been
contented with it. But far from this, he not only

K

was not content with putting hardships upon the
Presbyterian ministers, but, prompted by an evil fate,
he fell upon a thing which even the Episcopal people
in Scotland could not bear ; this was imposing the
English liturgy upon the Scots.   This was not only
the most rash and impolitic part in the Court, but it
was the most unkind and ungrateful part to his friends
in Scotland ; for now the Episcopal party themselves,
who had done every violent thing he had desired for
his service, were fallen upon, except they would comply
with the Service-Book, which abundance of them refused.   And thus he made his friends his enemies.

This was the project of Archbishop Laud in England,
who afterwards made *l'amende honorable* for these
and several other English extravagances of like nature with the loss of his head.   This bishop had introduced several novelties in the Church of England
itself, encouraged and proposed the Book of Sports,
persecuted the Puritans, and insulted with unheard
of pride several of the clergy of the English Church,
particularly, in a visitation of his clergy, he took upon
him to remove the communion table in all the
churches, which, from the Reformation, had always stood in the body of the church, and to place it
altar-fashion at the upper end of the chancel, on an
ascent, and railed about, exactly after the manner of
the Church of Rome.   " This," says a learned historian of those times,* " was opposed by divers of the
clergy, and the Bishop of Lincoln wrote a book,
called *the Holy Table*, shewing the practice of the
Primitive Churches, and with arguments against this
innovation."

Had he contented himself to have introduced his
petty-popery into the Church of England, and let
the Church of Scotland alone, his worthless name had
had no place in these memoirs ; but whether put

* Whitelock's Memoirs, fol. 24.

upon it by his own mischievous, turbulent spirit, which was always restless in tyrannizing over others; or, as some have suggested, invited to it by some of the prelates in Scotland, it was not long ere he began to intermeddle with his neighbours in Scotland: and the occasion seems to be as follows.

King James had, says the English historians,* so good success in pulling down the Presbyterian Church in Scotland, and setting up an Episcopal hierarchy, that he had conceived what they call in England a farther reformation of that Church, meaning the Church of Scotland, by bringing them to a conformity in worship, as well as in government, to the Church of England; and for that purpose had ordered some of the Scots Bishops to compile a book or form of common-prayer, &c., to be used in Scotland, which they did; but the death of that prince, and the opposition made to it from the most learned even of the Episcopal ministers themselves in Scotland, occasioned that no more was done in it at that time. This is taken from the accounts given in our English Histories of those things,† for the Scots either never knew any thing of it, or did not own it.

King Charles I. falling in with the pernicious counsels of Archbishop Laud, as above, renewed this project, if it was such, of his father, and gave direction to the said Bishop Laud, and several other of the English clergy, to revise that liturgy, which they did; and forming another out of it, with several material alterations, and even more distasteful to the Scots than the English liturgy itself, they advised the King to send it down into Scotland, and to command it to be read in all the churches there, and that it should be conformed universally to as it was in England.

---

* Coke's Detection, vol. i.
† Whitelock's Memoirs, fol. 25, col. 2.

The people of Scotland were greatly alarmed at this innovation; and it is said that several of the Episcopal clergy took the freedom to remonstrate against it, to whose memory I would not fail to do justice had history recorded their names.

But the bishops and some Lords of the Council, both approving the design, and having received the King's positive directions for it, set themselves immediately to work, to cause this common prayer-book to be read.

It is said,* that before it was admitted, some of the bishops in Scotland objected against it, that though they liked the book, yet they were disgusted at its being imposed by the English; also, they objected against the translation of the Psalms, Epistles, and Gospels, which were differing from their Bibles; and that this, to satisfy them, was amended.

Now, as if they were resolved to irritate the people of Scotland to the utmost, this service-book was not only appointed to be read, but the minister officiating was to have on the surplice, according to the English custom, which was a new and uncouth sight to the people of Scotland, hateful to the knowing, and next to frightful to the ignorant, well-meaning people, and which tended to make the thing itself to the last degree odious to the whole nation.

It was first set up in the chapel royal at Holyroodhouse, where none being obliged to go but the King's servants, it being no parochial church, it was not so offensive; for though the people abhorred the thing itself, yet as it was not imposed upon them, they concerned themselves the less about it; but this was only an introduction to the rest, and the using it there was to make it a little familiar to the citizens, who flocked thither to satisfy their curiosity. But this was upon a wrong supposition, viz. that as the fox, by often

---

* Whitelock's Memoirs, fol. 25, col. 2.

seeing the lion, was less terrified, so the more the people were acquainted with this innovation, the more they would like it; whereas, on the contrary, the more the people saw this service performed, the more hateful and abominable it appeared to them.

It was on the 23d of July 1637, when the Dean of Edinburgh, who was appointed to preach in the great church in that city, resolved before sermon, in his habit and surplice, to read the service-book, as he had done before in the royal chapel.

There was a great concourse of people in the church, expecting what would be the end of this matter, and some guards were placed at hand, to prevent any disorder in the town; but no one expected anything like that which happened, neither could it be suspected, or was there ever afterward any ground to believe that anything was concerted before, except that it was in the appointment of Divine Providence to bring forth what followed by these unforeseen accidents.

The hour of service being come, the Dean, in his surplice, came out of the vestry, the people gazing as at a great show, and making gestures of contempt enough, but no noise or disorder. He passed through the crowd to the reading-desk, and began to read, the people still continuing quiet, when, on a sudden, at some words that disgusted her, an old woman, in a rage, started up, " Villain !" said she, " dost thou say the mass at my lug ? " * and taking up a little stool which she sat on, she drave it full at his head, raising a most hideous noise in the church by it. Some that sat next her, following her example, did the like, till, in a word, the whole church was in an uproar, and the Dean was fain to come down out of the desk, and pull off his surplice, for fear of being torn in pieces. The Bishop of Edinburgh being present, went up into the

---

* My ear.

pulpit, and, beckoning for silence, offered to speak ;
but it was all to no purpose, neither did they spare ;
but sticks, stools, and anything that came to hand,
flew at him from all quarters, till at last both Bishop
and Dean were obliged to give over, and retire into
the vestry.

The Lord Chancellor called to the magistrates to
come down and appease the people, but it was all
ineffectual ; for by this time the tumult was as great
without as within, and showers of stones, sticks, &c.
assaulted the church windows from the street.

Nor did it end here ; for the multitude increasing,
went to all the churches where the curates had designed to read the service-book, and set all in an
uproar in every quarter of the city.

The Dean and clergy in the great church, with the
magistrates and the courtiers, having gotten rid of the
rabble for a while, locked themselves in, and went on
with their liturgy by themselves ; but the mob, who
waited for them in the street, assaulted the Bishop
as he came out ; and it was not without difficulty that
he got safe to the palace.

This was the beginning, and at that time it went
no farther, the care of the magistrates and power
of the court overawing the crowd. But the harvest
being over, and people more at leisure, it was soon
found that the generality of the nation—as well the
gentlemen as the old women—were disgusted at the
imposing this liturgy upon the Church ; and about
the middle of September, great numbers of gentlemen being, with their servants, come to Edinburgh,
a petition was drawn up, and handed about to be
signed, requesting the council, in their own names,
and the names of all the noblemen, gentlemen, and
others, who should agree to the same, that the service-book might be no farther pressed upon them till
these things might be represented to the King, and
his Majesty's pleasure be farther known. An infinite

number set their hands to this petition, and among
them several gentlemen of good rank, and their number increased every day.

The council, instead of showing any concern at
these things, pretended to resent it to the gentlemen
that presented the petition, and threatened them to
give the King an account of their names, as disorderly
and disaffected persons, and to take order with them
as such ; and, instead of an answer to their address,
they published a proclamation to remove the session—
that is the term—to Linlithgow, thinking thereby to
take away the pretence for people to flock to Edinburgh, as they usually did at that time on their law-
business. They also dissolved all meetings on church
affairs, &c.

This increased the rage of the citizens of Edinburgh ; for the removing the term was a ruin to the
city, as it hindered the concourse of people there on
those occasions.

The very next day after this, the mob gathered in
Edinburgh to a prodigious multitude, and there is no
doubt but that, whatever it was before, this new tumult
was concerted among those gentlemen who had petitioned as above ; nor was it long ere they publicly appeared with and at the head of them in the street.

The first thing the people did, was to surround the
council house, the privy council being sitting, and
demand a better answer to their petition, and that
the service-book be laid aside till the King was fully
informed of the matter. The Bishop of Galloway,
going to the council, was assaulted in the street,
though with words only, and followed to the door.
The Earl of Traquair had the same fate, as had also
the Lord Treasurer. The last was, indeed, insulted
particularly, and his white-staff taken away in the
street.

At the same time another part of the rabble beset
the magistrates of the city and the town-council, and

demanded of them to join with them in opposing the
English liturgy or service-book, and, threatening to
pull them out by the heels, they obliged them to draw
up a paper and sign it, engaging not to permit the
idolatrous service-book—so they then termed it—to
be read in any place within their bounds, and to recal
their banished ministers.

It was in vain that the Lords in the Privy Council
Chamber sent expresses to the town council house
to the magistrates, to come and rescue them ; who
could only make return by telling that they were in
the same condition, and what they had been obliged
to do.   The Lords had then no remedy but to send
to some of the better sort of those of the other side,
to come and relieve them.   Upon this request, several lords and gentlemen, of good quality, of those
who opposed the service-book, came and spoke to the
people, and desired them to let the bishops and lords
quietly depart.

To these the people immediately yielded, and they
guarded their enemies to their own houses through
the rabble.   And now it was easy for them to see
that the people were no more to be imposed upon :
for the very next day a petition was presented to the
Privy Council against the service-book ; and this was
not a petition of the rabble, but signed by nineteen
noblemen, three hundred gentlemen of good note,
and by the principal inhabitants of the city of Edinburgh.

This petition was sent up to the King, but no
favourable answer was obtained ; but to show the
resentment of the Court against the citizens of
Edinburgh, the session was removed to Stirling, by
proclamation ; and another was published to forbid
all tumultuous resorts or meetings, on pain of rebellion.

This served to unite the people, who, having made
themselves obnoxious by appearing in these things,

were obliged, for their own security, to go through with their work ; and therefore, taking no more notice of the Council than as enemies that did them ill offices with the King, and resolving to defend their liberties at whatever hazard, they now began to form themselves, and to consider their strength, the generality of the nation being really on their side.   In the first place, the Earl of Hume, the Lord Lindsay, and abundance of lords and gentlemen, drew up a protestation, under their hands, against these proclamations, and having sent it to the Council, they from that time met in a body, *de die in diem*, to consider the state of the nation.

Here the famous tables were formed, of which our histories are so full ; by the order of which every degree sat by themselves—1. the nobility ; 2. the gentlemen ; 3. the boroughs ; 4. the ministers.   And yet all communicated their resolves ; so that every thing was done with unanimity and agreement.

They were no sooner put into this posture, but being sure of the concurrence of the people, they took no notice any more of the persecuting Council ; no, nor of the King himself, as to his menaces or missions ; but taking the administration so far into their hands, they proceeded to redress the grievances of the state.

They began, *a Jove principium*, with the restoration of the Church.   All the Episcopal pomp and ceremony vanished at once.   The bishops stood at Gaza, or fled, not daring to show their persecuting faces, and the meeting of the general table renewed the ancient Confession of Faith and Presbyterian Church government, entering into a solemn Covenant, one with another, to defend and preserve the said profession of the true Protestant reformed religion, and likewise the person of the King.

The King had a particular account of all these things laid before him, and they were let know that his Majesty resented it highly, which was nothing more or less than to animate them in the prosecution of their new undertaking.

They proceeded, therefore, with all the resolution and vigour possible, to settle and establish the liberties and constitution both of Church and State ; and that in such a manner as not to be again supplanted or disappointed by their enemies. In order to this, the imprisoned ministers were everywhere set free, the banished called home, and all restored to their livings, to the inexpressible joy of the people of Scotland, who forebare not upon all occasions to express their detestation of the innovations which had been put upon them before.

It would take up a long history by itself to record the restless endeavours of the bishops, and their dependents, as also the Episcopal clergy in England, by any means to bring themselves in again ; but alas ! there was not the least room to thrust the notion of it into the people's heads. They were everywhere overjoyed to see their poor banished ministers return, the Church restored to her liberties, and to enjoy her General Assemblies, regular judicatories, public communions, &c., without disturbance as before.

The other party had but one way left, which was to provoke the King to the highest resentment, so as to embark the power of England in support of that resentment, and to bring down a formidable army to chastise them as rebels against his royal authority. This they threatened the Covenanters with, so the Presbyterians were then called in England, because of the covenant taken as above.

It was certain that a King of England, at the head of all the powers of that opulent nation, was a most formidable thing ; and as the King had troops ready about him, these people perfectly naked, unprovided, undisciplined, and the like, the resentment of the King was the more terrible, and it occurred often from Solomon's words, " That the wrath of a king is like the roaring of a lion."

But the covenanted lords, far from being dismayed at all these threats, stood boldly to what they had done; and when the Marquis of Hamilton, whom the King sent to them, proposed two things, their answer will sufficiently acquaint us, that they acted as men under no apprehensions of the powers of their enemies.

The Marquis, vested with the power of High Commissioner to settle the peace, entered into a treaty with them on two heads,—viz.

1. What it was they expected from the King in satisfaction of their grievances.

2. Whether they would, after such satisfaction, return to their obedience and renounce their Covenant?

To the first they answered—They expected a free Parliament, and a legal General Assembly, and to that they were willing to refer all their demands. To the second—That they had not forsaken their obedience, and therefore needed no terms of return; but that, as to their Covenant, they would as soon renounce their baptism; nor would they enter into any treaty if it were mentioned to them a second time.

There were long and tedious debates between them upon these things, and many expedients the Commissioner offered, in the King's name, to keep, if possible, the bishops in their seats. He went back to the King; returned again with new concessions. He offered a declaration from the King, consisting of eleven heads, all granting things to the Covenanters which they would have rejoiced at a little before, but now rejected. In this declaration the King granted,

1. To annul the Service-book.
2. The Book of Canons.
3. The High Commission.
4. The Five Articles of Perth.

5. That all persons, whether ecclesiastical or civil, should be liable to censure of the Parliament and General Assembly.

6. That no oath be imposed upon ministers at their entry but what was contained in the act of Parliament.

7. That the ancient Confession of Faith should be renewed, and subscribed as it was in his father's reign, with the band thereto annexed.

8. That a General Assembly be holden at Glasgow the 21st of May.

9. And a Parliament at Edinburgh the 14th of May after.

10. That therein a general pardon of all offences shall be granted.

11. That he will appoint a general fast.

These were great things; but as the main thing was left behind—viz., that Episcopacy was left in the Church, the bishops to remain and to sit in Parliament, and those things left to the King's nomination which, of right, belonged to the Church, nothing could be done. They protested against these concessions as king-craft to delude them; and, claiming the right to call a General Assembly themselves, as by act of Parliament formerly mentioned, then in force, they rejected any accommodation without a perfect restoring the Church of Scotland to all her powers and privileges, and the total abolishing Episcopacy in that nation—choosing to run all hazards, and to put things to the last extremity, rather than abate one tittle of it.

Such zeal and such faithfulness to the principles they professed, could not fail to prompt them to all proper means to support what they had undertaken; wherefore the Marquis of Hamilton, being gone back in disgust, and having used some threatening speeches at his parting, they resolved not to be surprised; but immediately to put themselves in a posture of defence, that they might be able to go through with what they had undertaken.

Accordingly they began to lay taxes for raising money; gave out commissions for levying twelve regiments of foot, and eight regiments of horse, making in all 18,000 men; sent over into Sweden and the low countries, to invite home the old experienced generals and officers of their nation, whom they could confide in, to come and take pay in the service of their country; and, in a word, made all necessary preparations of war.

As this arming in Scotland was not without very good intelligence from England of the resolutions taken there to reduce them by force, and the threats of the Marquis of Hamilton to their faces, when he went from them, who told them insultingly, " that they must not think to use their kings now as they did formerly, when they were only kings of rebels; that the King had another loyal and warlike nation at his command, and that they should soon feel it to their cost." As I say, these things went before their arming, the English historians are manifestly partial, who say the King armed only in his own defence, and in charging the Scots with a design to begin the war; it being manifest they were capable of no other design than of securing themselves against being trampled on by a bigotted court and an incensed clergy.

It is also evident that this vigilance was, under God, the means of their preservation; for, when the King advanced forwards to York, and from thence to the Border, they were ready in the field before him, and that with such a resolute countenance, as that the English army cared not to attack them; and when the Earl of Holland, general of the horse to the King, advanced in a bravado with a strong brigade of horse and a detachment of foot, he was driven back faster than he came, by half the number of the Scots

cavalry, with musketeers in their intervals, a manner
of fighting which the English had not seen, and which
some Scots officers had learned under the great Gus-
tavus Adolphus. It would make too much sport with
English courage and bravery, which is so well confirmed in the world, to give an account how like
scoundrels this army behaved. An English historian
of note says in a manuscript which I have seen, they
were raised by the clergy, and imitated their masters ;
for as the clergy, who prompted this war, accompanied the King to York, but left him when he came
into the field, so the raw and undisciplined army accompanied him to the field, but left him when they
should have engaged ; in a word, none of the troops,
after the first skirmish, cared to engage, or to look the
Scots in the face ; who, on the other hand, though
they would not attack the King, yet stood ready,
and showed all the forwardness in the world to give
battle.

The King's generals finding the disposition of their
men, told the King very plainly, it was not his best
way to engage ; upon which notice was given the Scots
army, that they might send some to treat with his
Majesty upon their demands, which was done, and in
which all possible artifice was used to make a super-
ficial agreement, that the Scots might be obliged to
disband, and so might be surprised again unarmed.

However, they made a pacification, and, according
to the terms, broke up their army ; but having certain intelligence from England of the treacherous
design, they kept the officers and generals in half-
pay, a practice to this day used when nations put an
end to a war with no very great assurances of preserving the peace.

As they had been informed, so it proved ; for the
King, fired by the clergy, sought occasions of new
quarrels, and declined establishing their civil and
ecclesiastic liberties according to their model, and then

pretending the Scots had not kept their articles, denounced them rebels both in England and Ireland.

This obliged them to restore their troops with all possible expedition, and so soon as they were completed, the zeal and alacrity of the common people furnished men even faster than they required, so that they were in the field twenty days before the King; and now they used no more ceremony about advancing beyond their own borders, as before, but finding no army ready, they entered England in order of battle, and advanced to Newcastle-upon-Tyne before any enemy appeared.

Here the royal army faced them, and it was thought impossible the Scots should pass the Tyne without fighting; but General Leslie, an old soldier, resolving to put it to the issue of a battle, passed the river at Newbourn, in the face of a strong body of the English army; beat them fairly by plain fighting from their post, and killed 300 of their men; which action so frightened the King, and his whole army, that they would not strike a stroke more, but shamefully retreated to York, leaving Newcastle and Durham in possession of the Scots.

Here began the English troubles and civil war, which, as they belong not to our story, I shall mention no farther than to make good what I observed before, viz., that God so ordered it even from the beginning of the Reformation in Scotland, that no men, or party of men, have ever yet fallen upon the Church of Scotland but it has been at length their own destruction; the Church has been like the stone in the Gospel, and on her religious Establishment may be written, as is upon her banners, *Nemo me impune lacessit.* Ever may it be so, and may her enemies take the warning, that they may never more make the attempt!

Now the Church of Scotland was arrived to her full grown state indeed. Her enemies were not only subdued, but all in her power ; her Assemblies were now revived, the Covenant, which had been the band of all this steadiness, was renewed ; all her Church judicatories were restored ; Episcopacy was entirely abolished, and all her persecutors fled, for fear of falling into the hands of that justice which they had before exercised to tyranny and oppression.

A few words will finish this part of her story. The King and his High Church army being retreated, after the action at Newbourn, it is impossible to express the consternation they were in. The Scots army being advanced to Durham, were now entire masters of England. If they had pleased to advance, nothing could have stood before them. They were entirely possessed of all the counties of Northumberland, Cumberland, and Durham, and began to extend themselves towards the west ; and as they received daily supplies of men from Scotland, they would, in six days more, have been possessed of Westmoreland and Lancashire, there being no forces to oppose them but at York, and those under the terrible apprehension of being attacked by our whole army, which, God and a just quarrel being on the Scots side, they were in no condition to oppose.

The King, in the utmost distress, here summoned a great council of his English nobility to consult what to do ; they advised him to what for fourteen years had been his aversion, namely, the calling a Parliament, and to send to the Scots to treat of a second pacification, which they, in the greatest prosperity of their affairs, readily consented to. This was the famous treaty of Rippon, where, granting a cessation of arms, contrary to the practice of all victorious armies, rating their contributions that the country might not be oppressed, and limiting their army to the banks of the river Tees, they sat still, waiting upon Providence, to see what would be the issue of those great things which were then in view.

I mention this as it concurs with what is observed
before, viz. that this arming in Scotland had nothing
in it of what the enemies of the Church of Scotland
charged upon them, viz. of a design against either
the person or government of their Prince; but was
nothing more or less than what the evident necessity
of their circumstances led them to, in defence of their
civil and religious rights, which were illegally overthrown by their enemies; which enemies had solicited
a foreign aid (for such even their own King, at the
head of the English forces, was) to subdue and destroy them.   Nor was their practice in this case
any thing but what has been practised and allowed
to be agreeable to the laws of nature, and of our
country, by both nations, on several occasions, less
urgent than this, as will, in part, appear in this
account.

It remains only to observe, that on the meeting of
the Parliament in England, the Scots being fairly
treated with, their just demands granted, and afterwards confirmed, they quitted England in August
1640 ; intermeddled not then with the quarrels and
divisions which, from that time, began to increase ;
but retired within their own borders, and laid down
their arms, till the flame of civil war, which afterwards
broke out in England, involved them of course in the
share of it, which they felt to their great loss and oppression, on many accounts.

But the story of those things not relating to the
Church affairs I pass over, referring to the histories
of both nations.   I have only to conclude this Part
with saying, that from this time to the Restoration
of King Charles II., the Church of Scotland, being
uninterrupted as to her ecclesiastical jurisdiction, subsisted in her full grown state, enjoying the full liberty
of her constitution, both in worship, discipline, and
government.   In civil affairs, their country was often
involved in war and confusion enough; but as to the

L

Church, which is the proper business of this tract, it suffered no considerable interruption.

Her next appearance will be a state of trial, the return of her implacable enemies the bishops and their hierarchy, where we shall see her again over-whelmed in blood, and suffering the most cruel and merciless persecution that ever Protestant Church endured—her neck being for eight and twenty years continually under the feet of tyranny and oppression.

CONCLUSION.

From this whole account, this just observation presents itself to our view.

1. That as the Church of Scotland reformed at first from Popery into Presbyterianism, so when the invasions of Episcopacy, supported by the tyranny of princes, had reduced her to the lowest ebb, yet whenever the hand of tyranny was taken away, and the people of Scotland were left to the freedom of their own choice in matters of religious worship, they never failed to demonstrate that Episcopacy was their aversion, and that they still retained a sincere affection to the model of their first Reformers; that the Presbyterian Church was truly national, and that they would always, by their choice, embrace the same, both in doctrine, discipline, worship, and government.

2. That Episcopacy never got ground in Scotland but by violence; and never failed to exercise what power it had there, to oppress and destroy its opposers; being always animated with a spirit of persecution in the Church, and absolute tyranny in the State, as will still more fully appear in that part of this work which is still behind.

ADDENDA TO PART II.

[Here follow some Original Papers, and accounts of things which are referred to in the foregoing Part.]

No. I.

The Protestation of Mr Andrew Hunter against the absolving the Bishop of St Andrews, without repentance.

In respect that the provincial Assemblie of the Kirk, gathered in Christ's name, holden at St Andrews, the twelfth day of April 1586, for manifest crimes and open contumacie, hath justly and formally, according to the Word of God, and sincere custom of this Kirk, excommunicated Mr Patrick Adamson; and that in this General Assemblie they take upon them to absolve the said Mr Patrick from the sentence of excommunication, the process not being tried nor heard in publick, the person excommunicated declaring no signs of true repentance, nor craving the said absolviture by himself, nor by his procurators, before the very time, wherein they absolve him; I therefore, for my part, and in name of all the other brethren and true Christians, who will be participant with me, take God to record of the dealing of that provincial Assemblie, and this Assemblie General; protesting also before the Almightie, his holy angels, and saints here convened, that I have no assurance in God's Word to my conscience to assent, allow, or approve this his absolviture. And, therefore, until the time I perceive his conversion to be true and effectual, I cannot but hold him as one justly delivered to Satan, notwithstanding of the said absolviture. [And this his Protestation, subscribed with his hand, he desired to be registred *ad perpetuam rei memoriam*; and withal gave his reasons moving him thereto.]

No. II.

The Recantation of Mr Patrick Adamson, Bishop of St Andrews, directed to the Synod convened at St Andrews, 8th Aprilis 1591.

Brethren, understanding the proceedings of the Assembly in my contrare, and being now withholden by sickness to present myself before you, that I may give confession of that doctrine wherein I hope God shall call me, and that at his pleasure I may depart in the unitie of the Christian faith ; I thought good by writ to utter the same unto your wisdoms, and to crave your godly wisdoms' assistance, not for the restitution of any worldly pomp or pre-eminence, which I little respect ; but to remove from me the slanders which are raised in this country concerning the variance of doctrine, especially on my part ; wherein I protest before God that I have only a single respect to his glorie, and by his grace I shall abide herein to my life's end.

First, I confess the true doctrine of Christian religion to be publickly taught, and rightly announced within this realm, and detest all papistrie and superstition ; like as (blessed be God) I have detested the same in my heart the space of thirtie years, since it pleased God to give me the knowledge of the truth, wherein I have walked uprightly, as well here as in other countries, as the Lord beareth me record, until these last days, wherein, partly for ambition and vain glory, to be preferred before my brethren, and partly for covetousness to possess the pelf of the Kirk, I did undertake this office of Archbishoprick, wherewith justly the sincerest professors of the Word have found fault, and have condemned the same as impertinent to the office of a sincere pastor of God's Word. And albeit men would colour the same, and the imperfections thereof, by divers cloaks ; yet the samine cannot be concealed from the eyes of the faithful, neither yet can the men of God, when they are put to their conscience, dissemble the same.

Next, I confess I was in an erroneous opinion, that I believed the Government of the Kirk to be like unto the kingdoms of the earth, plain contrary t the command of our Master Christ (as it is) ; but also in ministers who are nothing but vassals under him in an equality among themselves.

Thirdly, That I married the Earl of Huntlie contrair the commandment of the Church, without the confession of his faith and profession of the sincere doctrine of the Word, I repent and crave God pardon.

That I travelled both by reasoning, and otherways, to subject Kirkmen to the King's ordinance, in things that appertained to ecclesiastical matters, and things of conscience, whereupon sundry great enormities have fallen forth in this country, I ask God mercy.

That I taught Presbyteries to be a foolish invention, and would have had it so esteemed of all men, which is an ordinance of Christ, I crave God mercy.

Farther, I submit myself to the mercie of God, and judgment of the Assemblie, not measuring my offences by myself, nor infirmities by my cwn ingine, but by the good judgment of the Kirk, to which always I subject myself, and beseech you to make intercession to God for me, and to the King, that I may have some moyen to live, and consume the rest of my wretched time, for winning of whose favour (which foolishly I thought thereby to obtain) I committed all these errors.

Whereas I am burdened to be the setter forth of the book called the *King's Declaration*, wherein the whole order of the Kirk is condemned and traduced, I protest before God, that I was commanded to write the same by the Chancellor for the time, but chiefly by the Secretar, another great courtier, who himself penned the second act of Parliament, concerning the power and authority of judicature to be absolutely in the King's power; and that it should not be lawful to any subject to reclaim from the same, under the penaltie of the act, which I suppose was treason.

Item, Where it is alleged that I should have condemned the doctrine announced and taught by the ministrie of Edinburgh, concerning obedience to the Prince, I confess and protest before God, that I never understood nor yet knew any thing but sinceritie and uprightness in the doctrine of the ministers of Edinburgh in that point, or in any other.

Farther, I confess I was the author of the act discharging the ministers' stipends that would not subscribe the acts of Parliament, wherewith God had justly recompensed myself.

As for any violent course, it is known well enough who was the author thereof, and my part was tried at the imprisonment of Mr Nicol Dalgleish, Mr Patrick Melvíne, Mr Thomas Jack, and others.

Moreover, I grant I was more busie with some bishops in England, in prejudice of the discipline of our Kirk, partly when I was there, and partly by mutual intelligence since, than became a good Christian, much less a faithful pastor. Neither is there any thing that more ashameth me than my often deceiving and abusing of the Kirk heretofore, by confessions, subscriptions, protestations, &c., which be far from me now and ever hereafter. Amen.—Your brother in the Lord,

M. PATRICK ADAMSON.

Where your wisdoms desire to have my own opinion concerning the Book of the Declaration of the King's intention, the same is at more length declared in the confession, which I have exhibited already, wherein I have condemned all the articles therein contained, like as by these presents I condemn the same.

Where you require, what became of the books of the Assemblie? I reserved them whole, until the returning of the Lords and the ministrie out of England; and if I had not preserved them, my Lord Arran intended to have made them to be cast in the fire. And upon a certain day, in Falkland, before they were delivered to the King's Majesty, the Bishop of N., accompanied with Mr Henry Hammiltoun, rent out some leaves, and destroyed such things as made against our estate, and that not without my own special allowance.

As for the books which I have set forth, I have set forth nothing, except a commentary upon the First Epistle of Paul to Timothy, which shall be directed to the King's Majesty, and keeped no exemplar beside me; and I understand that Mr John Geddie got the same from the King, and lent it to Mr Robert Hepburn.

Farther, I wrote nothing, but only made mention, in my preface upon the Apocalypse, that I should write a book called *Psillus*, which (being prevented by disease) God would not suffer me to finish, and the little thing that was done I caused destroy it. I have set forth the Book of Job, and the Lamentations of Jeremie, all in verse, to be printed in England.

As for my intention, I am not disposed, nor of abilitie, to write any thing at this time; and if it please God I were restored to my health, I would change my stile, as Cajetanus did at the Council of Trent.

As for Sutlivius's book against the form and order of the Presbyteries, so far am I from being partner in that work, that as I know not the man, nor had ever intelligence of the work before it was done, so if it please God to give me days, I will write in his contrarie.

Prays the brethren to be at unitie and peace with me, and in token of their forgiveness, because my health suffereth me not to go over to the College where ye are presently assembled, which I would gladly do to ask God and you forgiveness, that it would please you to repair hither that I may do it.

Moreover I condemn, by this my subscription, whatsoever is contained in the epistle dedicatorie to the King's Majesty before my book upon the Revelation, that is either slanderous or offensive to the brethren. Also I promise to satisfy the brethren of Edinburgh, or any other Kirk in this realm, according to good conscience, in whatsoever they find themselves justly offended, and contrarie to the Word of God, in any of my speeches, actions, or proceedings which have past from me.

And concerning the Commentary upon the First Epistle of Paul to Timothy, because there are diverse things therein contained offensive, and that tend to allow the state of bishops otherwise than God's Word can suffer, I condemn the same.

The pages before written, dicted by me, Mr Patrick Adamson, and written at my commandment by my servant, Mr Samuel Cuninghame, I subscribe with my own hand, as acknowledged by me in sinceritie of conscience, as in the presence of God, before these witnesses, directed to me from the Synodal Assemblie, because of my inabilitie to repair towards them, James Monipennie, younger of Pitmillie; Andrew Woode of Stravethie; David Murray, portioner of Ardeit; Mr David Russel; Mr William Murray, minister at Dysert; Mr Robert Wilkie; David Ferguson, with diverse others.   M. P. ADAMSON.

David Ferguson, *witness.*
M. Nicol Dalgleis.
James Monipennie, of Pitmillie, *witness.*
Andrew Woode of Stravethie, *witness.*
M. Robert Wilkie, *witness.*

David Murray, with my hand, *witness.*
M. David Russel.
M. David Spence.
M. John Caldclough.
M. William Murray.

Mr Patrick Adamson's own Answer to, and Refutation of, the Book falsely called, the King's Declaration.

I have enterprised of meer remorse of conscience to write against a book, called *A Declaration of the King's Majesty's Intention*, albeit it containeth little or nothing of the King's own intention, but my own at the time of the writing thereof, and the corrupt intentions of such as for the time were about the King, and abused his minoritie. Of which book, and contents thereof, compiled by me at the command of some chief courtiers for the time (as is before written), I shall shortly declare my opinion, as the infirmity of sickness and weakness of memory will permit.

First, In the whole book nothing is contained but assertions of lies, ascribing to the King's Majesty that whereof he was not culpable; for albeit, as the time went his Majesty could have suffered these things to have been published in this realme, yet his Majesty was never of that nature as to have reviled any man's person, or to upbraid any man with calumnies, whereof there is a number contained in that book.

Secondly, In the declaration of the *second* act of Parliament there is mention made of Mr Andrew Melvine and his preachings, most wrongfully condemned, in special as factious and seditious; albeit, his Majesty hath had a lively trial of that man's fidelity and truth, in all proceedings from time to time. True it is, he is earnest and zealous, and can abide no corruption (which most unadvisedly I attributed to a fiery and salt humour) which his Majesty findeth by experience to be true; for he allowed well of him, and knoweth things that were alledged upon him to have been false and contrived treacheries.

There are contained in the second act of Parliament, and declaration thereof, diverse other false calumnies to defame the ministrie, and to bring the Kirk of God in hatred and envy with their prince and the nobility, burdening and accusing falsely the ministers of sedition and other crimes, whereof they were innocent. As likewise it is written in the same act and declaration thereof, that sovereign and supream power, in matters ecclesiastical, pertaineth to the king, which is worthy to be condemned, and not to be contained among Christian acts, where the power of the Word is to be extolled above all the power of princes, and they are to be brought under subjection to the same.

The fourth act condemned the presbyteries, as a judgment not allowed by the king's law, which is a very slender argument. For, as concerning the authority of the presbytery, we have the same warranted in the Gospel (Matth. ch. xviii.) where Christ commanded to tell the Kirk,—which authoritie being commanded by Christ, and the acts of Parliament forbidding it, we should rather obey God than man: and yet the Presbytery wanted never the king's authoritie for allowance thereof from the beginning, saving only at that hour of darkness when he was abused with evil companie. As for any other thing that is contained in this act, against any order or proceeding of the presbytery, it is to be esteemed that nothing was done by the presbytery without wisdom, judgment, and discretion, and so hath received approbation again by the Kirk, whereunto also I understand his Majesty hath given allowance, hath ratified and approved the same, which should be a sufficient reason to repress all men's curiositie, that either have or yet would find fault with the same.

The last act containeth the establishing of a bishop, which hath no warrant in the word of God, but is grounded upon the policie of man's invention, whereupon the primacie of the Pope, or Antichrist, is risen, which is worthie to be disallowed and forbidden; because the number of the eldership, that hath jurisdiction and oversight, as well of visitation as of admission, will do the same far more authentickly, godly, and with greater zeal than a bishop, whose care commonly is not upon God and his dutie but upon the world, whereupon his chief attendance is. Consider how that office hath been used these five hundred years bygone, with what crueltie and tyrannie it hath been exercised; ye shall find it to have been the chief mean that hath in every country suppressed the Word of God, which shall be evident to all that read the storie of the Kirk. As for my own opinion, it seemeth to be nearest to the truth, and farthest from all kind of ambition, that the brethren in equal degree assemble themselves under the head Christ, and there every man discharge his office carefully, as he is commanded. And because weakness of memorie and sickness suffereth me not at length to discourse upon these matters as I would, I must request the good reader to assure himself that I have written these without compulsion or persuasion of any man, with an upright heart, and have delivered the same with perfect sinceritie of mind, so far as infirmitie of flesh and blood did suffer, as God shall judge me at the latter day; and that the same reader account, that whatsoever things are omitted is to be imputed to the imbecilitie of my memory and the present sickness, and not to any good will, which I protest was to have condemned every point, yea, even to the false narration of the banquet and all the rest contained in the little treatise called *The Declaration of the King's Majesty's Intention*, as I acknowledge they deserve to be condemned by the censure and judgment of the Kirk, to the which also I submit myself, in whatsoever thing I have, either in word or writ, attempted in that foresaid declaration or otherways:—By these presents, subscribed with my hand, at St Andrews, the twelfth of May 1591, before these witnesses—Mr David Black, minister at St Andrews; Mr Robert Wilkie, principal at St Leonard's College; Mr John Aitoun of Enmath; Mr William Russel.

PATRICK ADAMSON.

M. David Black, *witness.*	William Learmonth.
George Ramsey.	Patrick Gutrie.
M. John Auchinleck.	Charles Watson, *scribe.*

I, M. Patrick Adamson, declare, that this confession and declaration before-written is my own confession, given with my heart, and subscribed with my hand, before these witnesses underwritten, under subscribing with me, at my request and desire, at St Andrews, the 10th of June 1591.

PATRICK ADAMSON.

David Carnegie of Colluthie, *witness.*	Alexander Bruce of Earlshal, *witness.*
William Scot of Abbotshal, *witness.*	Borthwick of Gordonshal.
William Learmonth.	M. William Russel.
Thomas Kingzo.	M. David Black.
M. Robert Wilkie.	M. Andr. Hunter, *Scribe of the Provincial Assembly.*
M. Andrew Moncrief.	

No. III.

[Here follows the account which the Episcopal party themselves give of the proceedings of the Scots bishops and Presbyterian Ministers, mentioned in this work, before the King at Hampton Court.]

The first audience was at Hampton Court the 22d of September, at which, besides the bishops and ministers from Scotland, were present the Earls of Dumbar, Argyle, Glencarne, Sir Thomas Hamilton, advocate; and Sir Alex. Straiton. Of the English, Dr Montague, Dean of the Chapel, was only admitted to stay. There the King declaring the purpose for which he had called them, spake a few words to this effect: That having left the Church of Scotland in peace at his parting forth of it, he did now hear of great disturbances in the same, whereof he desired to understand the true cause, and to have their advice how the same might be removed. This being, said he, the errand in general for which I have called you, I should be glad to hear your opinions touching the meeting at Aberdeen, where an handful of ministers, in contempt of my authority, and against the discharge given them, did assemble; and though they were neither a sufficient number, nor the accustomed order kept, they would take upon them to call it a General Assembly, and have since proudly maintained it by declining my council and such other means as they pleased to use. The rather I would hear your minds, because I am informed that divers ministers do justify that meeting, and in their public preachings commend these brethren as persons distressed, which in effect is to proclaim me a tyrant and persecutor.

Mr James Melvill, answering first, said, that there was no such discharge given to those ministers that met at Aberdeen, as was alledged, adjuring Sir Alexander Straiton, who was said to have given the charge, to declare in his Majesty's presence how that matter was carried. As to the absence of moderator and clerk, he said that none of these were essential parts of an Assembly, and that the moderator absenting himself of purpose, and the clerk refusing to serve, the brethren convened might lawfully create others in their places, so as the ministers having warrant to convene from the Word of God, and from his

Majesty's laws, as also coming thither by direction of their Presbyteries, he could not in his conscience condemn them.

Well, then, said the King, I shall desire you to answer me three things that I will ask.   First, if it be lawful to pray publicly for persons convicted by the lawful judge as persons being in distress and afflicted ?   Second, whether I may not, being a Christian King, by my authority royal, convocate and prorogue, and desert for just and necessary causes known to myself, any assemblies or meetings within my dominions ?   Third, whether or not may I by my authority call, and convene before me and my Council, whatsoever person or persons, civil or ecclesiastical, for whatsoever offences committed by them in whatsoever place within my dominions, and if I may not take cognition of the offence, and give sentence therein ?   And further, whether or not are all my subjects, being cited to answer before me and my Council, obliged to compeer and acknowledge me or them for judges in these offences ?

Mr James, answering, said that the questions were weighty, and craved a great deliberation, wherefore he would humbly entreat his Majesty to grant them a time to confer and advise together, that they might all give one direct answer.   This desire granted, they were commanded to advise and meet together that night, and be ready to answer the next day.   At this meeting the Earls of Salisbury and Northampton, with divers of the English clergy, were present.   The ministers desiring to have the meeting more private, requested the Earl of Dumbar to move the King therein, and that none but Scotsmen should be present ; fearing, as they said, that some unseemly words might escape them ; but this was denied, and they warned to speak with that respect which became subjects.   It was believed that the King should have begun with the questions proponed in the former meeting, but his Majesty taking another course, required them to declare one by one, their judgments touching Aberdeen Assembly.   The bishops, being first asked, did all condemn the meeting as turbulent, factious, and unlawful.

Mr Andrew Melvill then being inquired, made answer, that he could not condemn the Assembly, being a private man ; that he came unto England upon his Majesty's letter, without any commission from the Church of Scotland, and though he had commission in *dicta causa*, and not hearing what they could say for themselves, he could not give his judgment; sentence, he said, was given against them in a justice court, how justly he did remit that to the Great Judge, but for himself he would say as our Saviour did in another case, *Quis me constituit judicem.*

Mr James Balfour, being next asked, did pray his Majesty not to press him with any answer, for that he knew nothing would be well taken that proceeded from his mouth, and that Mr Andrew had answered his mind sufficiently.

Mr James Melvil, without giving a direct answer, began to tell that, since his coming to London, he had received divers letters, and with them a petition, that should have been presented to the late Parliament in behalf of the warded ministers, which he was desired to offer unto his Majesty, and, as he thought, the petition would make all their minds known.

The King, taking the petition, and falling to read the same, willed the advocate to go on and receive the answer of the rest. And as the advocate was questioning Mr William Scot, and urging him with a distinct answer (for he used many circumlocutions, according to the custom), Mr Andrew Melvill, in a great passion, said that he followed the instructions of Mr John Hamilton, his uncle, who had poisoned the north with his Papistry, and that he was now become κατηγορος των αδελφων. Northampton asking what he meant by that speech? the King said, he calleth him the mickle Devil; and then, folding up the petition, said, I see you are all set for maintaining that base Conventicle of Aberdeen. But what answers have you to give to the questions I moved? It was answered that they had conferred together, and finding them to concern the whole Church, they would not by their particular voices prejudge the same. But you will not, I trust, said the King, call my authority in question, and subject the determination of the same to your Assemblies. This they said was far from their thoughts, but if his Majesty should be pleased to set down in writing what he required, they should labour to give him satisfaction.

Thus were they dismissed for that time; and being the next day called before the Scottish Council (for after this they were no more admitted to his Majesties presence), they were enquired, whether they had, in their publick prayers, prayed for the warded ministers, as persons afflicted, and sufferers for God's cause. Some of them confessed that they had prayed for them as persons in trouble and distress; others, that they had commended them to God, but remembered not in what words.

The 20th of October, they were again brought before the Scots Councill, and had the three questions delivered to them in writing, which they were commanded to answer severally. Meanwhile, they were discharged to return into Scotland without his Majesties license, and prohibited to come towards the Queen and Princes Court. The bishops and others of the clergy that assisted them were permitted to return.

[Having thus given a summary of this eminent story on one side, it follows to see how the other side relates it.]

~~~~~~~~~

No. IV.

[Here follows the account which the Presbyterian party give of the same conference, extracted from the memorials of some of the persons present, and from Calderwood's History of the Church, &c.]

Upon the 22d of September, they were sent for to the King; and when they came, they were admitted to the chamber of presence, where they were courteously received by the Bishop of Canterbury. The King came to the chamber of presence, accompanied with the Earls of Dumbar and Orknay; Lord Fleeming; the Laird of Laurestoun; Sir Thomas Hamiltoun, the King's Advocate; Mr John Spotswood, Bishop of Glasgow; Mr George Gladstones, Bishop of St Andrews; Mr James Law, Bishop of Orknay; Mr James Nicolson; Mr Robert Howie; Mr Patrick Sharp; Mr Andrew Lamb. None were suffered to stay within but the Scotish Counsellors and Ministers, except only that of Montague, who kept the door. The King opened up the causes which moved him to write for them, almost conform to the tenor of the proclamation, and the missive sent unto them. In end, he gathered all his speeches to two heads, wherein he said, he would be through with them for the peace of the Church. The one about the pretended General Assembly (so he termed it), holden at Aberdeen, and the proceedings which followed thereupon. The other, how there might be an ordinary and peaceable Assembly holden, to set all things in quietness and good order. They had agreed among themselves to give no present answer, but to take all to advisement. Mr James Melvine was chosen to be their spokesman. After he had expressed, in a complementing manner, their joy for his inclination to intertain peace, &c., he desired time to advise; because his Majesty's letter did bear no particular, neither heard they of any before that time. Thereafter there was much time spent upon sending of commissioners from presbyteries, after receiving of his Majesty's Commissioners' letter, discharging any Assembly to be holden at Aberdeen. Item, upon the proceedings of the Synod of Fife, praying for the convicted brethren in prison, and upon Mr James Melvin's letter directed to the Synod of Fife. For the present they answered thus much : Many of the presbyteries had not received advertisement before the day; these who had received, considering that there were weightier reasons for holding the Assembly than for deserting of it, resolved to send their commissioners to keep the day appointed by his Majesty the law standing, which is the most authentick testimony that a king can give, as his Majesty himself declared in open assembly holden at Dundie; for the enemies were bold and busie : many references, appellations, and other matters, were lying not taken order with, which could not be ordered without a general assembly. The greatest motive was a fear to lose the right and possession of a general assembly, which would expire of itself, if there were not a set day appointed. The words of the letter, sent by the Synod of Fife to other synods, were, in their judgment, so conceived, that it could neither prejudice the General Assembly, nor his Majesty's royal power, nor the brethren who were in ward under his Majesty's mercy. They confessed they prayed for the imprisoned brethren, and professed they could not omit that duty to their brethren, which was extended even to malefactors for their amendment. As for Mr James Melvin's letter, the King said, I heard, Mr James, you wrote a letter to the Synod of Fife, holden at Couper, where there was much of Christ, and little good of the King. By God, I trow ye were raving or mad.; for ye speak otherwise now. Was that a charitable judgment ye had of me ? Sir, said Mr James, I was both sore and sick in body when I wrote that letter; but sober, and sound in mind. I assured myself and the brethren that these articles, a copy whereof came in my hands, could not come from your Majesty, they were so strange. Sundry of the bishops and commissioners of the General Assembly that were present confessed that many wrong copies were sent abroad, and some very odious, whereof one might have come in Mr James his hands. The King, resuming the first two heads, willed them to advise upon an answer against the next day.

They were scarce entered into their lodging at Kingstoun, when they received a letter from Mr Alexander Hay, Secretary fcr the Scotish Affairs, warning them in the King's name to come to sermon to-morrow. So, upon Tuesday the 23d of September, they went to Hampton Court, and sat in the place appointed for them in the chappel, the King and Queen being present. Doctor Buckerage taught upon Rom. xiii. 1. He joined pope and presbyteries together, diverse times, as enemies to the King's supremacy.

After dinner, they resolved upon this answer to the first head, which they appointed Mr James Melvin to deliver. They could not judge of the Assembly of Aberdeen, for these reasons :—1. His Majesty had indicted, by proclamation, a general assembly, wherein his Majesty expected a reparation of all disorders, in so far as belongeth to the censures of the Church. If they should now condemn, or resolve, having committed such a prejudice, they could not be heard. They called to remembrance his Majesty's practice, at the Assembly holden at Montrose, where the Commissioners of Lothian and Merce were rejected upon the like ground. 2. *Res non erat integra*, but judged already by the Council; but they would be loath to contradict. 3. The judgment thereof could not appertain to them. *Nam quis constituit eos judices?* 4. Put the case they could be judges, and that the matter might be committed to them, they could not do it *indicta causa, et reis non citatis nec auditis*. But the King took another course, which was to pose every one in particular, and so to catch advantage, if it were possible.

The ministers were sent for after dinner. The Prince stood at the King's left hand, with the abovenamed Scottish noblemen, counsellors, bishops, and commissioners of the General Assembly. The Archbishop of Canterbury stood at the King's right hand, the Earls of Salisbury, Suffolk, Worcester, Nottingham, Northampton, Lord Stennop, Lord

Knolles, and sundry other noblemen. Some bishops and deans stood at the door, behind the tapestry, who now and then discovered themselves. Mr Andrew Melvin desired the Earl of Dumbar to request his Majesty that the English might be removed, lest his Majesty should offend at anything spoken in a homely manner in their presence; but it was not granted. The King, after resuming of the points left the last day, came at last to be resolved in this particular, whether the Assembly holden lately at Aberdeen was a lawful assembly or not? and whether the proceedings of the ministers at it and afterward were justifiable or not? Mr George Gladstones, John Spotswood, James Law, Andrew Lamb, bishops; Mr James Nicolson, Patrick Sharpe, Robert Howie, and Laurestoun, were first asked, and answered, they ever damned that Assembly, and the proceedings of these brethren as unlawful. Then the King demanded at Mr Andrew Melvin, what say ye; whether think ye, that where a few number of eight or nine do meet, without any warrant, wanting the chief members of an assembly, as the moderator and scribe, convening unmannerly without a sermon being also discharged before by open proclamation, may make an assembly or not? He answered to the first objection thus: That in an assembly of the servants of Christ, whereof the number is not prescribed by a law, it is not lawful for any to disallow thereof for the number, seeing two or three (which is the smallest number) convened in the name of Christ, have the promise of his presence, who is their Lord and Ruler. Beside, rareness maketh not unlawfulness in an ordinary meeting, established by law and practice. Lastly, all that was done might lawfully have been done by a fewer number, authorized with commission, as they were; for continuation requireth not full conventions. As for their warrant. 1. They have warrant from God's Word. 2. Your Majesty's laws. 3. Their Presbyteries sent them in commission to that effect, and therefore approved the prorogating of the day, which was all they did; and therefore these Presbyteries were to be blamed if anything was done amiss, and not the persons who were executors only of their Presbyteries' will and commission. To the second he answered that the absence of a moderator and clerk were not *de essentia synoda*, and therefore the one, to wit, Mr Patrick Galloway, the mo-

M

derator of the former Assembly, absenting himself; the other, to wit, Mr Thomas Nicolson, being present, but craving leave to be absent for that time because of his weighty affairs, they might create others in their places according to the practice of the Church of Scotland, as is to be seen in the register of the General Assembly. To the third he answered, his Majesty was misinformed. For the ordinary pastor of Aberdeen, to wit, Mr James Ross, had a sermon before the meeting. As for the pretended charge given the night before, turning himself to Laurestoun, he said, I adjure thee in the name of the Kirk of Scotland as you will answer before the great God in the day that Christ shall appear to judge the quick and the dead, to declare the truth, and to tell whether there was any such charge given or not. Laurestoun answered not one word. Then the king asked what reasons he had not to condemn the ministers. He answered, if it please your Majesty to hear, I have these. 1. I am but a private man, come upon your Majesty's letter without any commission from the Church of Scotland; and, therefore, seeing *nemo constituit me judicem*, I cannot take upon me to condemn them. 2. Your Majesty, by virtue of your proclamation, dated here at Hampton Court (which he then produced), hath remitted their trial to the General Assembly, expecting reparation of wrongs if any be done. I cannot therefore prejudge the Church and Assembly of my vote there, which, if I give now, I shall be sure to have my mouth shut up then, as by experience I and other brethren have found before. 3. *Res est hactenus judicata* by your Majesty's Council, whether rightly or not, that I remit to the Lord the searcher of all hearts, before whom one day they must appear and answer for that sentence. Shall I then take upon me to contradict your Majesty's Council and their proceedings? I think your Majesty would not be well content with it. *Lastly,* how can I condem them *indicta causa*, not hearing their accusers objecting against them? This was the substance of his answer which he uttered after his own manner, roundly and freely. Mr James Balfour, standing next in order, was urged to declare his mind. He answered in effect as Mr Andrew did. Mr James Melvine answered, their proceedings are already censured by your Majesty and Council, wherein I am resolved with the peril to obtemperate either by obedience or patience. If your Majesty be pleased to have it farther judged by an

Assembly of the Church, which is our wish, I cannot prejudge the judgment of the Church.   If in the mean time
your Majesty will urge me to deliver my judgment of the
matter according to my conscience, unless the wrongs
done to them, and given in writ to your Majesty's estates
at the last Parliament holden at Perth, be considered and
discussed, I would not for all the world condemn them.
A copy of the wrongs we have earnestly desired of themselves, that we might present them to your Majesty; with
this he stepped forward, and delivered them to the King
in his hand.   While the rest were sporting, the King read
them over, and, smiling in discontented manner, he said,
he was glad they were given in.   Mr Robert Wallace followed.   He regrated some delations that were given in
against him, and then answered as the former did.   Mr
William Watson was sharp against Laurestoun, and laid
the burden of all upon him, but he never replyed one
Word.   Mr William Scot delivered his judgment in few
words, agreeable with these that preceeded.   The advocate craved licence of the King to deal with him, but Mr
William had the upper hand to his shame.   Because much
time was spent, Mr John Carmichael and Mr Adam Colt
were desired to be short.   They answered in few words
conform to the rest.   Their harmony moved the English and others to admiration.   In end, Mr Andrew Melvine brake out, in his own manner, and plainly avowed
the innocency of the brethren in all their proceedings at
Aberdeen.   Thereafter he recounted the wrongs done to
them at Linlithgow, whereof he was an ear and eye witness.   He laid to the Advocate's charge his favouring
and sparing of Papists, his crafty and malicious dealing
against the ministers; so that κατηγορος τῶν αδελφῶν could
not have done more against the saints of God than ye did
at Linlithgow against the ministers.   Ye would do God
and his Majesty better service, my Lord, if you bended
your forces and speeches against your uncle, Mr John
Hamiltoun, a seminary Priest, and Mr Gilbert Brown.
Abbot of Newabbay, who have infected a great part of
the country with Popery.   But these men's heads ye
have clapped, and shut up the faithful servants of Christ
in prison; and still ye shew yourself possessed with the
same spirit: for ye think it not enough to have pleaded
against them in Scotland, with all the cunning and skill
ye had, but still continue κατήγορος τῶν ἀδελφῶν.   At which

words the King, turning him about to the Archbishop of
Canterbury, said, What is it he saith? I think he is calling him out of the Revelation, Antichrist; nay, by God,
he calleth him the very devil. Well bourded, brother
John, said the King. In end, he demanded what overture they would give him for the other point. They answered, their best overture was to have a free General
Assembly, by which all jars would be removed and quickly
quieted. The King riseth, and they were dismissed, not
without great applause of the English, for their gravity
and boldness in the cause of God. The truth was cleared
unto them, which before was obscured by misreports. What
was omitted by one was remembered by another, every one
of them having a pretty space to advise upon his answer.

When the ministers were gone out of the palace, and a
little on their way to Kingstoun, Mr Alexander Hay sent
for them, readeth to them a charge from the King not to
return to Scotland, nor to come near the King's, Queen's,
or Princes' Court, without special licence and calling for.

Upon the 24. of September, M. Alexander Hay willed
them to return to Court with all convenient speed.
When they came, he shewed to Mr James Melvine that
he was directed by his Majesty to crave his subscription
to the sheet of paper which was given in by him to his
Majesty concerning the cause and manner of the delivery.
So he gave him it to peruse; which being done, Mr James
wrote the answer, and manner of delivery of them in the
King's hand. Within an hour after, the Earle of Glencarne and Mr John Gordoun came to them, directed from
the King, desiring their answer in writ, and subscribed, to
his question—What the King may do in matters ecclesiastical? And whether or not he had wholly the power of
conveening and discharging of Assemblies? They craved
the question to be set down in writ, and subscribed as
from his Majesty, and sufficient time to advise, and so the
matter deserted at that time.

Upon the 28. of September, they were again written for
to come to Court. The end was to hear Doctor Andrews,
Bishop of Excester, who, teaching upon the tenth of Numbers, discoursed upon the Two Trumpets, and proved, as
he could, the convening and discharging of councils and
assemblies to belong to Christian Kings and Emperours.

At supper, they were again warned to be at Court the
day following by eight o'clock; because the Scotish Coun-

cil was to deal with them. But when they came, they were willed by the King's express command, to come to the King's Chappel, namely, Mr Andrew Melvine and Mr James Melvine. Mr James warned Mr Andrew by the way that they were to be trapped, and to have their patience tried. There they saw the King and Queen offer at the altar, whereupon were set two books, two basons, and two candlesticks, with two blind candles. This was a day solemnly keeped in honour of St Michael. A German being present said, *Ego nunquam vidi talem cultum : nihil hic prefecto deest de solenni missa, præter adorationem consecrate panis.* Upon the occasion of this solemnitie, Mr Andrew Melvine made the epigrame, for which he was afterward troubled.

That day afternoon, the Earles of Argile, Glencarne, Orknay, Wigtoun, Dumbar, the Comptroller, the Advocat, the Abbot of Lindorse, Mr Peter Young, the Laird of Kilsyth, conveened in the Earle of Dumbar's lodging. When the ministers compeared, Dumbar shewed unto them, that it was his Majesty's will that the Council there conveened should deal with them severally, and crave their answer to certain heads, whereunto they prayed them to give clear answers for satisfaction of his Majesty, and to go forth and come in as they were called on. Mr James Melvine was first called on, and being demanded by the Advocat, 1, Whether he prayed for the imprisoned brethren ? 2, Whether he allowed the holding of the Assembly at Aberdeen, and the declinature given in to the Council by them who held it ? 3, Where was his letter, written to the Synod of Fyfe, &c. He answered, I am a free subject of the kingdom of Scotland, which hath laws and priviledges of their own, as free as any kingdome in the world, to which I will stand. There have been no summons lawfully execute against me. The noblemen here present, and I, am not in our own countrey. The charge *super inquirendis* was declared long since to be unjust. I am bound by no law to accuse myself, neither to furnish dittay against myself. He desired the noblemen present to remember what they were, and to deal with him, howbeit a mean man, yet as a freeborne Scottishman, as they would be content to be used themselves, that is, according to the lawes of the realme of Scotland. The Advocat, notwithstanding, urged him to answer, with whom he interchanged some sharp speeches, and told him, that howbeit he had not studied the lawes, as he had done, yet he had learned his logick, and taught it in the schooles. Will ye not daigne his Majesty with an answer? said Dumbar. With all reverence, said Mr James, if I might know the question, and have time to advise upon a good answer. Ye shall have that, said Dumbar; and desired him to give in his supplication, which the ministers imprisoned had sent to the King, which Mr James delivered unto him, and entreated him to present it to the King, and to assist it. He was removed, and the rest were called on by course. At last Mr Andrew Melvine was called, and told them plainly, they knew not what they were doing; they had degenerated from the ancient nobilitie of Scotland, who were wont to hazard their lives and lands for the freedom of their country and the gospel, which they were betraying and overturning. Night drawing on, they were dismissed.

Upon the thirty of September, they were again called on to sermon. Doctor King had a most virulent invective against the Presbyteries, crying to the King, down, down with them.

Upon the second of October, the eight ministers were again called before the Scotish Councellours. Three articles were delivered to them in writ, whereunto they were called to give answer in writ, every one of them severally, and to take as much time to advise as they pleased; and, indeed, the chief drift was to drive time till the Convention at Linlithgow were past. It was permitted to them to go where they pleased, provided they went not far from Court, and made the place of their abode known, that they might be found when it pleased his Majesty. The tenor of the articles, subscribed by Mr Alexander Hay, here followeth:—

1. Whether they had not transgressed their dutie, in making publick prayers for the brethren in ward, as being afflicted; and are willing to crave his Majesty's favour for the same, seeing their said brethren abide in ward for just causes, and by a just sentence of a lawful judge, standing unquarrelled and unreduc'd?

2. Whether they acknowledge his Majesty by the authoritie of his prerogative royal, as a Christian king, to have lawful and full power to convocat, prorogat, and cause desert, upon just and necessare causes known to him, the Assemblies of the Kirk, within his Majesty's dominions.

3. If his Majesty by his authoritie Royal, hath not sufficient and lawful power to call, and conveen before him and his Councel, whatsoever person or persons, civil or ecclesiastical, for whatsoever faults, and give sentence thereanent? And if all his Majesty's subjects be astricted to compear before his Majesty and Councel, to answer, acknowledge, and obey his Majesty and Councels judgment, in the said offences? 2d October, 1606.

The articles above-written, appointed by his Majesty's Councel to be delivered out of my hand to the ministers above-mentioned, by his Majesty's special commandment.

ALEXANDER HAY.

Upon the fourth of November, Mr William Scott, and Mr John Carmichael, went to Westminster, and confered with Mr James Nicholson, whom they found to be a man far changed, and resolved to accept the bishoprick of Dunkelden, bought to him by the King from Mr Peter Rollock for twenty thousand pounds. They delivered to him their answers to the three articles, and with all their grievance, which the King desired them to give up. They agreed in substance; howbeit some were more ample than others. Mr James Melvine answered thus:—

With all submission, humilitie, and reverence to the King's Majesty, and with all hearty affection to his grandour, James Melvine giveth answer to the questions proponed by his Majesty's most honourable Councel.

1. I cannot conceive a transgression of dutie, in praying for our brethren, the command and warrant being so clear in the Word of God, 1 Tim. ii. 1; 1 John v. 16; Heb. xiii. 3. And, if I could conceive any, prostrat at his Majesty's feet I would most willingly crave pardon and favour.

2. The lawes of the realm, the judgment, practice, and constitution of our kirk are clear hereanent; and, if there remain any doubt, let it be resolved in the next General Assembly, to the which by the whole Synod it is referred.

3. The third is civil, for the most part of many interrogations, and cannot, therefore, be simply answered; and, if to be doubted of, it is to be resolved by lawyers and the estates of the realme. And as for judging of ministers in matters merely spiritual or ecclesiastical, such as concerne their calling, and points of their ministrie, which

they have of and in Christ Jesus, and of his Kirk allanerly, together with the jurisdiction of the Kirk, what it is, and how it differeth from the jurisdiction and power of civil magistrats, the statutes of the realme, the judgment, practice, and constitutions of our Kirk, the Kings Majesty's declaration at Linlithgow, and at diverse General Assemblies, are most clear and evident; to which I stand till God teach my conscience better. Protesting before that great God of heaven and earth, that if I thought it not a sinne against Christ, the Lord of lords, and King of kings, and so most dangerous to the Kings Majesty's person, crown and estate, to ascribe and give any farther to him, there is none living would be gladder, according to his abilitie, for avouching, maintaining, and standing for the same to the uttermost than poor James Melvine.

No. V.

The first Commission of the King, called the High Commission.

James, by the grace of God, King of Great Britain, France and Ireland, defender of the faith, to our lovits, &c. ' Messengers, our sheriffs in that part, conjunctly and severally, specially constitute, greeting. Forsameekle as complaint being made to us, in the behalf of the ministry of this our kingdom, that the frequent advocations purchased by such as were either erroneous in religion or scandalous in life, not only discouraged the ministry from censuring of vice, but emboldened the offenders to continue in their wickedness, using their advocations as a mean to delay and disappoint both trial and punishment. We, for eschewing of this inconvenient, and that the number of true professors may be known to increase, the antichristian enemie and his growth suppressed, and all sorts of vice and scandalous life punished; and that neither iniquitie nor delay of trial and punishment be left by this subterfuge, or discouraging of ecclesiastical censures to proceed in things so meet and proper for them, have, out of our duty to God and love to his Kirk, being the nourish-father of the same in earth within our dominions, given power and commission to the reverend father in God, and our trusty and well-beloved counsellour, George, Archbishop of St Andrews, primat and metropolitan of our kingdom; and to our right trust cusine and counseller, Alexander, Earle of Dumfermline, Lord High Chancellour of this our kingdom ; George, Earle of Dumbar, Treasurer ; George, Earle Marchal ; John, Earl of Mar : John, Earle of Montrose ; Patrick, Earle of Kinghorne ; to the reverend fathers in God, Alexander, Bishop of Dunkelden ; Peter, Bishop of Aberdeen ; Alexander, Bishop of Murray ; Andrew, Bishop of Brechon ; David, Bishop of Ross ; George, Bishop of Dumblane ; Alexander, Bishop of Caithness ; and James, Bishop of Orknay ; to our trustie cusins and counsellours, ——— Lord Lindsey ; Simon, Lord Fraser of Lovat ; David, Lord of Scoone ; and to our trustie and well-beloved counsellours, Mr John Prestoun of Pennicook, President of our College of Justice ; Sir Richard Cockburne of Clerkingtoun, Knight, Lord Privie Seal ; Sir Alexander Hay, Knight, our Secretarie ; Sir James ——— of Kingaskon, Comptroller ; Sir Thomas Hammiltoun of Binning, Knight, our Advocate ; and to our lovit Sir David Carnegie of Kinnaird, Knight ; ——— Dundas of that Ilk ; Alexander Iruing of Drumme ; ——— Ramsey of Balmaine ; Mr John Arthure, Mr Thomas Henrison, Mr Adam King and Mr James Bannatine, Commissars of Edinburgh ; Mr John Weemes, Commissar of St Andrews ; Mr James Martine, Rector of the Universitie of St Andrews ; Mr Robert Howie, Principal of the new College there ; Mr David Monnipennie, Dean of Facultie ; Mr Patrick Galloway ; Mr John Hall, Mr Peter Hewat, Mr John Mitchelson, Mr Robert Wilkie, Mr John Strauchan, Mr Andrew Leitch, Mr Henry Phillip, Mr Arthure Futhie, and Mr Patrick Lindsey, ministers, or to any five of them, the Archbishop being always one, within the whole bounds of the province of St Andrews ; and to the reverend father in God, and our trusty and well-beloved counsellor, John, Archbishop of Glasgow ; Alexander, Earle of Dumfermline ; George, Earle of Dumbar ; John, Earle of Cassils ; James, Earle of Glencarne, John, Earle of Wigtoun ; James, Earle of Abercorne ; and to the reverend fathers in God, Gawin, Bishop of Galloway ; John, Bishop of Argyle ; Andrew, Bishop of the Isles ; and to our trustie cusine and counsellour, Walter, Lord of Blantire ; and to our lovits, Mr John Arthure, Mr Thomas Henrison, Mr Adam King, Mr James Bannatine, Commissars of Edinburgh ; David Forsyth, Commissar of Glasgow ; Mr James Halyday, Commissar of Dumfries ; Mr John Humiltoun, Commissar of Hamiltoun ; Mr J.

Hamiltoun, Commissar of Lanerk; Sir George Eldhin-
toun of Eastwood, Knight; Mr Patrick Sharpe, Principal
of the College of Glasgow; Mr William Birnie, minister
at Lanerk; Mr John Hay, parson of Ranfrew; Mr James
Hammiltoun, Dean of Glasgow: Mr David Sharpe, and
David Walkinshaw, Subdean of Glasgow; Mr Thomas
Ramsey, minister at Dumfreis; Mr John Bell, minister
at Glasgow; and Mr Walter Stewart, minister at ————;
or any five of them, the said Archbishop being always
one, within the whole bounds of the province of Glasgow :
To call before them, at such times and places as they
shall think meet, any person or persons dwelling or remaining within their provinces respective abovewritten,
of St Andrews or Glasgow, or within any diocies of the
samine, being offenders either in life or religion, whom
they held any ways to be scandalous; and that they take
trial of the same; and if they find them guiltie and im-
penitent, refusing to acknowledge their offences, they
shall give command to the preachers of that parish where
they dwell to proceed with the sentence of excommunication against them, which, if it be protracted or delayed,
and if their command by that minister be not presently
obeyed, they shall conveen any such minister before them,
and proceed in censuring of him for his disobedience,
either by suspension, deprivation, or warding, according as
in their discretion they shall hold his obstinacie, and refuse of their direction, to have deserved.   And, farther, to
fine at their discretions, imprison or ward any such persons, who, being convicted before them, they shall finde
upon trial to have deserved any such punishment.   And
a warrant under the hand of any five abovenamed of every
province respective abovewritten, the said Archbishop of
the province being one, shall serve for a sufficient command for the captains, constables of our wards and castles,
and to all keepers of ales and prisons, either in burgh or
land in any part of the provinces respective abovewritten,
for receiving and detaining such persons as shall be unto
them directed to be keeped by them, in such form as by
the said warrant shall be prescribed, as they will answer
upon the contraire at their perils.   And of all such fines
as shall be imposed upon any offender, the one-half to
pertain to ourself, and the other half to be employed upon
such necessare things as our said Commissioners shall be
forced unto, by charging of parties and witnesses to com-

pear before them; and the superplus to be bestowed at
the sight of the said Commissioners, by distribution among
the poor; commanding the Lords of our Privie Council,
upon sight of any certificate, subscribed by any five of the
said Commissioners within every province, as said is, the
said Archbishop of the province being one, either of any
fine imposed by them upon any party compearing and
found guiltie; or of the contumacie and refusal of any to
compear before them, that the said Lords of our Privie
Council direct a summar charge of horning upon ten days
only; and that no suspension nor relaxation be granted,
without first a testificat under the hand of the Archbishop
of the province, containing the obedience and satisfaction
of the partie charged, be produced. And in case of farther disobedience or rebellion of the partie who shall be
charged for his fine or not compearance, the said Lords of
our Councel are then to prosecute the most strict order as
is usual against rebels for any cause whatsomever, with
power to our said Commissioners to proceed herein; as
also to take trial of all persons that have made defection,
or otherwise are suspected in religion; and as they find
any just cause against them, to proceed in manner foresaid. And also whensoever they shall learn or understand of any minister, preacher, or teacher of schools, col-
ledges, or universities, or of exhorting or lecturing-readers,
within these bounds, whose speeches in publick have been
impertinent, and against the established order of the Kirk,
or against any of the conclusions of the bypast General
Assemblies, or in favour of any of those who are banished,
warded, or confined for their contemptuous offences, which
being no matter of doctrine, and so much idle time spent
without instruction of their auditorie in their salvation,
ought so much the more severely to be punished; in
regard that they are ministers, who of all others should
spend least idle talk, and specially in the chair of veritie;
and, therefore, after the calling of them before the said
Commissioners, they are to be questioned and tried upon
the points of that which is laid against them, and punished
according to the qualitie of their offence. And, whereas
complaint shall be made unto them by any partie that
shall be convened before any ecclesiastical judicatorie,
for any such crime as he shall be then suspected of, or
that the partie doth alledge always the matter itself to
be improper to their judicatorie, or the proceeding to have

been informal, or that the judicatorie itself hath been too partial; and when the Commissioners shall see any just cause, they are then to take trial and cognition thereof themselves, and to discharge the said judicatorie of all farder proceeding. Giving power also to the said Commissioners to make choice of a clerk, and other members of court; and to direct precepts in name of the said Archbishop and his associates within every province, for citation of any parties before them, within the bounds of the said provinces, in any of the said causes above-mentioned; which precepts to be sealed with a special seal, containing the armes of the said bishoprick. Giving also power to charge witnesses to compear before them, under the pain of fourtie pounds Scottish money; and, upon the certificat of the said Commissioners, that any of the said penalties are incurred by them, the said Lords of our Councel are to direct the like charges for payment of the same, as is appointed for the fines, as in the said Commission past our great seal, containing diverse other heads, clauses, articles, and conditions, and bearing date, at our Court at Roystoun, the 20 day of January last, at length is contained; whereof necessare it is that publication be made to all our lieges, that none pretend ignorance thereof. Our will is, herefore, and we charge you straitly, and command, that incontinent these our letters seen, ye pass to the said burrowes, within the provinces above-written, and there by open proclamation that ye make publication of the premisses, that none pretend ignorance. And also, that ye, in our name and authoritie, command and charge all our lieges and subjects to reverence and obey our said Commissioners, in all and every thing tending to the execution of this our Commission, and to do nothing to their hinder or prejudice, as they and each one of them will answer to us and our Councel, upon their obedience at their highest charge and peril. The which to do, &c. Given under our signet at Edinburgh, the fifteen of Februar, and of our reigne the 47 year, 1610.

PER ACTUM SECRETI CONCILIJ.

PART III.

OF THE CHURCH IN HER PERSECUTED STATE.

Bishop Spotiswood, in his History of Scotland, says, that the persecution of Dioclesian was a great means to farther the first propagation of the gospel in Scotland; which persecution being but in the south parts of Britain, it brought a great many Christians, as well preachers as professors, into Scotland, where they were kindly received by King Cratilinth, and the Isle of Man given them for their retreat, where he erected a magificent Church, and called it "The Temple of our Saviour." This is said to be in the year 277.

Like instances might be found in all the tracts of antiquity from thence to the present time, where persecution has spread and established the true religion, but no where so eminently as the persecutions of Presbyterians has done in Scotland.

It was with respect to the several troubles, divisions, wars, and interruptions which the establishment of the Church of Scotland met with, even in her most flourishing condition, that the last Part of this Work was called "The Growing Estate of the Church."

I would have been very well pleased to have called it the complete or finished state, and to have represented the Church in the perfection of her desires, arrived to the top of her own views, and in the full enjoyment of her just privileges, supported by her own power, and the majesty of her constitution.

But the Divine Wisdom which has always thought fit to exercise his Church with tribulation and affliction, as the best foundation whereon to build her temporal establishment, had otherwise determined ; and all that strength which the Church of Scotland had gained in the short intervals of peace which she had enjoyed in the last period of her circumstances, was little enough to carry her through the fiery trial she had now to endure.

No sooner was the restoration of King Charles II. brought to pass in England, but the enemies of the Church of Scotland began to lift up their heads, and the black cloud which did but hover over them, as it were for a while, and threatened them with destruction, being big with storms and furious thunders, broke upon them all at once.

There had some things passed in the English Parliament which had deeply affected the people of Scotland, and had given them a clear view of what they were to expect, though it was not yet fallen upon them, and this is what I mean by the black cloud which hovered over them for a while.

These were, 1. The declaring the Solemn League and Covenant to be unlawful, and obliging all people who held any office, &c., to subscribe to the said declaration, 13 Char. II., cap. 1. 2. The Act of Uniformity, and by which the Episcopal hierarchy in England was restored, and the ministers who would not conform to the liturgy and ceremonies of the Church of England before Bartholomew Day, 1662, were deprived of their livings, 13 Char. II., cap. 11.

These were preludes to what was to be expected in Scotland, and yet, albeit, the acts in England were made before those in Scotland ; yet the Privy Council, or Council of State in Scotland, took upon them to begin with the Presbyterians as soon, or rather sooner, than the Parliament in England began there. So that the Church of Scotland saw early what they had to expect; and thus we are led, without any other need of introduction, into the history of fact.

When the King was restored, the Church of Scotland was in its best and fullest possession of legal power. The professors of the Presbyterian doctrine had, by their adherence to the royal family, laid in as good a loan of obligation upon the generosity of the King as any party in their circumstances could have done. And if but the interest of that debt had been paid, or if gratitude had been the fashion of the times, they had some reason to expect a little consideration to be had for them.

It was indeed upon some expectation of such a return, that immediately on the first news of the King's restoration, the ministers, in conjunction with some of the nobility and gentry, resolved to present a paper to him, which was called a *monitory supplication*. It was a new term, perhaps, made for the occasion. And they did the Presbyterians much wrong, who told King Charles that it was a *minatory supplication;* for the contents of it prove the contrary, which are too long for the brevity of this tract, but in a word, is contained as follows :—

1. A very hearty and solemn congratulation of his Majesty's restoration to the throne of his ancestors, recognising his right, and extolling the goodness of God in returning him to his people, praying that it may be a blessing to his Majesty and the whole nation, and assuring him of their ready and dutiful submission to his authority.

2. Reminding his Majesty with great humility of his covenant engagement—mark that—to God and the nation, and his solemn promises to put forward the work of reformation in the kingdom, as the only thing in which his Majesty might expect the blessing of God upon his reign and upon his people.

This supplication was never presented, nay, it was not signed by many of the persons who had promoted and recommended it. But while it was a mere embryo the Council of State sent their officers, and as if it had been an act of rebellion, surprised and seized upon such as they had information were concerned in it, and clapt them in prison, having no other pretence against them but this supplication, which they told them was seditious, and tended to disquiet the minds of the lieges, and render his Majesty's government uneasy to them. Most of those they seized upon were eminent ministers.

It was alleged by the persons that were thus taken up that there was no law against supplicating their prince, and that where there was no law there could be no transgression; that they had not acted unpeaceably or undutifully to his Majesty in anything, and desired to know upon what law they were committed to prison. The Council let them know no other law at that time but their arbitrary pleasure, against which the poor gentlemen had no remedy but submission.

And this was the first article of persecution in that reign, viz., imprisoning without a law—a thing they reduced into a most general practice presently after.

The Government themselves acknowledged the injustice of this afterwards, by procuring an unrighteous law to be made to take away the subject's liberty of petitioning the sovereign, declaring it unlawful and seditious, (vide 2 sess. of the 2d Parliament of King Charles II., act 2), by which act even prisoners were denied the liberty to petition for their deliverance; nay, or a condemned person for his pardon, or his life—a cruelty scarce heard of in any nation before, which made many good people afterwards endure the most intolerable cruelties in their imprisonment, for fear of having them doubled by the crime of petitioning for mercy. But this was but the beginning of the afflictions of the Church of Scotland.

In the beginning of the year 1661, the first Parliament of King Charles II. sat down; and that they might lay a ground plot of that bloody persecution which they had resolved to raise, so they immediately applied themselves to make such laws, and make void such already made, as they well knew would be intolerable to the Presbyterians.   They knew the Presbyterians would neither obey the one or bear the other, and consequently would render themselves obnoxious to the penalties and punishment of those laws, and give the people in power a sufficient pretence for falling upon them, with all that violence and inhumanity which they had resolved to treat them with.

To bring the account into some method, it will be needful at once to give a detail of these persecuting laws as they came to be made, or at least of so many of them as were made upon these occasions.   And this I shall do in order to enter into the history of the sufferings of the people in the consequence of those laws, the more regularly; and this method I shall repeat again, as other and subsequent laws were made for the like purposes.

Some of the several new laws made after the Restoration, which were the beginning of the persecution, were as follows:

1. Act imposing the Oath of Supremacy.   This was directly contrary to the Presbyterian principle.   [This was the very first act passed after the Restoration, and it was called the Oath of Allegiance only to render the refusing it the more odious, but it contained also the oaths of supremacy in express words, and without the ancient limitations formerly granted.— 1 Act, 1 Par. K. Char. II.]

2. Act obliging all people in office to acknowledge the Prerogative of the King.   [This was in such terms as they had then advanced, above and against all former engagements, and which they knew conscientious people could not comply with.]

N

3. Act declaring void and dissolving the obligation of the Solemn League and Covenant. This the nation having sworn to, the good people could not be convinced that an act of Parliament could dispense with the obligation of their oath in the sight of God ; and therefore chose death, rather than comply with it.— Par. 1, sess. 1, act 2, Char. II.

4. Act declaring the National Covenant to be an unlawful oath, and that the same is not of any force to bind those that have taken it.—Par. 1, sess. 2, act 2, Char. II.

5. An act, not of Parliament, but of Council, to burn both the said Covenants by the hand of the common hangman.

6. Act to restore Episcopacy in Scotland ; striking at the root of the Presbyterian Church, and over-throwing all the settlement and establishment of the said Church at one blow.

(First act of the second session of the first Parliament of King Charles I. anno 1662.)

It may be truly said that some of these acts not only surprised the Presbyterians, but even filled the whole nation with horror, partly at the unheard of attack made upon the solemnity of the National Covenant, which most people there esteemed sacred, and wondered how their temporal power, or indeed any power upon earth, could take upon them to discharge the people of the obligation of an oath ; and partly at the dreadful things which they evidently foresaw would be the consequence of such proceedings.

It is not my business here to enter into the question whether the Parliament could dispense with the obligation of this oath or no, much less will I offer, till I see the affirmative better proved, to condemn the opinion of those who think the nation of Scotland guilty by that act of a most horrid national perjury.

Having gone this length on the one side, let us see

what course the poor people took who were to suffer for the least step they took in opposing these furious proceedings.

The first thing I find which the government laid any hold on was the ministers preaching against them. This was the least thing they could expect, and yet for some time was the greatest opposition they met with, and which way to deal with this they hardly knew ; for it would seem exceedingly tyrannical to attack the ministers for words spoken in their pulpits, which it would be hard to ascertain, and against which there was yet no law. Besides, having put so many hardships already upon them, it seemed very unlikely but these losers would have leave to speak, and very hard to deny it.

But they soon got over this ; and being resolved to use no ceremony, but to fall upon the kirk by all the violent methods they could devise, they published a proclamation, discharging, as they call it, that is, prohibiting and forbidding every one to speak against the proceedings of the State.

This opened a door to fall upon the ministers, for many of them being zealous for the Reformation and for the Covenant, which they believed was an oath of God, and could not be dissolved by man, could not, therefore, in conscience, but declare against the attempt made in the aforesaid law, to set up the power of man to dispense with the authority of God. For maintaining this, and opposing the act of the king's supremacy, a thing which they believed was no less than a rebellion against the regal authority of Christ Jesus, the only head and government of his church, many of the ministers were imprisoned, and some without hearing, or leave given them to make their defence, were, *indicta causa*, sentenced to banishment.

The number of these was seven at one time. They were not, indeed, sent or transported to any particular place into slavery, was as afterwards practised, but they were obliged by sentence to quit the country in a certain time upon pain of death, and never to return upon the like penalty ; and, accordingly, they took shipping for Holland, to the great grief of their flocks, who mourned for the loss of them, being left destitute as sheep without a shepherd.   But one was singled out from the rest to bear his testimony against them in another manner—this was Mr James Guthrie, the proto-martyr of this persecution, who was condemned to death, and accordingly was hanged at Edinburgh as a traitor ; whose behaviour during his imprisonment and trial before those tyrannical judges, and afterwards at the place of execution, might have convinced them that the blood of these men would be the seed of the Church of Scotland, and that torments and death would not weaken the cause of religion in Scotland, or advance them one step towards the conquest they aimed at.

Having now tasted blood, their fury seemed to increase ; and now, in consequence of the act for restoring Prelacy mentioned before, they advanced such principles as they knew were directly contrary to the Presbyterian doctrine, and such as they knew no bonds, no affliction, no, nor death itself, would ever bring them to comply with.   These were—

1. A declaration in the preamble to the act for establishing Episcopacy, signifying that the disposal of the government of the Church is in the King, as an inherent right of the crown.

2. Depriving the Church of the freedom of calling and choosing their own pastors.   This was included in an act for restoring patronages.

3. Dispossessing the ministers who would not conform to Episcopacy, and this without legal prosecution, by a mere act of Council, passed in October 1662.

I think it very necessary to set down these first measures of the persecutors of the Church, in order to remove a certain slander raised by the enemies of these poor suffering Christians, and which too many good people are prepossessed in this nation, viz., that the Scots Presbyterians suffered upon trifling punctilios not essential to religion, or upon points which the Christian Church have in all ages submitted to, even under the government of heathen emperors and the like; such as acknowledging the King, swearing allegiance to him, living peaceably, paying taxes, tithes, &c. Whereas, on the contrary, it is evident that the sufferings of the Church of Scotland, and the persecution which her faithful confessors have laboured under, have been occasioned for maintaining the essential points, both of doctrine and government, which she has held ever since the Reformation, and without which no true Church can be established, viz., (1) such as the refusing all usurpations upon the sovereignty of Christ, as king and head of his Church, in opposition to Erastianism and Episcopal supremacy; (2) the unsupportable yoke of what they called unscriptural Prelacy, which neither they or their fathers were able to bear; (3) the right of calling their own ministers in opposition to the pretences of lay patronages, &c., and the like; and (4) for opposing the tyranny and injustice of the proceedings of those in power, who condemned men unheard, sentenced men at pleasure, without examining into the facts or hearing legal witnessess, and punished men to death for such crimes as were not punishable with death by the laws of the land.

These and such as these were the points upon which the people of Scotland suffered the most bloody persecution that has been heard of in this age, or for the last hundred years passed in the world—the persecution of the Protestants in France being, in proportion to this country, and the number of people, and the blood spilt, no way to compare to it.

But to come now to the suffering party. The

Government having thus, by their unrighteous laws, made way for all the oppressions which they designed —having established Prelacy, and dispossessed the Presbyterian ministers of their kirks, filling their places with a race of men who, for ignorance and wickedness, were scarce to be equalled in the world, I mean as ministers, — the poor people were immediately scattered and dispersed in a dreadful manner. The new set of men were so weak in capacity, and so abominable in their known practice and conversation (speaking without the least prejudice of the most of them), that the people abhorred to hear them, or to come into the churches where they were.

This occasioned them to follow their own ministers, though dispossessed, into private places and corners, and to hear the Word preached, and have their ordinances administered, in private houses and meetings, as was soon after the practice in England by the Dissenters there.

The ministers, on the other hand, thinking it their duty not to forsake their people, kept themselves concealed and retired, and went from house to house, preaching and praying, visiting, baptizing, and, in a word, performing all the duties of their office, as opportunity would allow.

This the Episcopal party could not bear, and therefore, in the first place, fell to their former custom of making laws against it in Parliament, and enforcing those laws by proclamation and acts of Council, which they soon brought to be of equal force with acts of Parliament, though by law it was quite otherwise. Vide 3d act, 1st sess., 1st Par. Char. II, entituled Act asserting his Majesty's royal prerogative in making laws.

These laws against non-conformity are so extraordinary, and savoured so much of a true spirit of persecution, were in themselves so unjust, and in some things so unnatural, that none can wonder if the execution of them sometimes drove the poor people to desperation, and made, as in far less moving cases has been said, nature rebel against principle, and drove the people, made thus distracted by their oppressions, to tumult and rebellion.

And because they have in these things also been rashly censured by some among us as a people suffering as evil-doers, it must be useful in their vindication to expose a little the inhumanity and barbarity of their persecutors; and this can be done in nothing better than in giving a brief account of the laws now made, which they expected, and rigorously exacted obedience to, and which it was impossible that poor people could obey, without making shipwreck of faith and a good conscience, abandoning their profession, inverting the rule of the Apostle, and obeying man rather than God.

These Acts are as follow :—

1. Act discharging (*i.e.*, *forbidding*) all writing, remonstrating, printing, praying, or preaching in such manner as should show any dislike (1) of the King's supremacy in causes ecclesiastic ; (2) of the King's absolute prerogative in appointing such government of the Church as he thought fit ; and (3) of the government of the Church by bishops.—Act 2, sess. 2, Par. 1, Char. II.

2. Act prohibiting any minister to preach in churches publicly, or privately in families, without license first had from the Episcopal ministers called curates, and forbidding all house meetings for religious exercise.—Act 4, sess. 2, Parl. 1, Char. II.

Both these Acts were so directly contrary to the principles of the Presbyterians, and it was so well known that they could not in conscience comply with them, that they were very justly called the persecuting laws, together with the following act, which gave the finishing stroke to the rest, viz.

3. Act declaring that all nonconforming ministers that shall presume to exercise their ministry in any manner whatsoever, shall be punished as seditious per-

sons; requiring all persons, in obedience to his Majesty's government ecclesiastic, to give their countenance to the established worship, by attending, &c. Ordaining penalties to all that should withdraw from the public worship, as follows:—

"Every nobleman, gentleman, or heritor, one-fourth of his yearly revenue.

"Every yeoman, one-fourth part of his moveable goods.

"Every burgess, the loss of his freedom or burgship, and a fourth part of his moveable goods."

Leaving it also to the Council to inflict farther punishment, and to provide for the most effectual execution, which they did by proclamations of the most arbitrary, illegal, and tyrannical nature imaginable, viz:—

Proclamation requiring all to keep to their parish churches, under penalty of twenty shillings every omission; they knowing, at the same time, the poor people could not in conscience spend the Lord's Day in such a manner.

Proclamation prohibiting all preaching, praying, or hearing in families, if above three more than the domestics of the family were present; punishing those who had more as unlawful conventicles.

Proclamation appointing all such meetings not authorized as aforesaid to be punished either by pecuniary or corporal punishments, at the pleasure of the Council.

Proclamation commanding landlords, masters of families and magistrates, to cause their tenants, children, servants, dependents, taxmen, or farmers of duties or revenue, and all under their charge, to submit and conform to the Episcopal government and worship, and making the said landlords, &c., answerable for the default of their servants, &c.; the punishment here also being left to the pleasure of the Council.

[They reserved here the cruelty of punishment to themselves; to be inflicted, not as the laws or the nature of the offence should direct, but as the person who they should have before them stood more or less in or out of their favour.]

Now, to finish all, and enforce these laws and proclamations, the King erected a High Commission Court, consisting of a medley of clergy, nobility, magistrates, and soldiers. This body was empowered to hear and determine causes without appeal, to execute civil and ecclesiastical authority. They could suspend and deprive clergymen, excommunicate like bishops, commit to prison like justices of the peace, sentence like judges, and put to torture and death like hangmen. In a word, as a known Scots author calls them, they were a hotch-potch-mongrel monster of a judicatory, authorized by the prerogative against the laws of God and man, illegal in its constitution, and arbitrary in its procedure, whereby persons brought before them were made to answer, *super inquirendis*, without either accusation or accuser, contrary to an express standing law—Act 13, Parl. 10, Jac. VI.

It is scarce to be related what innumerable oppressions fell upon the people, but especially upon the poor ministers, in the prosecution of these laws; for the ministers, finding themselves bound in conscience not to abandon their flocks for any persecution or bodily sufferings whatsoever, exposed themselves freely to the worst that their enemies could do, and failed not at the greatest and utmost hazard to discharge their duty; and the people flocking after them, they preached to them with what privacy and caution they were able, but at the extremest hazard. Nor was it possible but that many would be daily falling into the hands of their persecutors, insomuch that the prisons were every where full of faithful ministers, whereof abundance died through the length of their confinement and the severity of their usage—some through cold and evil lodging, having contracted diseases and infirmities, and others for want of conveniences, and even necessaries; whose blood is no doubt to be esteemed as shed in the cause of religion, as much as if they had been brought out to execution, as several of their brethren afterwards were.

By this scandalous judicatory, called the High Commission Court, many innocent men, as well ministers as others, were prosecuted even after a manner near a-kin to the Spanish Inquisition; and, as an author well observes, having no other precedent in the Christian world but the said Spanish Inquisition, being neither suffered to know their crimes or their accusers —never suffered to come to a hearing, or to make any legal defence. But when they demanded their accusation or judicature indictment, and leave to answer to the same, they were told they could not be admitted to any defence, unless they would first take the oath by which they were to acknowledge and submit to the jurisdiction of their judges; and then without hearing their offence, or having leave to answer, they were sentenced to scourging, stigmatizing, banishment, transportation to slavery in Barbadoes, perpetual imprisonment, and the like, as the commissioners thought fit; and this to such a degree that the people fled before them, and the whole country-sides, as they are called there, became depopulate for nonconformity. As this High Commission Court is justly represented to be the most arbitrary, illegal, cruel, and unjust judicatory that ever was set up in a Protestant nation, and imitated by none but the bloody Inquisition aforesaid; so it cannot be unacceptable, in our relating the sufferings of the good people of Scotland, to give some few instances, out of an innumerable crowd of oppressed suffering Christians, of the vexations, barbarities, inhuman and illegal practices of this court, in pursuance of the commission given them to put the aforesaid acts in execution.

The author of a book entitled, "The Wrestlings of the Church of Scotland," has touched at the irregularities and inhumanities of their proceedings; but alas ! what are they to the innumerable examples which living testimony are yet able to give, and which the collector of these particulars has received from the mouths of many of the sufferers themselves.

I have already mentioned how persons were brought before these new judges without any notice—without information, accusation, witness, or accuser ; but being fetched in, were instantly charged by way of inquiry, and therefore was it that this Court was not improperly called a Court of Inquisition—the Arch-Prelate or Bishop of St Andrews, the same who was afterwards killed, presiding therein.

Upon the bringing any person before them, he was required immediately to answer such questions as were propounded to him, being allowed neither council to advise with, nor time to consider. If he answered satisfactorily to one question, they would still find others to ensnare him. If he refused to answer, and pleaded the great law of nature, *Nemo tenetur seipsum accusare*, they set him by instantly as convicted, and proceeded to sentence. If he answered boldly, and perhaps smartly, they immediately sentenced him for contumacy and disrespect. A minister was sentenced to banishment for calling the Archbishop " Sir," and not " My Lord." One Mr Porterfield, a gentleman, of a loyal family, was brought before them, and asked, why he did not come to his parish church to hear the curate ; to which he gave them a very pertinent answer—viz., Because the curate had abused him, and slandered him in such a manner as was both scandalous to him as a minister, and just ground of resentment to any thing of a gentleman. The Court, upon his exposing and proving the fact, were ashamed of the curate ; but being resolved to revenge it on the gentleman, they put several other questions to him, all which he answered so as no advantage could be gained of him. At which the Archbishop being enraged, asked him if he would take the oath of supremacy, which, when he modestly declined, they immediately sentenced him to banishment and confinement to the town of Elgin, far north, and fined him almost to the full value of his whole estate.   And this was the constant method when any person convened before them could no other way be laid hold of ; nor in their sentence did they confine themselves to suit the punishment to the offence, or consult the power of their commission ; but frequently sentenced people to the severest punishment for the smallest offences, and frequently passed such sentences as they had no power by their commission to pass.   One famous example, among a great multitude, is left upon record, as follows :—

Mr John Livingston, a most eminent and reverend minister, particularly famous in the Church of Scotland, had been banished the kingdom for no other reason but his refusing the oath of supremacy.   There was collated to that benefice, a curate or Episcopal minister, one Mr Scott, who it seems stood excommunicated before, and continued under that sentence. Besides that, the people had other objections against his morals and good name, insomuch that they publicly opposed him at his coming to preach ; and it seems there were some warm expressions used by some of the people against him, which he complained of to the High Commission Court.   Four poor men of the parish where hereupon convened before them, and being not charged with any thing by the said Scott ; but being interrogated, they acknowledged they were present when the parishioners did declare their dissatisfaction at Mr Scott's coming to their Kirk, but said, that they did not speak what was said.

This the Commissioners, contrary indeed to several of their own body, voted to be a confession of guilt, and immediately gave this barbarous sentence, That the four men should be scourged through the town, stigmatized on the forehead with the letter T, at the Cross of Edinburgh, and be transported to the island of Barbadoes; all which was rigorously executed. Nor was this enough to satisfy the rage of the persecutors, even in so trifling an offence. But a few days after, two brothers, and a young maiden their sister, inhabitants of the same parish, were sentenced on the same account, the two men to be banished to Barbadoes, and the young woman to be whipped through the town of Jedburgh; all which sentences were executed accordingly.

Two more examples we have of their justice which are very eminent. The one of Mr Smith, a learned nonconforming minister, who was brought before them for praying and preaching to a few of his friends, met privately in a friend's house. They had, it seems, no evidence of the fact, much less any thing to object against what he had spoken.

When he came before the Commissioners, he did not speak disrespectfully at all, but he declined giving the Archbishop the title of "Lord." At which, one of the Bench asked him very scornfully, if he knew who it was he was speaking to, and what character he bore. To which he answered, he did know him to be Mr James Sharp, once a minister, as he himself then was, and that he knew no higher character any Christian man could bear than to be a minister and ambassador of Jesus Christ. This he spoke, directing his words to that Commissioner who had reproved him, and gave him the titles he was known by.

This so enraged the Archbishop, that he knew not how with violence enough to wreak his malice on the poor man ; but, to shew his willingness to destroy him, he sentenced him, besides his sentence for conventicling, as they called it, to be led by the hangman to the place in the Tolbooth, called the Thieves' Hole, and there laid in heavy irons, there being a raving creature, who was an idiot, and furious, confined in the same place, and left loose with him. Here the godly minister lay some days in danger of being destroyed by the poor demented wretch, who every moment threatened to kill him ; but God, that stopped the mouths of Daniel's lions, restrained him, so that he hurt him not ; and these merciful judges hearing, that by the grate of this hole, which looked to the street, he was relieved and comforted by the charity and compassion of many good people of the city, many were threatened for relieving him ; and at length the poor man was carried away to a place called the Iron House, in the same prison, where none could come at him. Here he continued close prisoner and in irons for many days. Besides this, they sentenced him for his private preaching to perpetual banishment to the Island of Shetland, the coldest and most unhospitable of all the Caledonian Islands, where his only relief, as to this world, was the society of our blessed sufferers, banished thither for the same good cause.

The next instance of their cruelty was one Mr Black, a layman, charged by the Commissioners with having been at a meeting of a few Christians in a private way for prayer. Whether any minister was with them or not was not alleged, neither had they anything else to charge upon him of any kind whatever. They could not prove his being at the meeting, but would have him confess, which he declined. Then they demanded him to give them an account, upon his oath, who was at the said meeting. This he declared was against his conscience ; and he would not be an accuser of innocent men. For denying this, they sentenced him to be scourged through the town, which he very patiently submitted to, and cheerfully suffered.

It would be endless to enumerate the names of the sufferers in this case, and it has not been possible for the author of these collections to come at the certain number of those ministers or others who died in prisons and banishment upon account of these persecuting laws, there being no record preserved of their prosecution in any court of justice, nor could any roll of their names be preserved in those times of confusion any where but under the altar, and about the throne of the Lamb, where their heads are crowned and their white robes seen, and where an exact account of their number will at last be found.

But, according to the reports of creditable and impartial people, who, upon our earnest inquiry, have, from their memories, as well as they could, recollected these things, and putting their several relations together, comparing them with what has been made public, we shall at the end of this part give the calculations which such have made of the numbers of those suffering Christians, who falling into, or flying from, the hands of their cruel persecutors, perished in prisons, and went into banishment, without any legal process, most of whom perished by the distresses and extremities they were reduced to by those means; and a surprising number it will be to those who have not inquired into these things, or discoursed with the people of Scotland about them, and all this before the year 1666—a time made remarkable upon the following occasion, and to which occasion these things have been the unhappy introduction.

If the poor people were by those insupportable violences made desperate, and driven to all the extremities of a wild despair, who can justly reflect upon them, when they read in the Word of God, "That oppression makes a wise man mad?" and, therefore, were there no other original of the insurrection, known by the name of the Rising of Pentland, it was nothing but what the intolerable oppressions of those times might have justified to all the world, nature having dictated to all people a right of self-defence, when illegally and arbitrarily attacked in a manner not justifiable either by the laws of nature, the laws of God, or the laws of the country.

But, besides all this, it is evident, that this insurrection was no premeditated design, but began in the violence of military execution committed by four soldiers, commanded by Sir James Turner, who, falling into some houses in Galloway without commission, or without order from their own officers—as Sir James afterwards alleged—were opposed, and driven out of their doors by four or five honest men of the inhabitants, in the just defence of their wives, children, and goods, unjustly insulted and offered to be plundered by the said soldiers. The more particular relation of this part is recorded as follows :—

Sir James Turner was an officer of dragoons, who was sent with his troops, by order of the Council, to quarter at discretion upon the poor western people of Scotland, because there they found the chief body of the constant sufferers for, and adherers to, the true religion were to be found.

This Sir James was a tool to their minds, a stranger in the country, being an Englishman, bred to plunder and rapine in the service of the French, perfectly void of the fear of God or man, and unacquainted either with religion or humanity. He had made three invasions into this part of the country, where his cruelty and exactions had been such as had almost stript the country, not of its substance only, but even of its inhabitants, who were obliged to quit their habitations to avoid the fury and brutality of the soldiers.

It is impossible to give the detail of the cruelties and inhuman usage the poor people suffered from this butcher, for such he was rather than a soldier ; neither is it the present purpose but to introduce what followed at this time.

The poor people had patiently suffered the merciless treatment this man showed them above seven months, and thereby testified more passive submission than most of those who have since upbraided them with resistance can pretend to; when Sir James Turner put an end to their patience by the following occasion.

On the 13th day of November 1666, he sent four soldiers from Dumfries, where he quartered, to a town called Dalray, in the shire of Galloway, with orders to seize upon a poor man's goods, who he pretended to have broken the laws by not coming to his parish church; and if he had no goods, to take the man, and bring him prisoner to Dumfries. The soldiers, as Sir James alleged after, beyond their instructions, not only seized his goods, but his person, too; and binding the poor old man hand and foot, like a beast, brought him out, and laid him on the ground till they rifled his house.

The neighbours, moved with compassion at the indignity of the usage, and at seeing a poor ancient man lie on the ground, bound like a beast, to be carried away to the slaughter; and with just indignation at the insolence of the four soldiers, came to the soldiers and calmly entreated them to unbind him, and to let him go with them like a prisoner, and like a man, not like a beast.

The insolent soldiers pretended to be affronted at this motion, and fell immediately upon the people with their swords, wounding two or three. This so enraged the rest that they attacked the soldiers immediately, wounded one, and made the rest throw down their arms, and beg quarter.

This breach, thus purely accidental, and by an unforeseen provocation being begun, the soldiers vowing revenge, and preparing to fall upon the whole neighbouring part of the country, drove the innocent people to the necessity of gathering together and standing upon their own defence; so that, when ten or twelve soldiers returned with their bloody resolution of plunder and desolation, they were likewise disarmed and made prisoners; and when, after this, three troops were sent, they found the people too strong to be attacked, upon which they cried presently, a rebellion, and sent for more forces, which, of course, obliged others to run into the aid of their brethren, all which was purely casual, till finding themselves reduced by this last gathering together to a circumstance which, stay or go, would be fatal to them, if they fell into the hands of the Government, they saw no remedy but to stand to it ; and, inviting all the injured and oppressed people to join with them, they declared for liberty and the Kirk of Scotland ; upon this, marching to Dumfries, they there seized their great persecutor, Sir James Turner, in his quarters.   Afterwards, they marched to Kirkcudbright, to Ayr, and from thence to Lanark, where they solemnly renewed the Covenant, and resolved to seal it with their blood, as we shall immediately find they were obliged to do.

The brief history of this rebellion is such as it can be no considerable interruption to our story, and is much to the purpose, to relate it.   The occasion being as above, the people having by necessity been driven to repel unjust violence by force, and seeing no room for mercy, but a certain destruction at hand, from the troops which were drawing about them, they resolved to stand to it ; they were not increased to above four hundred men, but those very well armed when they marched to the town of Dumfries, where, as I have said, they seized upon Sir James Turner, who was the commanding officer of the persecuting troops which had oppressed them ; him they carried away prisoner, though, as he confessed, they used him very civilly.   From thence, gathering and increasing in number, they marched to Kirkcudbright and Ayr, principal towns and sea-ports on that side the country, where they seized upon all the arms and ammunition they could find, but in no other thing offered any injury to any man.   From thence they advanced, being, as was reported, increased to the number of above two thousand, though that was a great mistake, to the town of Lanark, where, on the 26th day of November, they had a great meeting, and in a solemn manner fasted and humbled themselves in behalf of the nation of Scotland for the great sin of national perjury in making void the Covenant ; and there in the most solemn manner possible they renewed the said Covenant with their hands and eyes lifted up to heaven.   From thence they advanced still towards Edinburgh, where they arrived the 27th of November 1666 ; but being not strong enough to attack the city, they posted themselves at the foot of the Pentland Hills on the south-west of the city, waiting the conjunction of other friends who they expected from the Border and from the city of Edinburgh.

Here they were attacked and surprised the next day by General Dalziel, even during a proclaimed cessation, with a body of the King's forces ; and after a very bold and resolute defence, they were at length overpowered and broken.   Many escaped, having dispersed themselves the two days immediately before the fight; about fifty were killed upon the place, eighty were taken prisoners, and the rest saved themselves by flight.

For this action, besides those slain, ten were executed at Edinburgh December the 7th ; and the 11th, Thomas Paterson by name, who was condemned with them, died in the Tolbooth before execution, being grievously wounded,   Five more were likewise condemned the 10th, and four of them executed the 14th.   Four more were executed at Glasgow the 19th of December, six more at Edinburgh the 22d, eight more at Ayr, two at Dumfries, and two at Irvine ; and fifty-five who had made their escape, were fore-faulted, as they call it, or outlawed, and proclamation with reward made for apprehending them, declaring it treason to harbour, relieve, receive, or so much as to see and speak to them.   Among these were several ministers, of whom more hereafter.

It will hardly be allowed us in England to call this persecution, or that the sufferers here put to death should be reckoned among the martyrs of Scotland, because (say they) these were men taken in arms against the King, and executed as traitors. But we leave all those who afterwards thought it lawful to join in the revolution, and in taking up arms against the oppressions and arbitrary government of King James, to judge whether these good men had not the same individual reasons and more for this Pentland expedition; and it is answer enough to all that shall read these sheets to say, that these men died for that lawful resisting of arbitrary power, which has been justified as legal, and acknowledged to be justifiable by the practice and declaration of the respective Parliaments of both kingdoms. But we leave all those disputes to the readers to determine, as truth and justice shall guide them, and return to the history of fact.

Besides the death of these poor men, we find upon record above eight hundred men proscribed and driven from their families by the violence of the proceedings of this High Commission Court, who, besides those afterwards fallen upon, of whom more remains to be said, these suffered in their flight all the miseries that tongue can express, even beyond what we read of in the 11th of the Hebrews. They wandered about in sheep's skins, and goat skins, in dens, and caves of the earth, being destitute, afflicted, tormented. They suffered extremities that tongue cannot describe, and which heart can hardly conceive of, from the dismal circumstances of hunger, nakedness, and the severity of the climate, where it is known how insufferable the cold is, lying in damp caves and in hollow clefts of the naked rocks, without shelter, covering, fire, or food. None durst harbour, entertain, relieve, or speak to them, upon pain of death. Many, for venturing to receive them, were forced to fly to them, and several put to death for no other offence; fathers were persecuted for supplying their children, and children for nourishing their parents; husbands for harbouring their wives, and wives for cherishing their own husbands; the ties and obligations of the laws of nature were no defence, but it was made death to perform natural duties, and many suffered death for acts of piety and charity, in cases where human nature could not bear the thoughts of suffering it. To such an extreme was the rage of these persecutors carried on.

Besides these eight hundred families, who I call proscribed, and who were obliged to fly from their habitations to avoid the cruelty and rapine of their persecutors, there were fifty-five eminent persons who were panelled, or, as we call it in England, arraigned, as being actually in arms in the Pentland expedition; and being prosecuted by the Advocate, were sentenced respectively to be executed to death when apprehended; and in the meantime their estates to be forfeited, and seized upon to the King's use. Among these were the following ministers, of whom more is to be said :—Mr John Welch, Mr James Smith, Mr John Cunningham, Mr Gabriel Semple, Mr John Guthrie, Mr Alexander Peddin, Mr William Veach, Mr John Crookshanks, Mr Gabriel Maxwell, and Mr John Cairstairs.

But God, in his infinite goodness, delivered these all out of their hands. Also, it is very observable that some of the above-named fifty-two outlawed persons being gentlemen of good estates, their said estates were seized on, and given by the King to the most violent of their persecutors, as an encouragement to others to imitate the inhumanity and butchery by which things had been thus brought to extremity.

Nay, some of them thought that the council had it in their real design to drive the poor people to the necessity of taking arms, in hope of getting their blood and estates more in their power.

Never more let us talk of Popish cruelties, or give

the Romanists the title of bloody ; let not the rigour
of the Inquisition any farther engage our pens, till
the barbarities of this Protestant inquisition, the merciless, unrelenting fury of these Protestant persecutors has been expiated by their being abhorred by all
mankind.

But to leave the generals, and descend a little to
particulars as they occur historically to our view.

It is proper to mention here, because we shall
have occasion to speak of their names again, that,
amongst the rest of the ministers who fled on this
unhappy affair, Mr John Welch and Mr Gabriel
Semple were two whose zeal and sincerity in the
cause of religion occasioned their being more eminent
than their brethren. These fled to the borders,
where they found shelter and friends to harbour them
in an unexpected manner, and where they were made
wonderful instruments in God's hand to plant the
gospel and the fear of God in the hearts of the most
bloody and barbarous of men, who were before robbers and murderers, who, by the preaching of these
banished ministers became eminent converts ; and
both them and their posterity were made eminent in
the knowledge of God, and in their love to his ways,
in so much that, to the praise of sovereign grace,
those rude and unguided Borderers are now the
most zealous professers of the true religion of Britain ;
and those places which were dens of robbers and re-
ceptacles of thieves and murderers, are now become
some of the best planted and most flourishing congregations of serious Christians, perhaps, in the world.

It must not be forgotten here to mention the methods taken after this to prosecute and follow those
that fled, which (it was said) was owing to the merciless disposition of the Archbishop of St Andrews—
viz., publishing a proclamation, prohibiting the con-
cealing or corresponding with any of those who had
escaped, and this on pain of high treason. In this

proclamation the fifty-seven gentlemen and ministers mentioned before were particularly named.

Thus the persecution of God's servants in one country has often been the means of calling of others, and perhaps is yet to be the means of spreading and planting the everlasting gospel in all corners of the world, of which this border of Scotland and the colony of New England has been such noble examples, as we need look no farther into history to multiply particulars.

But before I quit this part, one thing cannot be omitted with relation to the good men who died thus on account of this rebellion. The persecutors, for such this very thing will prove them to be, as if they were fond of having it said that these men died for religion, and not for being in arms, and as if they scorned the excuse which the affair of Pentland put into their mouths for putting them to death, causes several of them to be offered their lives, if they would take and subscribe the declaration to renounce the Covenant. Whether they did this fraudulently or sincerely, Providence never gave them an opportunity to discover. Nor whether, if the weakness of any had brought them to yield, they would have performed their promise to them or no. For, not a man they ever offered it to (I mean of those condemned to die for the rebellion of Pentland) but received it with indignation, and choose to die, rather than to yield to that unconscionable proposal. So that in that point they gained an undeniable testimony, that they suffered for religion, not accepting deliverance; for none of them esteemed renouncing the Covenant to be anything more or less than renouncing God and his Church, to whom and for which that Covenant was first entered and engaged in.

The cruelty of these executions was attended with one piece of inhumanity, which we believe no Protestant ever practised before; nor was it practised in all the Popish persecutions in England in Queen Mary's days,— a barbarity beyond the cruelty of death, namely, causing the drums to beat round the scaffold all the while the executions lasted, that the people might not hear what the sufferers had to say to them, and to discompose and disorder them as much as possible in their last moments.

It is very remarkable that the like of this was never read of in any modern history, except in the history of that bloody tyrant and persecutor, the Duke d'Alva, Governor of the Netherlands for the King of Spain.

From this time we may date the persecution to be in its height of fury. For the rage of the persecutors extended every way, provoked by the constancy of the sufferers, until it came to such a height as was never yet heard of in any Protestant country in the world.

The poor people were driven from their habitations and from their families. This was indeed in their power, and they did it with the utmost cruelty; but they could never drive them from their principles. Nor while ministers were to be found, who durst preach to them, was it ever possible to prevent the people assembling to hear them, were the penalty loss of goods, liberty, imprisonment—nay, even death itself. And, which was still wonderful, the more their persecutors multiplied laws and penalties against them, and the more they were punished by those laws for those assemblies, the more numerous they grew, and multitudes were added to the Church every day by the sufferings which they met with.

But the subtle enemy finding this, fell upon a stratagem which did more harm to religion in Scotland, as it made a breach and division among the sufferers, than all the cruelty of the persecutors could ever do; and this was what they called the indulgence. The history whereof is necessary to the justification of the suffering people, as well against the reproaches of their friends, who were not rightly informed of their circumstances, as against the slanders of their enemies.

The short account of the affair is thus:—

"King Charles II. was a prince not naturally inclined to cruelty, not a man of blood by his disposition, and had, it seems, some about him who had taken the freedom to let him know more of the inhumanity and barbarity of the Archbishop and his accomplices than these were desirous he should have heard of; and particularly, what was alleged by the friends of the Kirk against that prelate's conduct, when the King had once before, upon the like representation, sent an express order to the Council that no more should be put to death, namely, that the Archbishop kept that order in his pocket until he had seen the execution of the last nine or eleven of the Pentland men who were condemned."

This being represented to the King, his Majesty began to resent it, and spoke some things which gave them reason to think that he would some way or other put a stop to their proceeding, if they did not find out some new method to impose upon him. This they wickedly but effectually did at the same time, and in the same act, and deed, by which they very fatally divided the Church of Scotland against itself in the manner following:—

First, they told the King that they (the Council) were not all prosecuting the whole Kirk, but only some few men that were enemies to human society, and not safe to be suffered in a civil government, who denied even the ordinance of magistracy itself; and would neither acknowledge or submit to his Majesty's authority, or the laws of the kingdom; a few obstinate rebels, who would neither obey the laws of God, or submit to the government of man. That to convince his Majesty of the truth of this, they had

resolved to publish an act of indulgence to all those
who would submit to the civil magistrate, and give
assurances of their fidelity to his Majesty's person and
government, allowing them the exercise of religion,
according to their consciences, and then his Majesty
would see that those people who would stand out
were not fit to be suffered in human society, were
irreconcileable enemies to his Majesty, and such as
no government could be safe until they were rooted
out and destroyed.   With this hypocritical shew of
clemency they satisfied that easy prince, a man given
up to his luxury and the effeminacy of his vices, and
who suffered the mildness of his disposition to be de-
luded with false pretences under the shadow of lenity
to all that were proper objects of compassion, and
leaving those who were misrepresented by his flat-
terers to the matchless rage of their irreconcileable
enemies.
     To carry on this farce, they passed an Act of Indul-
gence, as they called it, anno 1669, after they had
wasted the west of Scotland by their soldiers, even
worse than an enemy's army would have done in time
of war ; and after the sufferers were so entirely scattered that few were to be found, and very little plunder left to satisfy the rapine of their dragoons.   By
their act of council—for they caused their acts of
council to bear the authority of laws—they proclaimed,
" That all such outed ministers as should take license
from the council, or the bishop of the diocess,"—which
licenses also had several limitations annexed, all of
them directly contrary to the Presbyterian principle,
and homologating, as they term it, the authority of
the civil magistrate in ecclesiastical affairs, even to
the height of Erastianism—" all such ministers were
allowed to preach and exercise the ministerial func-
tions in private houses or meetings, and their people
allowed to attend them with a *non obstante*, to all
acts of Parliament then in force to the contrary." So

that here was not only an invasion of the Church, but the exercise of the dispensing power in the extremity, setting aside the established laws made in Parliament, by the authority of the council.

This indulgence kindled a terrible flame of division and breach of charity among the suffering good people, a schism that is really such, carried on even to excommunicating one another, and the effects of which is felt even to this day.

Many ministers, upon principles to themselves perhaps satisfactory, came in and accepted this indulgence ; being willing to go any length that their consciences could be satisfied with, in order to preserve the privilege of exercising their ministry and preaching the gospel to their people.

But the prosecuted people, whose zeal commanded them not to do the least evil to reap the greatest good, began to protest against this compliance of their brethren as wicked and detestable, declaring not only against the indulgence itself, but against all those who submitted to it, as guilty of yielding to the power of the prelate's homologating the supremacy, forsaking their principles, and breaking the Covenant.   In a word, they not only refused to accept such a sinful toleration, but protested against the making it, as void in its own nature, and this in the warmest manner ; and being thus effectually secluded from the advantage of worshipping God in their houses, even in the most secret manner possible, they took to the fields.

Now their persecutors obtained what they desired ; for now they thought they might with assurance boast to the King of having made a right judgment in these affairs ; and having said many favourable things of those they called the sober Presbyterians, whom now they cajoled, in order to bring them to accept of the indulgence, and to take licenses ; they represented those who remained, who were now called Whigs, as a party, who were not to be suffered in any government, but that ought to be rooted off from the face of the earth ; and this is the first time that the name of a Whig was used in the world, I mean as applied to a man, or to a party of men ; and these were the original primitive Whigs, the name for many years being given to no other people.   The word is said to be taken from a mixt drink the poor men drank in their wanderings, composed of water and sour milk, but that by the way.

At the same period began the field-preachings, or field-conventicles, of which I shall have frequent occasions to speak more largely.

And at the same period also the people frequenting these meetings, or field-preachings, were first called Cameronians, from one Mr Cameron, a zealous assertor of the sovereignty of conscience over the laws of men, of whom also we shall have occasion to speak hereafter.

If the persecution was cruel and furious before, it was now raging and insufferable, carried on with such madness and with such an unsatisfied thirst of blood, that I believe none of the heathen persecutions in the primitive times could go beyond it in all its parts. It is true, they did not immediately torment the body by fire, by racks, and a vast variety of instrumental tortures, though they had cruelty enough that way too, as in those barbarous engines of cruelty called the boot and the thumbkins, than which a more exquisite torture could not easily be devised.

But they had torments beyond the cruelty of death, which they drove the poor persecuted people to suffer, namely, the driving them from their habitations into mountains and hills, into dens, and holes, and caves of the earth, attended with unsufferable, unsupportable hunger and cold, in a climate the most unhospitable, and places most barren, and empty of sustenance or relief of any in these parts of the world.

It is not to be calculated how many were starved

in this manner, and whose bones many of them were found afterwards who had perished in the most deplorable circumstances, and were not discovered by any other remains. It would make the heart of any considering Christian bleed to contemplate the miseries of those people who perished in this deplorable manner, when such was the cruelty of their persecutors that even the parents durst not relieve or entertain their children, or children harbour, or nourish their parents; but, if the person was accused of having been at one of these field-meetings, they were immediately proscribed and intercommuned, by which it was made death for any one so much as to speak with them, much more to harbour or relieve them.

It has been inquired why these people would so obstinately continue to assemble in these field-meetings; and I have heard them censured by many who did not understand the circumstances which they were reduced to; which, therefore, it is necessary a little to describe.

It is mentioned before how severe the laws they had already made were against those who did not come to church; and how none were permitted to exercise the ministerial office but upon such and such limitations. This they found embarrassed them, with the whole body of the Kirk, and begun to appear too rigid and severe; and for this reason, as before, the indulgence was set on foot. After which lenity, as it was called, they supposed nothing would be called cruelty upon those who would not accept of liberty upon their terms; and, therefore, no sooner was the indulgence granted, but they began to persecute with the utmost fury all those who either would not or did not accept of their benevolent indulgence.

Immediately sanguinary laws were made to fall upon those they had now doomed to destruction, for not complying with their most merciful toleration;

and first, all such who thought fit to take licenses from the bishops, were admitted, or indulged to meet, &c., in such and such places. So all other were immediately sentenced, by a law to suppress conventicles; whereby all those ministers, who presumed to preach, expound, or pray in any house where were more than the family, were to be imprisoned till they gave security never to offend again, or to depart the kingdom; and every person presented in such house to be fined a fourth part of their annual rent, if gentlemen, and in proportion for others; but for field conventicles, the preacher was to be put to death, and his goods confiscated, and 500 marks reward was given to the person that should apprehend them, the hearers also to be fined double to what the hearers in house conventicles were fined. This is that famous persecuting law, intituled, act against conventicles, 6 act, 2d sess., 2d part., Char. II., anno 1670, and was continued afterwards for three years more, and after that continued again, and the fines doubled.

The ministers who could not accept of this indulgence, had now their sentence. If they thought fit to lay aside their office, and neither be minister nor hearer, they were indeed tolerably safe, but this they could not yield to. What was then before them, as ministers, was clear; for house meetings, imprisonment and banishment; for field meetings, immediate death. This, however, did not deter the poor people to assemble themselves together, or the ministers to attend and perform the duty of their office at first in houses, but afterwards their numbers increasing, they assembled in the fields or mountains rather, and that in such numbers, and so well prepared, as that their persecutors often paid dear for falling upon them.

But this enraged them the more, and occasioned the persecution to rise to such a height, as can scarce be equalled for its cruelty and variety in any history.

As I have said, the numbers of the people flocking to the ministers were not to be concealed, indeed, not to be contained in houses; so that it presently became so dangerous to meet in that manner, that few, if any such meetings, could be held, without being discovered, in which case the minister was sure to suffer imprisonment and banishment, and the poor people were as sure to be ruined by fines.

This caused them to quit their houses, and go to the hills, the beginning of field conventicles, as I said before, where they had more convenience of meeting, were much easier concealed, and had more opportunity to make their escapes, if delivered. Before this had been long practised, the Council took the alarm. It is true, as soon as ever the poor people took to this method, their numbers increased to a prodigious degree, for thousands of people who durst not distinguish themselves in appearing at house meetings, finding more safety, and almost an impossibility of being discovered in these field meetings, crowded thither, so that it was very frequent to have seven, eight, to ten thousand people at a time at those meetings.

Upon this method, the Council being, as I said, alarmed, resolved to raise forces, and to put the kingdom at the expense of keeping and supporting a standing army, on pretence of supressing the Cameronians—a people who all that while desired no more than a quiet, peaceable enjoying the liberty of serving God, free from the impositions of men—and who, although they had already suffered all kinds of oppressions and injustice, yet offered violence to none. What provoked their enemies on this occasion was, that they could not fall upon them now in the usual manner by their civil officers and persecutors, for the people having been before dispersed from their habitations, and not daring to appear where they were known, yet now gathered together from all parts to the solemn occasions of worshipping God without any fear, and in a posture not to be easily disturbed. This their persecutors presently called rebellion, and represented it as well to the Parliament there, as to the King himself, in the most formidable appearances, as a thing threatening a civil war, and which, if not timely suppressed, would embroil the whole kingdom.

As it was easy for them to impose by these things on the most credulous prince in the world, so they had their agents ready at Court to aggravate and expatiate upon every article, and by this means they brought the Court into all their most sanguinary resolutions; and having, as is said, obtained an act of Parliament, whereby they made it death and confiscation of goods for any minister to preach or pray at these field meetings, they had this specious pretence to raise forces to put that law in execution. The number of soldiers they raised was not great at first, amounting in the whole, not to above 2500 men, most dragoons; but they afterwards thought fit to join 3000 Highland thieves to them, by which they completed the ruin of the country. With these forces they pursued these poor people through the hills and mountains, to disturb and separate their assemblies; to which purpose they were ordered to seize, secure, and apprehend all they could lay hold on, to murder and destroy all that made resistance; and to plunder and waste the goods of those who they could not apprehend. Nor was any cruelty omitted by these dragoons which it was in their power to inflict, till their masters obtained by them the great end which they always aimed at—viz., to make the poor people desperate, and drive them to take arms. This was the case, and this issued in the rising of Bothwell; of which in its place.

These troops were immediately dispersed over the whole country; I mean that part of the country where the things were chiefly transacted viz., the western

and southern shires.   They were empowered to apprehend and bring, dead or alive, such ministers as
they had given them by name; and at length they
had a power to apprehend all people that they had
reason to suppose were present at any of those meetings, or were going to them, or coming from them.
This last clause gave them such an unlimited extensive power, that no person was exempt from their
enquiry; and if they found any person upon the road
that had but a Bible in their pockets, they took it for
a sufficient proof that they either had been at or were
going to one of those meetings, and accordingly they
sent them to prison, where they seldom failed of finding some pretence or other to ensnare them, and draw
them into some acknowledgment of what they called
a crime, so to keep them in custody.   For, as the
honest people would not lie to save themselves, they
failed not to purge them with questions whether they
had been or intended to be present at any field conventicles; and many times the people so questioned would
boldly acknowledge, though to their own hurt, that they
both had been at them, and intended as often as might
be to be present again at them; defying the power of
their enemies, and bidding them do their worst.

By these things the prisons were filled with great
numbers of faithful confessors; and many were confined in the island of the Bass, the castles of Dunnotter, Blackness, and other unwholesome places,
where they perished with distempers and in misery,
occasioned by want of conveniences, by severity of cold
and length of time; and others languished without
hope, or at least without prospect of deliverance, seventeen or eighteen years, until their persecutors were
supplanted by heaven at the glorious revolution effected by King William.   Many likewise were banished in this part of the persecution, and hundreds,
nay thousands, were driven from their dwellings, outlawed and intercommuned.

P

The reader is desired to observe now that the persecutions of the Church of Scotland may be divided into two parts, and they have their respective periods of time—to wit, (1) the persecution of the whole Presbyterian Church, as described from the time of the act restoring Episcopacy, anno 1662, of which mention has been made; and (2) the persecution of the Cameronian Presbyterians (so they were then called), which began at or immediately after the declaration of indulgence, to wit, in the year 1670. This indulgence was called a declaration, because it was not done by act of Parliament, but by the King's council, upon a letter from the King himself. And to give it an equal sanction as a statuted law, an act was immediately passed in the Parliament, by which it was enenacted that the government of the Church and the ordering thereof does of right belong to his Majesty and his successors, by virtue of his supremacy, and is inherent in the crown, and that the King may set forth such constitutions concerning ecclesiastic matters as he shall find proper, which are to be obeyed and observed by all his subjects as law.

Upon this indulgence, those ministers who submitted to accept of licenses to preach from the bishop, and to take the oaths therein prescribed, to wit, of allegiance and supremacy, were allowed to set up meeting-houses for religious worship, and to exercise all the parts of their ministerial office to such congregations as gathered to them for that purpose. And it is acknowledged that in the east and north parts of Scotland, many, perhaps the greater part of the Presbyterian Dissenters did comply and accept of this indulgence, esteeming it better so do to than to leave the people as sheep without a shepherd; and better than to be utterly deprived of the means of preaching the gospel at all. For though they should have suffered the greatest extremities, and had been willing to endure the worst their enemies could inflict, yet could they not have had the least opportunity to have preached, or the people to have heard them in those parts where the country, being fully inhabited, and chiefly by their enemies, they would have been certain at all times to have been disappointed, and fallen upon.

But there were a body of people, especially in the west and southern parts, whose zeal carried them beyond all such compliances, and who, esteeming the accepting of the indulgence as homologating (to use their own words) their solemnly abjured Prelacy, and detesting every thing that looked like a yielding up the cause of God, as they really believed theirs to be, stood out, and would by no means accept of deliverance in a sinful manner.

It is too long a subject to enter upon in these Memoirs, to set down the reasons that one side gave for their complying with, and the other for their rejecting this indulgence; it is sufficient to the case in hand that these men declared they thought the terms sinful ; that the good pretended was by no means equivalent to the evil that was to be committed ; that it was against the Covenant, by which they were engaged to God to endeavour to their utmost the extirpation of Prelacy ; that they ought to suffer the greatest torment rather than to commit the least sin ; and that as this was, in their opinion, a great sin, they could not in conscience comply with it.

What they denied, or refused to do, may be comprehended in these heads, with the reasons they have for it :——

1. They would not accept of an indulgence for worshipping God by the licence of the bishops, because, they said, they had abjured Prelacy in the Covenant, and had declared the bishops to be anti-scriptural and anti-christian, and to take licence from them was to homologate their authority as legal, which they detested and abhorred.

2. They would not take the oath of supremacy, because they could not in conscience allow any king or head of the church but Jesus Christ.

3. They would not pray for the King, or swear to him, because he was a persecutor of the Church, and thereby an enemy to God ; because he had renounced the oath of God in the Covenant, and till he had repented, they would have nothing to do with him.

4. Being debarred all manner of liberty to worship God in public, and on the severest penalties forbid to assemble themselves together, either in the churches or in private families, and believing it at the same time their duty, according to the Scripture, not to forsake assembling, &c., they could not satisfy their consciences to obey man rather than God.

These things, however condemned by others who thought the suffering people strained their matters too high, were yet principles which those people could not in conscience abate or go from ; and it was apparent they would lay down their lives rather than abate or go from them.   And this makes the proceedings of the council against them be justly esteemed the height of persecution.   Nor were the methods taken with them such as could be justified either by the laws of God or man, especially Christians, though their principles had been really worse than their enemies ever pretended they were; for they were treated not only with all manner of cruelty, barbarity, and inhumanity, but with treachery, perfidy, and breach of even the laws of nature.   They were abandoned to the mercy of every common soldier to kill and destroy them, upon even suspicion of guilt, without trial, evidence, or examination ; they were made witnesses against themselves, and against one another ; and methods were taken to try, convict, and execute them in a few moments without law, order, judge, or magistrate.

The merciless rage of their persecutors was come

to such a height, that they would frequently contrive to surprise them, so as that they might put them to death, without giving them time so much as to pray to God, as if they thought their rage could extend beyond death, and that, if possible, they would punish their souls as well as their bodies; and I think it is no breach of charity to say, that if they could have made an act of Parliament, that they should have had no mercy shown them in the next world, any more than in this, they would not have failed to have passed it.   Few persecutions in the world have ever been circumstanced with such particular marks of inveterate malice; they have even envied them the prayers of others; and if upon their trials any one had but said, " Lord comfort them," they were sure to be taken up and questioned for themselves.

Such inhumanities have not been paralléled in the world as has been used here, particularly, that when two hundred and fifty of them were put on board a ship for transportation, and the ship was cast away upon the rocks, so hardhearted and inhumanly-cruel was the officer who commanded, that he would not suffer the hatches to be opened that they might be saved, though to be still banished according to sentence; but stood over them till they were all drowned in the hold of the ship, except fifty who miraculously escaped, some of whom are alive at the publishing of this account.

These, however, are generals, I shall meet with them all again in their course.   I return to the field-meetings; for it is of these, and of the people frequenting them, that all that is now to be said is to be understood.

After the poor people had thus adjourned their meetings to the hills, as is said, and the council had obtained those laws above mentioned, declaring it imprisonment, death, &c., to be found at any of them, and troops were levied to put those laws in execution, there could be nothing expected on any side but blood, and the fire of persecution was but then said to be kindled.

The first civil or pretendedly legal step was an act of Parliament, 2 sess. 2 Parl. Char. II., anno 1670, by which every person, of what quality, age, or sex, soever, was obliged to answer upon oath, and depose all that they knew of such field-meetings, and of what persons were thereat, and to answer to the questions that should be asked them upon oath, upon pain of imprisonment, fine, corporal punishment, or banishment, at the pleasure of the Council. By this act, fathers and mothers were obliged to betray and accuse their own children, and children to betray and accuse their parents, husbands their wives, and wives their husbands ; and many for refusing thus to betray their nearest relations, have been transported to the plantations from their country, relations, and interest, where they have been sold for slaves, and have perished by the severity of labour, violent cold, or violent heat, not having been used to such hardships.

A serious and judicious writer of those times says, Such havock was made by the cruelty of the soldiers, and by the furious executions of their arbitrary and tyrannical laws, that greater could not be found in the reigns of Nero and Caligula, Roman emperors most infamous for cruelty.

Nor were these violences exercised for a little while, as in several of the most cruel of the primitive persecutions was the case ; but for eighteen years together, the poor people had no redress, no relaxation, but that every day matters grew worse and worse, and more and more desperate, their enemies always contriving some new and unpracticed severity, and acting something never known before, in order more and more to exasperate and oppress them. This account of eighteen years' persecution is to be reckoned from the time of the indulgence, or at least from the year after, viz. 1670.   But the whole persecution continued twenty-eight years—viz., from May, the beginning of the year 1660, being the first of the Restoration, to November, the latter end of the year 1688, being the beginning of the Revolution.

Things were now come to the utmost extremity, and the sufferers being treated thus with all manner of cruelty, had, as is said, taken to the hills, where they worshipped God with more freedom and with gladness of heart, but not with much less hazard at the last; for they were then fallen upon as rebels by troops of dragoons, who executed the bloody orders of the council with such rage over the poor defenceless people, riding over the poor flying women and children, and dragging them like beasts up and down the fields till they brought them to prisons, that it was no wonder the men took measures to meet together with more safety to themselves.   From this time it was resolved, that seeing self-defence was a natural law, and that every man had a right to preserve his own life in the performance of any lawful action, and likewise that the worship of God was not only lawful, but their indispensable duty, which no human power ought to restrain, or had a right to forbid; it was lawful therefore for them to defend themselves from violence, and preserve their liberty in the exercise, and during the time of worship.   And therefore they resolved, that at their said field-meetings, as many of the young men that had fire-arms should come armed; not to use violence against any, but to resist the dragoons, in case they should fall upon the meeting, or lay hold of any of the people going to or coming from it.

This was the famous resolve of the great meeting at Lanark, and, for a time, was some surprise to the persecutors.   For, indeed, after this they were often beaten back by the courage of much inferior numbers of the people, notwithstanding their rage and fury. And at other times the persecuted appeared to guard their meetings with such numbers, and so skilfully posted, that the dragoons durst not attack them : though, on all these occasions, the persecuted kept themselves on the defensive, never offering any more than to stand firm, facing their enemies till the poor frighted women and children were separated, and gotten safe from the place.

I cannot refrain from giving some few instances of the behaviour of these people when power was in their hands, which may serve to let posterity see whether they were rebellious by their inclination, or whether they were driven to take arms in their hands for their own just defence or not ; and to prove that, even when it was in their power to have cut their enemies in pieces, who well had deserved it for their cruelty, yet they contented themselves with bare rescuing their brethren from the butchery of the dragoons, and let the murderers escape.

There had been a meeting in the fields in Nithsdale, not far from Drumlanrig Castle, the seat of the late Duke of Queensberry. The assembly was very numerous, and there were about sixty men with firearms, who placed themselves at convenient distance so as to keep off their enemies, if they should come to disturb the assembly till the people might disperse ; and these also had scouts out every way at great distance to discover, and give notice, &c. It was not long before an alarm was given that they were betrayed, and that two parties of dragoons were marching to attack them. Upon this the poor people, as was always the method, separated, and went every one their own way, so that the soldiers found them entirely dispersed, and no meeting in appearance except of about 300, who were gotten together where their men were posted that had arms, who, presenting their pieces at the dragoons from the side of a steep hill, where their horses were useless, they did not think fit to dismount and attack them.

The soldiers, however, grown furious and enraged, spread themselves over the fields in pursuit of the poor straggling people, and seized several of them ; and, amongst the rest, they unhappily fell upon six men naked and unarmed, one of whom was the minister. These they took ; and after having abused, bruised, and wounded them, though they offered no resistance, they bound and dragged them along with them, making the poor men go on foot at their horses' heels as fast as they rode. They carried these prisoners directly for Edinburgh, where also they were sure to be put to death as soon as they arrived.

As the ministers on these occasions were very free to hazard their lives in the work of their office, and for the comfort and edification of their people ; so the people again were remarkable for their love to their ministers, and their concern for their preservation. No sooner, therefore, was it known among them that their minister was taken, than the men began to gather together in several parties with their arms, resolved, whatever it cost, to rescue their minister. To this end they dispersed themselves into all the ways by which they thought the dragoons might march ; by which it happened that the smallest number of them, not being above thirty-seven men, who lay on the side of Entrekein Hill, met with them, that being the way the enemy really went with the prisoners.

This Entrekein is a very steep and dangerous mountain ; nor could such another place have been easily found in the whole country for their purpose ; and had not the dragoons been infatuated from heaven, they would never have entered such a pass without well discovering the hill above them. The road for above a mile goes winding, with a moderate ascent on the side of a very high and very steep hill, till on the latter part still ascending, and the height on the left above them being still vastly great, the depth on their

right below them makes a prodigious precipice, de-
scending steep and ghastly into a narrow deep bottom, only broad enough for the current of water to
run that descends upon hasty rains.   From this bottom the mountain rises instantly again, steep as a precipice, on the other side to a stupendous height.   The
passage on the side of the first hill, by which, as I
said, the way creeps gradually up, is narrow, so that
two horsemen can but ill pass in front; and if any
disorder should happen to them so as that they step
but a little awry, they are in danger of falling down
the said precipice on their right, where there would
be no stopping till they came to the bottom.   And
the writer of this has seen, by the accident only of a
sudden frost, which had made the way slippery, three
or four horses at a time, of travellers or carriers, lying
in that dismal bottom; which, slipping in their way,
have not been able to recover themselves, but have
fallen down the precipice and rolled to the bottom,
perhaps tumbling twenty times over, by which it is
impossible but they must be broken to pieces before
they come to stop.

In this way the dragoons were blindly marching
two and two with the minister and five countrymen,
whom they had taken prisoners, and were hauling
them along to Edinburgh.   The front of them being
near the top of the hill, and the rest reaching all
along the steep part, when, on a sudden, they heard
a man's voice calling to them from the side of the hill
on their left, a great height above them.

It was misty, as indeed it is seldom otherwise on
the height of that mountain, so that no body was seen
at first; but the commanding officer hearing some
body call, halted, and called aloud, "What do ye
want; and who are ye?"   He had no sooner spoke,
when twelve men came in sight upon the side of the
hill above them, and the officer called again, "What
are ye?" and bad stand.   One of the twelve answer-

ed, by giving the word of command to his men,
" Make ready ;" and then calling to the officer, said,
" Sir, will ye deliver our minister ?"   The officer answered with an oath, " No, sir, and ye were to be
damned."   At which the leader of the countrymen
fired immediately, and aimed so true at him, though
the distance was pretty great, that he shot him
through the head, and immediately he fell from his
horse.   His horse, fluttering a little with the fall of
his rider, fell over the precipice, rolling to the bottom, and was dashed to pieces.

The rest of the twelve men were stooping to give
fire upon the body, when the next commanding officer
called to them to hold their hands, and desired a
truce.   It was apparent that the whole body was in a
dreadful consternation—not a man of them durst stir
a foot, or offer to fire a shot.   And had the twelve
men given fire upon them, the first volley, in all pro-
bability, would have driven twenty of them down the
side of the mountain into that dreadful gulph at the
bottom.

To add to their consternation, their two scouts who
rode before, gave them notice that there appeared
another body of armed countrymen at the top of the
hill in their front, which, however, were nothing but
some travellers, who, seeing troops of horse coming up, stood there to let them pass, the way being
too narrow to go by them.   It is true, there were
about twenty-five more of the countrymen in arms,
though they had not appeared, and they would have
been sufficient, if they had thought fit, to have cut
this whole body of horse in pieces.

But the officer having asked a parley, and demanded, " What it was they would have ?" they replied
again, " Deliver our minister."   " Well, sir," said the
officer, " ye's get your minister, and ye will promise
to forbear firing."   " Indeed we'll forbear," says the
good man, " we desire to hurt none of ye.   But sir,"

says he, " belike ye have more prisoners ?"   " Indeed have we," says the officer.   " And ye mon deliver them all," says the honest man.   " Well," says the officer, " ye shall have them then."   Immediately the officer calls to bring forward the minister; but the way was so narrow and crooked he could not be brought up by a horseman, without danger of putting them into disorder; so that the officer bade them loose him, and let him go, which was done.   So the minister stept up the hill a step or two, and stood still; then the officer said to him, " Sir, and I let you go, I expect you promise to oblige your people to offer no hindrance to our march."   The minister promised them he would do so.   " Then go, sir," said he, " you owe your life to this damned mountain."   " Rather, sir," said the minister, " to that God that made this mountain."   When their minister was come to them, their leader called again to the officer, " Sir, we want yet the other prisoners."   The officer gave orders to the rear where they were, and they were also delivered.   Upon which the leader began to march away, when the officer called again, " But hold, sir," said he, " ye promised to be satisfied if ye had your prisoners—I expect you'll be as good as your word."   " Indeed shall I," said the leader, " I am just marching away."   It seems he did not rightly understand the officer.   " Well, sir," said the officer, " I expect you call off those fellows you have posted at the head of the way."   " They belong not to us," says the honest man, " they are unarmed people waiting till you pass by."   " Say you so," said the officer, " had I known that, you had not gotten your men so cheap, or have come off so free."   Says the countrymen, " And ye are for battle, sir; we are ready for you still, if you think you are able for us, ye may trye your hands; we'll quit the truce, if you like."   " No," says the officer, " I think ye be brave fellows, e'en gang your gate."

The case was very clear, and the officer saw it plainly. Had those thirty-seven men, for that was the most of their number, fired but twice upon them, and then fallen in sword in hand, or with the club of their muskets, not a man of them could have escaped. Nay, they must have destroyed one another, for they would have thrust one another down the hill with but the least offer to move, or turn, or do any thing but go forward; nor could any dragoon apply himself to any thing but to govern his horse, so as to prevent his falling over the edge of the way down the hill. Indeed, the persecuted had them all at mercy; and had they commanded them all to lay down their arms, and surrender themselves prisoners at discretion, they must have done it. But these testified by their moderation that they sought no man's blood, and that they took arms merely for their own defence, and yet four of these were afterwards executed for this fact.

This little affair made a great noise. The officer of the dragoons was threatened with a council of war; and whether he was not broke for cowardice I am not certain; but this I am certain of, that had the best of them been upon the spot, they must have done the same, or have resolved to have made a journey headlong down such a hill as would have chilled the blood of a man of good courage but to have thought of. As to the mistake of not discovering the place before they entered the pass, that fault lay upon the officer who was killed, who had already paid dear for his omission.

There was another occasion in which the persecuted people had let the soldiers know, that they were not always to expect their blood so cheap as they had formerly had it. And this had been much to their advantage, had they not carried it on afterwards to an enterprize, which neither their numbers nor circumstances were by any any means equal to.

John Graham, Laird of Claverhouse, the same who was famous afterwards by the title of Viscount of Dundee, and was killed at the battle of Killicrankie, in the year 1689, was a furious persecutor, and an implacable enemy of these poor innocent people upon all occasions. He had, among the rest of his cruelties, barbarously murdered several of the persecuted people with his own hands, as after this action he did several more, particularly one of his own name—viz., Graham of Galloway, who fled from him out of a house where the said Claverhouse had pursued and beset him. The young man being forced to quit the house, and run to save his life, Claverhouse rode after him and overtook him ; and though the young man offered to surrender, and begged him to save his life, he shot him dead with his pistol. This, with several other like barbarous things, he practised upon the poor persecuted people ; of which hereafter.

There was a great meeting of the persecuted people in the fields near Loudon Hill, where, by report, many thousands were met together. I think they had intended to have the communion, and to have made it a day both of humiliation and rejoicing—a day of humiliation for the apostacy of their brethren, and for the sins of the land—and a day of solemn joy for the liberty of and affection of the people to the service and worship of God.

As it was a very great meeting, so the number of men was greater than were in arms for their defence, than as usual on other and ordinary occasions ; there being about 200 men with fire-arms prepared for and resolved to do their parts with the enemy if they came, as was threatened, to disturb them.

The Laird of Claverhouse having information of this assembly, prepared to attack them ; and had boasted what havoc he would make of the Cameronians on that occasion. It seems he said that he heard they had some firemen among them, but if they offered to make one shot at his men, he would save the council and courts of justice the trouble of prosecuting his prisoners with the formality of the law, for he would immediately hang up every one that fell into his hands, if he should take 500. It was confidently reported that some of the soldiers of his own troops gave private notice of this, and of the measures he had taken for assaulting the meeting, as also of the menaces and boasts he had made. Compassion, indeed, might move some of the soldiers; for though, generally speaking, the soldiers were barbarous and cruel as their officers could desire, yet oftentimes it was found they were less so than their officers.

However it was, the persecuted had received information that Claverhouse, with 300 dragoons, was resolved to surround the meeting, and put them all to the sword. This account came not to them till after they were assembled, and their worship was actually begun; whereupon the men who had the guard of the meeting, far from being surprised, consulted together what they should do, whether they should disperse for that time, and appoint another meeting at another place and time, or what course they should take.

They had not many hours to deliberate, much less to put in execution, what they should resolve on. But, in a word, it was concluded the people should be desired to sit still and compose themselves, whatever should happen, leaving the event to the providence and good pleasure of God; and that they should send for help to all the neighbouring places, and in the meantime to meet Claverhouse and his men, if they came to attack them, and do as God should direct.

Upon mustering their men, they found their number increased to about 250 men, well armed, besides several that came in afterwards; and before the action began it is thought they were near 400. The assembly was great, and the people sat all on the ground on the side of a steep hill, the minister preaching to them from a little tent near the bottom of the hill. The Laird of Claverhouse, with his dragoons, came on with great fury, like a troop of wolves to fall upon a naked and defenceless flock of sheep, and not expecting any resistance kept no scouts out before him ; when on a sudden they were challenged, and bid stand, by an outguard of the persecuted, who finding them come on, fired at them, and retreated to the main body.   But the dragoons were a second time surprised, when they found a large body of men advantageously posted, the first line of whom fired a volley of shot upon them, and killed and wounded sixteen or seventeen men, and some horses.

This brought them to halt and prepare for battle. They took not much time for it, but came on again with great fury, but found that the persecuted had a large ditch cast up in their front, with a low old ruined wall, which served them as a parapet, from whence they fired with more security ; and so well they plied them with their shot, that, after two or three attempts, they gave it over, and retreated, having lost about fifty men, killed and wounded ; and found that they had to do with men resolved to die, and sell their lives as dear as they could.   There were some of the persecuted who signalized themselves upon this occasion ; and who, leaping over their works, advanced so near them, as that once a young gentlemen laid hands on the bridle of Claverhouse's horse, and had certainly taken him prisoner if he had been well seconded.   This was Mr Cleeland, who, eighteen years after, was Lieutenant-Colonel to the Earl of Angus's regiment, which was raised among these very people at the revolution, and was called the Cameronian Regiment, being raised and completed in one day without beat of drum.   This was the same regiment, now called Preston's, which was at the attack of the late rebels at Preston in Lancashire. And this gentleman, Lieutenant-Colonel Cleeland, was unhappily killed at Dunkeld against the same Claverhouse, then Viscount Dundee.

This action began to make the persecuted terrible to the Council ; and had they continued to have acted thus upon the defensive only, it was thought they would in time have ruined the troops of their persecutors. But their pushing things to extremity afterwards ruined them and all their friends.

It is easy to believe, that this check enraged the soldiery to the last degree. Many of the persons who had thus appeared being known, were after this obliged to fly for fear of falling into the hands of their persecutors ; but the heads of the actors finding there was no going back to their own houses, they unhappily resolved to keep together ; and this began the rebellion of Bothwell Bridge. For, encouraged by success, and made desperate by the extremities they were driven to, they, in less than four days, found themselves near 2000 men, very well armed and furnished. Upon this they marched to Glasgow, and were increased in a few days more to between 6000 and 7000 men.

Their friends now began to be in pain for them, because England was more immediately concerned to reduce them now, as well as Scotland. And the Duke of Monmouth was sent down from thence to command the army.

This was, I say, that well-known insurrection of Bothwell Bridge ; and it was called rebellion, because they declared against the King. They were afterwards attacked by the Duke of Monmouth, while they were irresolute, and consulting whether to yield or defend themselves, and were defeated.

It is not any part of the present work to give the particulars of this rising. From the action mentioned

Q

to the defeat, it is sufficient to observe, that, in this action, there was between 300 and 400 killed, and about 1200 taken prisoners. The rest escaped, and dispersed themselves as well as they could ; nor were the persecutors at all satisfied with the Duke of Monmouths conduct, who refused, at their request, to let the poor people be pursued and massacred by the dragoons—not failing to make a complaint against him to the court of England on that head, and to have it improved to his disadvantage.

Many were the unhappy consequences of this insurrection, as well to those who were not concerned in it as to those who were ; for, though the Duke of Monmouth, as general of the army, restrained the rage of the soldiery, as above, from the inhumanity of a hot-blood execution, yet, his command ceasing, and himself returning immediately after to Court, the persecutors took pains to shew the world that they could act with more cruelty in cold blood than men of honour and of Christian clemency could find in their hearts to suffer, even in the heat of victory.

For now they gave themselves a full swing in all their bloody measures, letting loose the most bloody agents of tyranny to execute whatever their private rage, as well as public, could dictate to them. Under the pretence of rooting out rebellion, and of executing justice, they pursued the innocent as well as the guilty, and put to death hundreds of people by all manner of cruelties, and on the meanest pretences imaginable—nay, often without any pretence at all, and that in the most barbarous manner.

It is impossible here to enter into the particulars of the murders committed upon this occasion. And if I should take all the verbal relations that I have met with in conversing among those that were eye-witnesses of the cruelties of that time, it would exceed, if we compare the smallness of the country and numbers of the people concerned—I say it would exceed all that ever was set down in any history of persecutions, whether of Popish or heathen tyrants.

The first year after this insurrection was wholly taken up in searching after and pursuing those who were actually in the army, but had, by the mismanagement, as they called it, of the Duke of Monmouth, made their escape. For, by the way, their desire was, that when the body that defended the bridge was defeated, and the rest began to disperse and fly, they should have been all surrounded and cut in pieces or pursued, and no quarter given them, till not a man of them had been left to carry news to Glasgow of the defeat; and, this having failed, they resolved, if possible, to find out every man that had been at Bothwell, and to put them to death wherever they found them upon the very spot.

In order to this, they neither required much evidence of the fact, nor took the pains to examine the persons themselves; but, if it was but said to them, that such a man, or such men, had been at Bothwell Brigg, they immediately sent the soldiers to their houses, who were to ask them no questions, but seize upon them, drag them just out of the doors, and shoot them dead in a moment. How many poor innocent men, after protesting in the solemnest manner, that they had not been any way concerned in the Bothwell affair, have they shot to death with those protestations in their mouths! and when they have fallen on their knees, and begged but for two minutes' time to recommend their souls to God, have denied them, and shot them kneeling as they were, with that request in their mouths.

It would make any Christian man's heart tremble to read the blasphemies, the oaths, the cursings, and the insultings of those people over the poor men and their families, when they dragged them thus out of the arms of their wives and children to massacre them.

Add to this, the usage others met with in order to

extort confessions from them of their being at Bothwell Brigg rebellion; obliging men by horrible tortures
to accuse themselves, and weak women and children
to accuse their husbands, fathers, brothers, and nearest
relations ; putting fire-matches between their fingers,
or under their joints; stripping stark naked the most
modest and tender women and children, and thrusting
them out in the extremity of cold, and a thousand other
violences, too many to give an account of, in order to
discover those who were at this insurrection of Bothwell.

Of the prisoners taken at Bothwell and executed
for rebellion, I shall say the less, because putting men
to death who are taken in arms is nothing but what
is usual in such cases; but that, as the occasion of
that insurrection was merely the cruelty and violence
of persecution for conscience, we must account those
who were executed in cold blood afterwards, as all
dying by the hand of persecution, and for the cause
of religion ; and this was fully demonstrated by Mr
John King and Mr John Kid, two ministers, taken
in the action at Bothwell, and put to death at Edinburgh on that account.

But when we come to speak of the usage given to
the rest of the prisoners who they did think fit to put
to death by the hangman, there we shall see the
spirit of persecution in the abstract, and such articles
of cruelty as are not to be equalled in Dioclesian or
Maximinian—such as are not to be found in the Irish
massacre, or perhaps in any of the most bloody and
barbarous persecutors,—no, not in D'Alva himself, or
even in the Spanish inquisition.

There was, as is said, about 1200 prisoners, few
more or less, taken at Bothwell. These were in
general stript by the soldiers of what clothes they
had upon them that were anything valuable, and
driven like a herd of beasts, bound two in two, to
Edinburgh, where they were kept several weeks in

a churchyard walled in, being strictly guarded, and allowed no lodging but the earth, neither any covering but the heavens, either to shelter them from wet, cold, sun, or wind, although many of them were very sore wounded. After this trifling severity, a pretended mercy was extended to them, namely, that such of them as would sign a bond condemning their whole cause, acknowledging it to be rebellion, declaring it unlawful to take arms against the King upon any pretence whatsoever, and binding themselves in a penalty not to do so at any time thereafter, were let go.

Many took this declaration and signed this bond, being not able to endure the severity of that usage which they were exposed to in the churchyard, which, however, others called trifling. But many of them refused to accept of deliverance upon such terms as were against their principles, and as trampled upon the blood of their brethren who had died in that quarrel. These were near 400; and the Council not thinking it proper to set the hangman to work upon them all—above fifty having already been put to death—found out new and unheard-of ways of murdering the greatest part of them altogether. About 300 of them having received a general sentence of transportation to the English colonies in America, a ship was found which, as was pretended, was bound to Jamaica, or rather was hired by the government to transport these poor victims to Jamaica, where they were to be sold as slaves. On board this vessel these people were shipped. Some have ventured to tell us that so great a number could not possibly have gone to Jamaica in that ship; that the vessel was by no means able to have carried fresh water and necessary provisions for so great a number, and so long a voyage; and moreover, upon examination, we have been told that it did appear that no proportion of provisions for such a number and such a voyage

was in the ship at that time ; all which, if true, serve
to prove that what was afterwards wickedly done was
the horrid contrivance and bloody instructions of the
persecutors, who had resolved the destruction of the
poor sufferers whatever it cost.

The ship sailed, as above, and whether by stress of
weather, negligence, or wickedness, it is not material ;
neither could the poor prisoners who were locked
under hatches judge of it.   But this is certain, that
coming near the northermost part of Scotland near
the Orkneys, the ship was driven on shore amongst
the rocks, and stuck fast.   The ship's crew saved
themselves and all that belonged to them ; and all
the prisoners, had they been allowed to shift for
themselves, would have been saved with ease enough ;
but the officer set over them would not suffer the
hatches to be opened, neither could any entreaty prevail upon him to let one soul of them out, till the ship
being dashed to pieces, they were all of them drowned
in the hold, except only that an honest seaman, seeing and being struck with horror at so barbarous an
act, ventured his life to go on board, and with an axe
cutting through the deck of the vessel, got forty-nine
of them out alive ; the rest, being about two hundred
and fifty, perished together. After this piece of cruelty
is related, I think I need make no apology for having said, that the reign of Dioclesian or any of the
most cruel persecutors of God's Church could not
match it ; for these were men delivered, men to whom
life was granted.   After the decimations and drafts
made out of them for the gibbet and scaffold were
over, these were sentenced to transportation, but
given up to be murdered in the most inhuman and
most unprecedented manner, such as I believe no history can shew the like of.

Another ship had sixty or more of these banished
men put on board her, whereof several were ministers, and being obliged by the act of navigation,

for she was really bound for Jamaica, to go first to
England, there, by the good providence of God, some
misunderstanding happening between the owners and
freighters of the vessel, upon the terms of charter-
party, the ship was not permitted to go the voyage,
and the poor sufferers got their liberty—no thanks to
their persecutors.

There was near an hundred others transported in
several ships—some to one country, some to another;
besides about thirty of the same Bothwell Brigg prisoners that died in prison, either of their wounds, or
otherwise by distempers contracted in their confinement and by the cruelty of their keepers.

But this was not an end of the Bothwell Brigg
affair; for, as I said before, it was made for some
years the subject of the strictest inquisition, and abundance of poor people were murdered in cold blood by
the persecutors, on pretence of their having been at
that rebellion, as shall appear in its place.

In the time of these transactions, the Archbishop of
St Andrews, the most fierce and cruel persecutor
of the good people aforesaid, and one who, as was
reported, had declared it as his opinion that they
were not a people fit to live, but ought to be extirpated from the face of the earth, was himself cut off
by the hands of some men, whose zeal carrying them
beyond their patience, took upon them this execution
as a thing they had a right to, as they supposed—there
being no way to obtain public justice any other way.

There have been several accounts given in public
of this man's death, the truth and impartiality of which
I have much reason to question; not only because I
have heard it otherways related, but because those
accounts have manifest contradictions in them, both as
to the manner and circumstances of the fact, and as to
the persons concerned in it.   Neither shall I say any
more than this for the relation here set down, than
that it came immediately from the mouth of one of

the persons concerned in it, and shall be repeated as near as possible in the very words.

" We were (says this person) a poor people made desperate by the violence of our persecutors, and still more so for want of opportunity and strength to resist them by force; which, in case of such manifest injustice as we daily received, we had very much will to do, and believed was not only lawful, but our duty. And on this principle we acted before at Pentland, and afterwards at Bothwell, which we believe were very lawful and justifiable actions : however, it pleased not the Lord to give us success therein.   In the pursuit of this opinion, it was proposed at a meeting, whether we being therefore, though suppressed by power, in a state of war with our persecutors, who had illegally vowed our extirpation, it were not lawful for us to destroy them by surprise, or by attacking them as well apart as together, wherever we could find them ; and it was unanimously agreed that it was lawful.   Next it was proposed, that whereas all appeal to the public justice being denied us, and all remedy against our oppressions—that is to say, such as the civil magistrate ought to yield us—being rendered impossible, we might, and ought endeavour to execute that justice which God himself had denounced against murderers, and which God had by his own law deputed to the next of kin.   That the persons here put to death were murdered, nay even butchered—many of them without so much as any pretence to the legal forms and ordinary course of justice, being killed in cold blood by the raging soldiers, or by bloody-minded persecutors, backed and supported by the said soldiers ; and this by mere surprise and ravenous unguided rage, being equal to assassination, or rather something like being devoured by wild beasts or savages.

" That upon such as murdered without law, justice was to be executed without law, and the sword of God was in every injured man's hand to execute the divine justice on such; no justice being also to be had from men—those who bore the sword not bearing it in vain only, but joining themselves to, protecting, and aiding these murderers, and therefore bearing equal guilt art and part with them.

" This likewise was resolved upon in the affirmative; whereupon we who were then present, and whose souls were fired with zeal for God's glory, resolved, with Phineas, to execute justice on those who had thus lifted up their hand against the Lord's people, wherever they might be found, and to place ourselves in the room and authority of the avenger of blood for our innocent brethren, who were destroyed and cruelly massacred for the cause of God and the testimony of a good conscience.

" In this our zeal, and fortified with such considerations as these, five men of our number arming ourselves, placed ourselves in ambush, with design to execute God's justice upon the Laird of ——, a cruel and bloody persecutor of God's people, and who had not many days before put to death several of our brethren in the province of Fife. This was our intent; neither had we at that time any thought or expectation of any other, when we were surprised with an account from one of our number, who was at a distance, that the arch-enemy of God and his people, the Prelate of St Andrews, was passing on the road in his coach.

" It was immediately suggested to us, that albeit we had missed of the man who we had sought for; yet God had, by a wonderful providence, delivered the great and capital enemy of his Church into our hands, and that it was a visible call to us from heaven not to let him escape. That he had been a notorious persecutor of God's people, and a vile murderer of our brethren; particularly in that, when the King himself sent his commands to the Council in the year 1666, after Pentland Rising, that no more should be put to

death ; which command was sent in writing, directed
to the said Privy Council, and was delivered to the
said bishop ; yet that he had kept the said written
order in his pocket till the last ten persons mentioned in this work, who were then in prison, were
put to death ; and that now was the time when that
Scripture was to be executed by them, 'He who
spilleth man's blood, by man shall his blood be spilt ;'
and that they ought not only to believe that God had
delivered him up into their hands ; but that, if they
let him escape, it should be required of them and of
their brethren, as in the case of King Ahab, 1 Kings
xx. 42, ' Because thou hast let go out of thy hand a
man who I appointed to utter destruction ; therefore
thy life shall go for his life, and thy people for his
people.'

"Fortified with these principles, and particularly
with this thought—viz., how wonderfully God had
delivered this great enemy into our hand, we resolved
that he should not escape.   However, one of our number declined acting therein, having a private reason
against his bearing part in this work ; but not prevailing with us to desist from our resolution, which
we thought we had a call from heaven to finish, he
withdrew from us, standing at a great distance, so as
to have no hand in the action, in which case the hand
of God was farther remarkably seen by the consequence ; for, that none of us ever fell into the hands
of the enemy, or were put to death for this fact, but
that one person, viz., Hackston of Rathillet, who
really had no share in the work, but refused to join
with us therein as before.

" Having resolved, as he said, that this enemy
should not escape the judgment of God by our hands,
we rode after him ; and, coming up to the coach,
quickly stopped the same, and, disarming his servants, we gave him notice of our resolutions, letting
him know his offences ; and, in serious terms, exhort-

ing him to give glory to God by confessing his guilt, and that he would repent heartily for the wickedness of his ways, and the innocent blood that he had shed; for that now his time was come to die for the same.

"It was some time ere we could convince him that we were in earnest resolved to put him to death; and he seemed to smile at what we had said about the wickedness of his life. His daughter also, who was with him in the coach, railed on us with much evil language. But thereafter, causing her to come forth of the coach, we let him know that his moments were very few, that we would wait for him yet a little while, and exhorted him not to trifle with his soul, but to call upon God for mercy. After which, seeing us indeed in earnest, he began to entreat for life. But we soon let him know we were not to be put by our purpose for any entreaties that could be used; and that there was no mercy to be shown to him, who had shown no mercy. Hereupon he began to think of death. But hear just the very words of the person who related the story: Behold! God did not give him the grace to pray to him without the help of a book. But he pulled out of his pocket a small book, and began to read over some words to himself, which filled us with amazement and indignation. However, waiting some time, and then calling again upon him to commend his soul to God's mercy, for that he should immediately die, we fired upon him with our pistols. When finding he was not yet dead, and remembering that it had been reported that he had used sorcery in order to defend his body, and that he was invulnerable; and withal, to rid him of life with as little torture as we might, we slew him with our swords, and departed."

This relation of the action coming from the mouth of one of the actors, has not only that authority for its currency, but even seems in itself to be most consonant with all the other accounts of it which have

been made public, and is believed to be a very just
and faithful account both of the killing of the bishop,
and of the circumstances going before it.

The reason why this account is made public in this
place, though some time after the fact, is on the following account :

The spirit of persecution was now come to the
height, and the persecutors seemed to have exerted
themselves to the uttermost.   The common methods
of cruelty in putting to death by process and by forms
of law were exhausted, and they behoved to find out a
more summary way to proceed ; for there were persons to be destroyed against whom they had nothing
to allege, nor any proof to be made against them of
any fact.   And it was necessary to find out some way
or other, first to make the whole body guilty, and
then to make men their own accusers, charging themselves with belonging to the body or society by owning the principles upon which they acted.

This is that unheard of part which constitutes this
persecution to be the most inhuman of all the persecutions which we read of, either before or since the
primitive age of the Church of God ; and by which
the sufferings of the Church of Scotland are distinguished from the sufferings of all that ever went before them.

And what reproach must the practice of these times
leave upon the Episcopal party now alive in Scotland ;
many of whom were real actors in the cruelest part
of this tragedy !   Nay, saving that the author of this
would not, by naming of names, load the heads of
some who are, at the writing of this, under the just
prosecution of the government for treason and real
rebellion.   He could single out the persons of some
that are now in the hands of justice, who were among
the most bloody and raging persecutors of those
times ; but omitting their names, however just the
reflection, he cannot but lead them by the hand to

this just observation—viz. How righteous is that Providence which causes them to lie at the feet of a provoked sovereign, crying for mercy *and to be denied*, who denied mercy to so many of their innocent neighbours and fellow-creatures, who were guilty neither of treason or rebellion, but only of worshipping the Great Creator of all things according to his command, and in such a manner as the authority of conscience made their indispensable duty.

But to return to the facts. Prosecutions in forms of justice, as I said, seemed now at an end ; the methods of drawing blood seemed to be exhausted, though the thirst for blood was not quenched. The number of prisoners to be dragged to execution, or informers to accuse particular persons either were few, or too few, to satisfy the voracious appetite of the persecuting party. Nor was it particular persons, but the whole body of Christians in the denomination of Whigs, whose blood they resolved to shed.

Being, therefore, unsatisfied with the personal guilt of such who had been at Bothwell Brigg, or such as could be found at field meetings, whose number, though daily great, were but few, when compared with what they resolved to fall upon, they proceeded now to sum up their profession into generals, to form them into principles, and then make those principles criminal. By which method they knew they should infallibly involve the whole body of those people in such circumstances as would entitle the Government to a right to put them to death. The case was thus—

1. They knew that these persecuted people esteemed themselves engaged by the National Covenant in the solemnest bond imaginable. That it was the oath of God ; that no human power could dissolve the obligation ; and that the breaking it as it had been broken, was no less a crime than a national perjury.

2. They looked upon the King as an enemy and

persecutor of God's people ; as a prince perjured by his breaking and renouncing the Covenant, and guilty of involving the whole nation in the same detestable crime of perjury ; also, they looked upon him as a persecutor of God's Church, and a bloody destroyer of his people ; and for these reasons they could not satisfy themselves to pray for him, or say to him, God speed.

3. As for the killing of the Archbishop of St Andrews, they did not esteem it a murder or an assassination ; but esteeming themselves to be in open war with him, and with all the members of that bloody society, called " The Council of Scotland," who had treated them and their brethren with barbarity as enemies to mankind ; and had, by all kinds of cruelty and inhumanity without law, except such as their lust of blood formed into acts of council and contrary to the constitution, had called laws, and to which they gave the force of laws ; put their brethren unjustly to death, which they esteemed murder of the vilest sort ; esteeming these men, I say, by their bloody doings, to be blood-suckers, murderers, and open-declared enemies to God and man, they thought it just, as in time of war, to pursue them to death in what manner they could, and wherever they could, and wherever they might be found.

4. As to the taking arms at Pentland and at Bothwell, and other places, they would by no means admit it to be rebellion ; because, nature dictating self-defence to all creatures to whom it has given a life to defend, and they being attacked by the armed troops of their persecutors, while they innocently and peaceably performed their undoubted and indispensable duty, viz. the worshipping God according to his own institution, they thought themselves bound by the laws of nature, and allowed by the laws of God, to defend their lives, and the lives of their wives and children.

As the poor people maintained these principles with the greatest exactness, and persisted to do so with the greatest constancy, so their persecutors knew well what use to make of this steady adherence to their principles, and how to make it a handle to them to take hold of the otherwise most innocent and inoffensive part of the people, and drag them to immediate execution without further process. And this device, they questioned not, would serve them to destroy and extirpate the whole body of the people, as they owned was their design.

To this wicked and barbarous purpose they framed four questions upon the heads above-mentioned, which they resolved to have offered to the persecuted people upon all occasions, and to which they should oblige the said people to give an immediate direct answer. On refusing which answer, or not answering to their minds, they were immediately to be put to death. And here is to be noted, that, as it was said, the late Archbishop of St Andrew's, General Dalziel, and several others of the fiercest of the persecuting Council had often complained, that the formalities of the law, that is to say, bringing men to the bar, and to be tried by judges, juries, hearings, pleadings, &c. were obstructions to the King's service; so the present Council, proceeding by the same rules of cruelty, resolved to make shorter work with them; and, therefore, that the forms of process, bringing to prisons and to trials, might not delay or encumber the execution, and prevent the dispatching the innocent victim fast enough, they decreed, that every private soldier, an army of whom they had now quartered upon the persecuted people, should have power to tender the said questions to every man they met, or to whom they pleased; and upon refusing to answer, the said soldier was empowered to kill them upon the spot. And lest I may be thought to do this General Dalziel an injury, and record of him any thing which was not

suitable to the rest of his practice, who, if fame belies
him not, was a man as void of humanity as most that
ever heaven permitted to live,—I say, that I may
not wrong him, I shall give the following brief account of an action of his, as a specimen of his compassionate temper, by which the character of the man
may be guessed at without breach of charity :—It
was soon after the rising at Pentland, when he had
been sent into the shire of Ayr to make search for,
and put to death, such of the poor people as he could
find were in the said rising.   He sent a lieutenant,
with a party of men, to Newmills, and ordered them
to seize and bring to him an honest poor man, whose
name was Finlay, and who was peaceably living in
his own house, nor had he been at all in arms. When
his men brought the prisoner to him, he examined
him privately, no witness being by, and with a kind
of civility unusual to him, whether he had been at
Lanark with the rebels ?   The man answered he was
at Lanark upon his private business when their army
came thither ; and told him what his business was,
offering to prove the truth of it, and declared that
he was not in arms, nor had any weapon with him ;
neither did he go among them.   Then he asked him
if he remembered any of those he saw among them,
and who they were ?   The man declared he did not.
Whereupon he called for the lieutenant, and ordered
him to carry that man to the gallows and have him
shot to death, for that he had confessed he was with
the rebels.   The poor man being brought to the place
in a great hurry and surprise, asked the lieutenant if
the General was in earnest.   The lieutenant said, he
feared he was.   However, being a civil man, and loth
to execute such a cruel commission, and the poor man
protesting his innocency, and entreating him as a
Christian, that at least he might have a reprive for
that night, that he might prepare for death and eter-
nity,—the lieutenant, I say, upon this goes back to

the General, and, laying before him the poor man's case, entreated him to grant him a few hours time to prepare for death ; but the General, flying out in a rage at the lieutenant, and with horrid oaths and blasphemies, commanded him to return, and told him he would teach him to obey his orders after a better manner than to come back and make himself an advocate for rebels. Upon this the lieutenant went back directly to the man, and immediately shot him dead upon the spot.

This, and such as this, was their temper at that time ; and I think I may say, they were now come to the height of their fury. The measure of their cruelty filled up apace. All the French dragooning, the Popish burnings, the Heathen torturings, that we read of in the world, scarce ever came up to this. In all those cases, the sufferers were brought before judges and magistrates, officers of justice and men in power ; but such was the thirst of blood here, that they appeared willing to strip themselves of their magisterial authority, and make every private sentinel, every musketeer, both judge, jury, and executioner.

Never was justice executed in such a summary way as on this occasion ; for now the soldiers filled the streets and highways with blood ; men, women, nay, and little children, were dragged out of their houses, from their shops, trades, and labour, to immediate death, without warning, without pity, and without time given them to call upon God for mercy to their souls.

Nor was the life of the most innocent person safe at this time from the rapine of the soldiers ; for now it was the easiest thing in the world for private revenge to be pursued to blood ; and it was in the power of the soldiers to execute the greatest villany with impunity. They had no more to do but to rob, ravish, insult, plunder, and commit what wickedness

R

they pleased, and, adding murder to the rest, say the person murdered refused to answer the questions.

These questions, modelled according to the heads before recited, were thus—

1. Will you renounce the Covenant ?

2. Will you pray for the King, or will you say, God bless the King ?

3. Was the killing of the Archbishop of St Andrews murder, yea or no ?

4. Was the rising at Bothwell Brigg rebellion, yea or no ?

It should have been observed before this, that, in order effectually to suppress these persecuted people, and to finish the ruin of the country, the Government had raised what the country people called the " Highland Host." The account the persecutors gave of this was, " That the loyal clans offered their service to his Majesty to bring into the field a body of men, from among their vassals and servants, completely armed, who were to march whither his Majesty should please to command them, for the suppressing of the rebellion, and for preventing the rebels and whigs from gathering in troops in the western shires."

On these pretences those Highlanders, little better than barbarians, and in some cases much worse, were armed and taken into the service of Satan, and some time after the Bothwell Brigg affair, were ordered, to the number of eight thousand men, to quarter upon the suffering people in the shires of Ayr, Galloway, and other of the western shires. There they exercised all the rapine, violence, robbery, and wickedness, over and above the murder and shedding of innocent blood, of which we are just going to speak, that may be expected from an ungoverned soldiery, or that could be practised upon or suffered by a people, given up to the lust and rage of a crew of savages.

In this posture stood the public affairs as to the persecutors, yet their rage received no abatement; the very thought of the spirit and undepressed courage of the persecuted galled and exasperated them. They saw a set of men living like wild creatures in the mountains, and yet there, in spite of human power, freely preserved the liberty of their principles, and met publicly and frequently in mighty numbers for the worship of God; and that it was impossible for them either to apprehend or prevent them. This provoked them to the last degree. They found now, that, as these wandering outlawed people must be, and indeed so they really were, harboured and relieved at the greatest peril by the people in the plain country, the only way left to extirpate them more effectually was to ruin and impoverish the whole country, that the banished proscribed refugees might have no relief from them; and to make it punishable in the highest manner, and as the most capital crime, for any so much as to talk with, much less entertain, comfort, relieve, and support, one of those who, as they call it, were intercommuned; and this was so severely put in execution, that we find among their lists of their butcheries by the hangman, one Ramsey executed only for going over a river in a ferry-boat with one who had been a rebel, and talking with him in common, as with other men in the boat.

But all these cruelties were not yet able to extirpate a race of men, by whose sufferings the grace and mercy of God was to be made so conspicuous in the world. Nay, so far was it from that, that on the other hand, the numbers of them daily increased, even under their very persecutions, as was the case in the primitive times of the Church; their field-meetings grew more frequented, and were more publicly held, and that with such multitudes as were scarce credible to relate.

Nor were the zealous persecuted people prevailed

upon to abate one tittle of the testimony which they thought themselves obliged to bear against the wickedness of their enemies, and that particularly in two points.

1. Their national perjury in breaking their oath to God and to his people—viz., in breaking and renouncing the Covenant.

2. Their erecting an Episcopal Church government, which they abhorred, and which these treated with no other name than an anti-christian Prelacy.

[They justified the term anti-christian, for the Prelatic hierarchy owned the supremacy of the King over the Church, whereas they allowed Christ Jesus to be the only Head and King of the Church on earth.]

On the other hand, those two articles, and especially the open and daring profession of them by these persecuted people, was unsufferable and to the last degree provoking to their persecutors; and the more in that they could neither, by all their cruelties and most inhuman usage, deter either those that died to abate their open detestation of these two things at their execution, or those that remained to refrain their open profession of the same abhorrences—no, not for fear of the same tortures.

Nor could they, by all their bloody prosecutions, prevent the field-meetings they so much exclaimed against, where the resolution of the persecuted peoto persevere to their death in their opposition to the Prelates and their adhering to the Covenant was always expressed in such terms; and the people were so confirmed in those resolutions, that the Council saw too plainly nothing but death could put an end to it, and the whole race of suffering Christians must be destroyed and extirpated, or they should never conquer the opposition they made to the planting of Episcopacy in that kingdom; and upon this resolution they proceeded.

In the meantime, the poor people, as if the heat of the persecution had but served to influence their zeal, thought themselves obliged to declare a war, though of a different nature, against their persecutors, and to let them see that, upon a just and equal principle, they could clear themselves of the guilt charged upon them of being rebels against lawful authority; and to this end, at one of their public and most numerous meetings in the west, they openly declared themselves revolted from the Government, "renounced and disowned all allegiance, obedience, homage, or duty, to the King and his administration, as being an enemy to God and to the Church of God, and therefore not legally constituted, or to be acknowledged as their supreme Lord. But, *ipso jure*, deposed from all regal authority over them, and divested of the office of a magistrate, and of the trust or charge of government which was reposed in and devolved upon him by express compact at his coronation, when he solemnly entered into an oath and covenant with God and his people; and which oath, covenant, and compact he had violated, breaking all the conditions, and impiously renouncing the obligation thereof, upon which oath and obligation thereof all his regal authority and their allegiance were entirely founded; and upon the breach whereof, their subjection, which was limited to the provisions of those compacts and covenants, was explicitly disengaged and remitted."

This was, it is true, a bold step, and many of their brethren seemed to censure them upon such a desperate proceeding; but it seems they were only such who had accepted the liberty mentioned before upon the terms of a license from the Prelates, which temporizing and cowardly compliance, these zealous people abhorred as sinful, and condemned as a fainting in God's cause, giving over their constancy, and, above all, as a wicked recognition of that Episcopal authority from which they received such license. This they called homologating the legality of what they themselves condemned as anti-scriptural and anti-christian, and which they were engaged in the solemnest manner by the Covenant never to permit, much less submit to in the nation.

The censure of such, therefore, was of no value to them, and they insisted upon the right they had to declare their revolt from their allegiance to King Charles II. as their natural privilege, and as the just consequence of his breach of the compact of government.

. The noise the council made of this declaration was strange indeed, how they declared these people rebels, mad, enraged, scelerates, &c., people to be abhorred by Christians, and to be rooted out from the general society of mankind, and the like ; and seemed to justify all the inhumanities they at that time resolved to practice upon them, and to legitimate all their extrajudicial measures by the clamour they raised upon them, for this one action ; not foreseeing that in a few years those same men should do the same thing with the next King of the same race, and call for a regiment of those same honest persecuted sufferers, whom they had thus damned for rebels and parricides, to guard them in the doing it, as was within the space of twelve years the very case, as I shall shew in its order.

In this solemn revolt, or renouncing their allegiance, they repeated the several acts of violence and oppression, which had been practised or authorized by the King, and by his wicked councillors, whereby he unhinged all the legal establishment of their religion, and subverted all their religious liberties. The King's supremacy they called a blasphemous and sacrilegious usurpation, being an illegal anti-scriptural dominion over the institution of Jesus Christ, and the ordinances of his own Divine appointment.

They proceed to declare that the King had overturned all the fundamental part of the civil constitution, subverting the laws and liberties of the people, destroying their civil and natural rights, and all the securities of life and enjoyment whatsoever ; and that all this was by claiming and assuming a right to an absolute, tyrannical, arbitrary government, by his pretended prerogative, independent of law, and superior thereto ; all which they declare to be illegal and inconsistent with the safety, freedom, and legal privileges of the people, and with the oath and obligation of a king.

These, and many other things, they gave as the reason of their revolt from, and renouncing allegiance to, the King, which I am the more particular in, because of their affinity to, and the sanction they soon after received from, the general practice of the whole island, and also to add this remark, viz., how these poor people were not only handled by their enemies, but even censured by their friends, for owning those very principles at that time, upon which the safety of the whole nation was found in a few years to depend ; and for professing such opinions, as in so little a while were judged essential to the public safety, and on which to this day our Protestant constitution is founded, viz., that tyrants and arbitrary persecuting princes may be renounced, the people may revolt from their allegiance to them, depose them from their usurped authority, and yet cannot be justly called rebels and traitors. Witness the Revolution and Protestant succession.

But, asking pardon for this needful digression, I return to the suffering people, who, however righteous the principles were which they acted from, were yet for some years to drink the dregs of Popish and tyrannical persecution, to the full trial of their faith and patience.   For example, after they had thus declared their revolt from, and renounced their allegiance to the King and his instruments of tyranny, they proceeded in a solemn manner to pronounce the

greater excommunication, in which they excommunicated the King and the bishops among the enemies
and contemners of God and his Church.   They likewise, in the same declaration, protested against a
Popish successor, and declared that they would never
receive the Duke of York in Scotland, nor admit him
to possess the crown.

Thus I have given the reader an abridged relation
of what was done on their part.   But what tongue
can express or pen describe the usage these poor
people received, and the cruelties they suffered on
this account.   "Not only time," says a solid writer of
that day, "but heart and tongue would fail any Christian to relate all the violences, murders, plunderings,
extortions, and insolencies, that from the beginning
of this persecution have been committed in a military
way, besides what has been done in the form and
course of public pretended justice.   If stabbing,
wounding, beating, stripping, and imprisoning men's
persons—if violent breaking into their houses in the
dead of the night, beating, wounding, ravishing, and
inhumanely abusing wives and daughters—if forcing
weak women by tortures, such as burning matches,
and other insufferable torments, to discover, nay accuse, their husbands, fathers, and dearest relations—if
driving away their cattle, spoiling their goods without
respect to guilt or innocence, and this in as cruel a
manner as ever Scotland had seen, or could have seen
had a foreign army been in the bowels of their country—if all these, and many more such, may express
our misery," says this author, "some guess may be
made at the sufferings of this Church, from the malice
and fury of this wicked prevailing Prelatic party."

But we now come to the methods taken with those
persons who they could by no other means lay hold
upon.   These consisted of two sorts.   (1.) Those who
having been in arms, and had escaped the sword of
battle, were fled to the mountains; or (2.), Those who,

having been marked out for destruction by their persecutors, were withdrawn to the other.   Those men holding fast their integrity, and having many ministers among them, kept up their field-preachings, and enjoyed the freedom of their religious exercises, notwithstanding the most inveterate rage of their enemies ; and this, as I said already, provoked the persecutors to such a degree that they were not able to contain themselves, but would fly at the innocent to punish the guilty, that is to say, who they supposed guilty, for other guilt they had none.

To punish them, then, as far as they were able, seeing they could do it no other way, first, they intercommuned them, as they call it, forbidding any person to harbour, hide, comfort, or correspond with any of them, or even so much as to salute, or talk with them on the way, on pain of treason and rebellion ; and of being prosecuted for the same crimes which those they so harboured, comforted, or corresponded with, were charged with.

In the next place, to disappoint them who were wandering about in sheep-skins and goat-skins, in dens, and holes, and caves of the earth, and effectually to prevent their being relieved or supported from their friends, relations, or otherwise, they found it absolutely necessary, by troops of soldiers who were subsisted by the poor sufferers, to ruin and impoverish the country by their various plunderings and depredations, rather like troops in an enemy's country than troops billeted and placed under discipline.

This was the case when justice was transferred from the judges on the bench to the soldier in the field, and this not to the officers, to the court martial, or assembly of officers, or generals, but to the brutal common soldiers, who neither had conscience to judge by, reason to judge from, sense to guide, humanity to spare, or temper to consider who to kill, and who to save.

It would be endless to turn this account into a
Scots martyrology, or a register of barbarities. These
sheets are no way equal to a history of such a length;
but, keeping myself to the brevity of memoirs, agreeable to my title, I shall give some specimens of the
bloody management of this part of the work, I mean
as to this new-fashioned way of persecution, by de-
livering a naked defenceless people up to the fury of
the common soldiers, and some flagrant instances of
this kind will be sufficient to describe the rest.

The first I meet with is the story of a poor woman,
and a young maiden of about sixteen years old, in the
west of Scotland, who were cruelly murdered by some
men belonging to Grierson of Lagg, an eminent persecutor in that part of the country.   They began by
putting the questions to them above-mentioned, and
the first they offered as what was most popular at
that time in the world, and best served, as they
thought, to expose the persecuted people to the
court, was that of—Will ye say God bless the king?
As I have received this story from creditable witnesses, take it as follows :—The woman told them she
would pray to God to forgive the King his sins.   The
maid she would pray that God would please to give
the King repentance.   But it would be an impious
thing, said the woman, to pray to God to save—that
is, to bless—a covenant-breaking, perjured-magis-
trate, and in the prosecution of his perjury too.   And
they both declared it was against their consciences,
their principles, and the covenant, and that, therefore,
they could not do it.   The woman said boldly that,
while the King was a persecutor of God's people, he
was an enemy to God and to the Church of God;
and she thought it was an abominable thing to ask of
any Christian to pray for prosperity to the persecutors of the Church of Christ—for that was to say God
speed to them, even in the very persecution itself.
She was an undaunted woman, and challenged them

to answer her in that particular ; but they had nothing to say to her arguments, but thought she would have some regard to theirs, which was, Pray to God to bless the King——or die.   Will ye kill me, says the woman, because I will not bless those who God curses ? the Lord forbid that I should do it, though I were to die a thousand times !   Upon this they fixed a stake in the sea at the low water-mark, and binding the poor woman and the young girl to the stake, let them stand there until the tide flowed over them and drowned them both, being also tormented almost to death with the cold by standing in the water so long as until the tide was high enough to drown them.   However, they both endured it with great constancy, and without the least offer of compliance with the barbarous adversary.

It has been matter of censure among some, and even of those otherwise in the same interest, and of the same doctrinal principles with those people, when they found that they were so severely nice in this particular of praying for the King, seeing that they are bid to pray for kings and all in authority. But not to make these memoirs enter into long disputes of the points between them and their persecutors, which is not the work of a historian, I shall only state and remove the question in few words from these poor sufferers to their enemies, and leave them to answer it if they know how.

In the first place, it is true they began with these poor women upon that question of praying for the King, which was a piece of wicked policy on their parts, because it was the most popular question, and by which they thought they made these people odious to the King, and represented them as his particular enemies ; and persuaded him by it to let them go on with their persecution, which by the way they had much ado to prevail in——for the King, who was in himself of a merciful disposition, being often shocked with the accounts of their cruelties, and often saying openly he would have no more blood shed—I say this was a wicked policy on their part; for it is known they had three or four questions more in their orders, any of which were of such a nature as that the poor people would have suffered death rather than to have complied.   For example, had these two poor women answered, Yes, we will say God save the King; the next question had been, Will ye renounce the Covenant?—a question which, if it were now asked in Scotland, I believe there are 50,000 people would as soon renounce the very name of Christians—that is to say, they would suffer all that human nature could suffer rather than do it.   So that, upon the whole, these people did not suffer for a single opposition of the King's lawful authority, as was wickedly charged on them; but they were given up to death by a party, and they singled out such points to question them upon as they knew they could not comply with, that they might destroy them; and if these questions would not have done it, they would have named others for the purpose.

Farther, it is evident that they refused praying for the King upon a religious principle—not upon a rebellious principle; and that as they believed the King, as before, to be an idolator, a persecutor, and an enemy to God and his people.   They believed that for them to pray for God to bless him would be either to mock God by seeming to pray for what they did not mean, or really to pray to God to bless the King even in his persecuting God's people, which would be impious, and was against their consciences.

As to the other part which the objectors allege—viz., it was a trifle, and a thing so small as that they could not answer to lose their lives for it—we answer that then much less could those cruel and inhumane persecutors answer to take the lives of poor innocent women and children away for so small a thing, which in the common judgment, and by their own confession, was but a trifle in its nature.

Likewise if it was against the consciences and principles of the poor people, though we were to suppose them misinformed or uninformed, yet they died in a righteous cause, not as they died for refusing to pray for the King, but as they chose to die rather than to violate their obedience to the sovereignty of conscience, which is a principle every Christian ought to adhere to.

Let these things serve for answers, till they can be confuted, to the persecutors themselves, and to all those who would blacken the memory of these conscientious and zealous people, pretending they were obstinate, that they threw away their lives, and that they died upon foundations and principles which are not to be justified.   It is evident they were right in their adhering steadfastly to the known duty of a Christian, viz., of suffering the greatest evil rather than committing the least sin.   Nay, though they were to have it granted that they were (as I said above) misinformed in the nature of the thing they suffered for, it might be observed here, that it was the very argument used with many of the primitive martyrs in the time of the ten persecutions—that it was a small thing but to take a censor in their hands, to seem as if they did sacrifice, though they did not ; that the prayer to the gods was made by the priests, and it was a thing of no consequence to bow the head, which they might do as to Cæsar, and not as to the gods above. Thus also in the case of the martyred Maccabees, their persecutors pretended in clemency to offer them their lives, if they would but take a bit of swine's flesh into their mouths, though they did not swallow it down. But with what abhorrence did they refuse ! with what joy and alacrity did they die !—I mean the primitive Christians as well as the Maccabees—insomuch that the wisest of the heathen condemned them as fools ; for that they cast themselves away and lost their lives, not for the essential parts of religion, but for trifles and circumstances of no consequence.

I might insist here upon the evident testimony that God was pleased to give even from heaven to these suffering people, that the offering up their lives in this case was an acceptable sacrifice to him, and a reasonable service in them. And this testimony was, by an almost universal assistance, given them in their sufferings, filling them with abundant strength to undergo, patience to bear, and comfort even to joy and triumph under the severest and cruelest torments that their most inhumane persecutors could inflict. I take this from an author who was an eye-witness of, and a fellow-sufferer in, much of it ; and therefore give the following account in his own words, and from his own observation, as follows.

" We shall not, indeed cannot, enter upon the particular declaration of that grace, constancy, and courage by which the Lord's faithful witnesses were sustained, and by which they did bear testimony to the Word of his truth. Only this is certain, that many of them, though illiterate and obscure men, and that when they came to the scaffold they were hurried and interrupted by the order of the prelates and council, and by the cruelty and inhumanity of the executioners and officers attending, yet they did bear witness to the cause of God, and of that grace and assurance whereby the Lord upheld them to the admiration and astonishment of all the beholders.

" That at Glasgow and Ayr, where eleven of them were executed, all mean countrymen, some very ancient, some not above seventeen years old ; and that their enemies caused drums to be beat round the scaffold that they might not be heard ; yet they were so little thereby amazed or disordered, that as well by words of praise and thanksgiving to God, when they might be heard, and by their countenances, gestures, and other carriage, they did bear such testimony to the truth, as that thereby many were confirmed, and their enemies were made ashamed.

" Likewise though some at other times did appear weak and faint-hearted at first, yet so powerfully and abundantly was it given to them in that hour, that out of weakness they were made strong, and declared often that they had such discoveries of God's glory between the prison and the gibbet, that all fear was thereby discussed ; and, particularly, a poor country boy, who they condemned at Ayr for refusing the declaration, which they told him was a renouncing the covenant that he had taken at Lanark. This child, through fear, and particularly ignorance of the grounds of Christianity, was in great agonies upon his soul's account, greatly fearing to die, yet not daring to redeem his life on the terms offered. But after the prayers and conference of some good people that had access to him at Irvine two days before he died, he appeared so much changed, that on the morning of his execution, instead of the depth of fear and perplexity, he obtained a full resolution and joy so much enlightened with the knowledge of God, in and through our Lord Jesus Christ, and with the hope of salvation through his name, that all saw him do bear testimony to the grace and wonderful work of God in his heart, whereby he went to the scaffold with joy, leaping and praising God.

" From all which, and the several testimonies and speeches which these left behind them in writing, we conclude and rejoice that God, out of the dark cloud of such a sad and astonishing providence which has now overspread us, hath brought forth so blessed and so bright a cloud of witnesses, strengthened and filled with so much grace and glory to bear testimony to his name, covenant, and cause, for the confirmation of all that love and wait for his salvation."

A further testimony of this will be seen in the speeches of some of the sufferers at the place of execution ; of which in its order.

But to return to our memoirs of fact.   The first thing the Highland forces were empowered to do, was to press from all the people, where they had any know-ledge of their being dissenters, or of their having dis-senters in their families, a bond of conformity, as they called it ; wherein every person entering into the said bond was bound, not only for himself, but all under him, viz., wife, children, and servants, to frequent and keep to his parochial kirk or parish church, and never to go either to any house or field-meeting ; nor reset, that is, receive or entertain any that did so on any pretence whatsoever ; also to inform against, and to deliver up, if in their power, all the ministers or preachers that exercised the office of a minister or preacher in any such meeting or assembly.

Many through fear complied with these unreason-able conditions, not being able to bear the ruin of their families, and the severity of a flight into the mountains in the winter season, where they had no comfort or relief, but struggled with the extremities of cold, hunger, and diseases, occasioned by damp places to lodge in, want of necessaries, &c.   But others, resolving to suffer every thing that nature was able to support to preserve a good conscience, fled to the mountains, where they had to their lot exactly what is described in the 11th of the Hebrews, verses 37, 38. " They wandered about in sheep-skins and in goat-skins, being destitute, afflicted, tormented ; they wan-dered in deserts, and in mountains, and in dens and caves of the earth."   This was their portion ; and by this means the towns were left uninhabited, the villages desolate, the lands unlaboured (i. e., unculti-vated), and the richest, most populous, and in propor-tion the most fruitful part of Scotland, became a kind of wilderness, and like a house without the inhabitant.

By this means, however, and by the rising at Both-well, mentioned before, the number of those refugees in the mountains increased, and the meetings in the

fields for public worship were more frequent, which
still exasperated the persecutors, and they being enraged, omitted no cruelty, no injustice, no inhumanity for the destruction of them. They very well
knew that the people lurking on the mountains must
of necessity receive supplies of food and clothes, either
from their own families and friends which were left
behind, or of charity from others; and, therefore, as
first they took care effectually, by plunder and rapine, to leave nothing in the houses of those that
were fled, so they persecuted with the utmost rigour
all that were but suspected of harbouring or relieving them.

I shall begin with the prisoners taken at Bothwell.
Mr Kid and Mr King, as has been said, and several
others, were executed as traitors; and, as if their
cruelty had been satisfied, it was resolved in council
to transport the rest into the English plantations.
Upon the King's orders, and under pretence of this
transportation, there were 300 of the said prisoners
put on board of a ship in order, it was said, to be
sent to the West Indies. These are those of whom
mention is made already, of whom this is yet necessary to be said, that although they were publicly
allowed transportation, yet it is certain nothing
less than so much favour was designed them. Some
have said that it was then publicly known that
the Council had, notwithstanding the order from
England, determined the transported people for death,
and, indeed, it seems more than probable, seeing,
besides what is said before of their not having sufficient store of provisions in the ship for such a voyage,
they sailed northward to go to the English colonies
in America directly from Scotland, which, by the
constituted law of those countries, called the Act of
Navigation, could not be done, neither would any of
those colonies have received them, but have seized
upon and forfeited the ship and goods that came with

s

them ; so that it is certainly more than a suspicion that the poor people were designed for destruction. The case was thus : when these poor people, I say, were put on board the ship, and sailed out of the Firth of Edinburgh, it was expected they should have gone directly to England, as ships bound to the English plantations were always used to do, and as indeed they were obliged by the laws of England to do, as above ; but, on the contrary, they sailed north-ward to the coast of the Orkneys, where, by stress of weather, as was pretended, the ship was driven among the rocks and broken to pieces. The master and seamen, and the persons, or murderers rather, who had the guard or conducting of the prisoners, easily got on shore, as has been said, and, had they been permitted, all the prisoners might likewise have done the same ; whereas the officer who had the guard of the prisoners, with the master of the ship, having, on pretence of securing them, locked them all down under the hatches, would not, upon the most earnest and moving entreaties of even the seamen and others, nor the shrieks and cries of the poor dying people, suffer the hatches to be opened, or one of them to be let out.

It seems there was one seaman who ventured his life on board, when the ship was just breaking to pieces, and, with an axe cutting his way through the side or deck of the vessel, let about fifty out, who were every one saved, but the rest all perished as before.

The best excuse that the murderers ever gave for this was, that they had strict orders, whatsoever port they should go on shore at, not to let any of the prisoners go out of the ship. But this was so trifling an excuse that none could be satisfied with it ; for either they had orders that though the ship was stranded or split they should not let the prisoners out, or they had not. If they had, it must be with an intent in those who gave those orders to have them perish in such shipwreck, as it happened, and would give a shrewd suspicion that such a shipwreck was intended, especially considering how it afterwards came to pass. If no such orders were expressly given, then were the officers murderers; for it could not be imagined that a general order not to let the prisoners go out of the ship, had any other meaning than that he should use all means possible to prevent their escape; but not that they should be drowned, or that they should be kept in the ship when she was sinking, any more than a mittimus to a jailor, wherein he is to have the prisoner in safe keeping within his jail (suppose of Newgate, or any other prison) gives him power or obliges him if the prison-house should be on fire, to suffer the prisoners to be burnt to death rather than open the doors to let them out.

It is therefore very reasonable to believe that this wretched instrument or executioner, for he could be no better, had his secret instructions from the bloody persecuting council for what was done, and that the ship was knocked on the head on purpose to drown and cause to perish the number of poor sufferers who the clemency of the sovereign had forbid to be put to death in a judicial way, and who yet the malice and rage of the persecutors would not suffer to live.

Moreover, it has been creditably reported that those who provided or furnished this vessel out for her voyage, acknowledged that she was not victualled at all in proportion to so long a voyage and so large a number of people as were on board—no, nor any thing like it; nay, it has been said that there was not provisions on board for the prisoners sufficient to keep them alive fourteen days, which, if it is true, would convince an atheist in such things, that the design in putting these poor people on board was not to transport but to murder them.

Another argument is still good also against the persecutors of that time, namely, if they did not approve of the officers murdering these poor people, why were they not prosecuted and punished for so horrid and inhumane a murder, the like of which no protestant age or country can give the history of? But, on the contrary, the master or skipper, the officer of the guards, and all the rest concerned, had no punishment, no reprimand, neither was any thing done to them, to let them or the world believe they had not done them very good service.

Thus perished 250 of these good people; I call them so on this most justifiable foundation, viz. because that though they might have their lives and liberties given them by the sovereign upon terms which, in conscience, they could not comply with, they loved not their lives to the death, they refused to accept of deliverance; and I call it murder, because, as it is well known, the King's express orders were that they should not be put to death, but be transported. The suffering them thus to perish, when it was apparent their lives might have been saved, was not a murder only in the officers, but a premeditated, malicious murder in the Council, who so far connived at and approved it, as never to offer any vindication of themselves from it, or any resentment against the guilty persons; for it is a murder of the blackest and most horrid kind, and which, I think, as before, has not its parallel in any history.

It has been mentioned also, that there were about sixty more of these prisoners put on board another ship for transportation, who, there being no secret design to murder them, were suffered to go by the ordinary method, and to sail the usual way, viz. to England; where, as it is already noted, some difference happening between the master and owner of the ship, so that the ship did not pursue her voyage, and the prisoners having been made the property of the owner, not of the master, the said master thereupon, being also a well inclined person, opened his hatches

and let them all go.   I mention this again here on this
occasion, viz. that it was very observable in their case,
that the government here took no notice of their
escape, nor did the King order any search after them,
or give any order to retake them, if found,—all which
evidently proves that the cruelties exercised upon
these sufferers in Scotland proceeded from the malice
and rage of their persecutors there, and neither by
the direction or with the approbation of the King
himself,—not that this clemency which, in the King,
was rather an accident to his nature than a virtue in
his government, can excuse his permitting these cruel
persecutions which he had, doubtless, power to prevent,
and therefore was doubtless guilty of the blood that
was spilt on that occasion, which, though his inclination led him not to delight in, yet his indolence in
government, and his apostate principles, suffered him
to permit.   But though it is no excuse to him whose
duty it was to have put a stop to the stream of innocent
blood shed under his authority, it was, on the other
hand, a convincing evidence of the bloody disposition
of his ministry in Scotland, who, thirsting for an occasion to extirpate the very name of a Presbyterian
Church out of Scotland, dipped their hands in blood in
that most inhumane and unnatural manner, till they
made all the West of Scotland a wilderness and a
desolation.

This was the proceeding against the Bothwell
Bridge prisoners.   We shall now see what usage they
met with who had not been any way concerned in it.

First, in their pursuit of the supposed parties they
established little inquisitions; and, indeed, they were
very properly called so, for they went round the country in circuits, where they inquired not only who really
and actually were in the rebellion, but who were suspected or believed to be so; and these they took lists of,
made their return upon, and after this they summoned
them to appear before them to clear themselves.

If they did not appear they reputed them guilty, and declared them to be rebel convicts.

If they did appear, they were examined why they did not go to the King's camp in order to fight against the rebels; and if they did not give a satisfactory answer to those questions, they were committed to prison in order to get others to accuse them, where many innocent persons perished by long and close confinement, though nothing could be laid to their charge.

If in these examinations they effectually cleared themselves of being in the rebellion, yet an incredible number were ensnared with other unforeseen inquiries; some were imprisoned, some fined above the value of their estates, others were condemned to death for having but seen and spoken to any of the escaped rebels, after they had fled from Bothwell Bridge, alleging that it was treason so to do, and not to discover and apprehend them.

If neither by examination, confession, or delation, *super inquirendis,* so it was termed in their law, they were able to reach them, yet many such were condemned and executed even for their simple-declared opinion of it, according to the questions mentioned before, and which we shall speak farther of presently.

Nor was the number small or inconsiderable of those who were thus dealt with. There is scarce a county or parish in those western parts of Scotland, where several have not been thus condemned; nor was it easy to prevent the poor people being drawn into this snare, for, when they were brought before the Council, or the Court of Justiciary, it was often extorted from them by threatenings of death, and sometimes by torture, and upon this single question, in their courts of justice, viz. " Whether the rising at Bothwell Bridge was rebellion, and a sin against God ?" I say many for refusing to answer it, waving the question, and declaring that they did not think themselves qu-

liged to answer, were condemned, and immediately led away to execution; for the mercy of those courts was such, that many were sentenced in the morning, and executed in the afternoon; nay, some were led immediately from the bar to the gibbet, where they were used again in the like cruel manner, being not suffered to declare their innocence, or to speak to the people, but the drums being placed round them, were kept beating all the time of their being upon the scaffold and ladder, as has been mentioned already.

But to return to the soldiers, to whom, as I said before, these cruelties not sufficing, justice was transposed. When we were talking of the severities of the courts of justice and the cruelty of their executioners, on pretence of rebellion, it was sufficient to call it murder (for injustice in form of law is the devil representing an angel of light, and killing innocent men by legal process is the worst sort of murder); but now we come from murder to massacre, for the soldiers, being now vested with judicial authority, went up and down like ravening wolves, with mouths opened to suck the blood of the innocent. They seemed like men clothed with more power than they understood, though not more than they desired—that had a loose given to the excess of what, by their occupation, they delighted in—I mean blood; had no sense of justice; they knew how to kill, but not how to save; they knew how to destroy, but not how to spare.

Their grand enquiry was for Bothwell-Brigg-men, as they called them. If they heard casually but the least report of a man that he was a Whig or a Cameronian (for so they began now to be called) their way of process was no more than to enter his house, seize upon his person, and, telling him he was a rebel, drag him immediately out to the street, and shoot him at a post.

If the soldiers saw a man in the road who seemed

in the least shy of them, or that endeavoured to shun them, they immediately pursued him like blood-hounds, and, if he fled, fired upon him without any further inquiry.

If, upon searching any strange person, they found a Bible about him, it was sufficient to charge him with having been at a field-meeting, or that he was going to one, either of which was sufficient to set them upon him like hounds upon a hare, when they never ceased pursuing till they had brought him to death.

If, when any were dragging thus to execution, a stander-by should offer to intercede for them, or look concerned, seem to pity them, or lift up a sigh for them, they would lay hands on them and cry, " What are you, sir, that you seem so much troubled at this ?   Wherefore do you pity them ?   Are they not the King's enemies ?   And they were all at the gal-lows, you should be glad if you were a friend to the King.   Come, can you answer the questions ? " And thus they have singled out honest men among the spectators, by the mere trouble which appeared in their faces and countenances for the suffering of those that have been thus cruelly handled.

And now, to confirm all these things by examples undeniable, the few that are made public are indeed sufficient to silence the tongues of any that pretend to deny the fact ; but, alas ! they are nothing com-pared to the number of those that many yet living can give an account of from their own knowledge and memories.

Besides the public accounts given by name, and of which lists have been printed, we find several in-stances of cruelty not made public, especially in this case of the soldiers having power given to kill and save as they pleased.

A lieutenant and three soldiers passing by the road, found a man sleeping on the side of a bank, and a small pocket Bible lying by him, whereupon one of the soldiers waking him, brought him to the lieutenant. The lieutenant asked him who he was. He told him his name, place of abode, and whether he was travelling, namely, going to Fife, being a weaver by trade. They asked him then if he would pray for the King. He said, Yes, with all my heart; upon which the lieutenant was about to let him go; but one of the soldiers unhappily put in—But, sir, will you renounce the Covenant? The man hesitated a little, but being urged and insulted, cries out, Lord, forgive me, that I feared to own thy work; and then speaking to the lieutenant—Indeed, sir, says he, I'll as soon renounce my baptism (or to that purpose), I know your power, work your will with me; upon which they shot him upon the spot.

A party of dragoons in Nithsdale had information that six Bothwell-Brigg-men, as they called them, were harboured in the house of a countryman near hand. They immediately beset the house, and, breaking in, they found four men there and the master of the house; and without enquiring whether they were guilty of the rising or not, brought them all out of the door, and shot them dead, refusing to give them a minute's time to pray to God, but swearing and blaspheming when it was but begged for by the persons.

The writer of this has heard the late Lieutenant-General Maitland express great abhorrence of the cruelties committed by Major Balfour, Captain Douglas, General Dalziel, and several others, who would take pains to search out such men as they thought did but shun to be seen, and, with little or no examination, shoot them upon the spot, which he, being then under command, could no way prevent; but many times, when power was in his hands, he either facilitated their escape or otherwise prevented the mischief intended.

In a village not far from Hamilton a poor tradesman was beset in his house while at his work by five soldiers, his name Lawson. They called to him to come down the stairs, which he refused to do ; upon which all the five soldiers fired at him, but he, being aware, stood by the wall of the chamber and avoided the shot, and then called to them and asked them wherefore they came to him, he was no Bothwell-Brigg-man. Well then, say the soldiers, come down, and we will do you no hurt. The man, however, knowing they were not to be trusted, came down, but got out of his back door, and, jumping over two or three low stone-walls of the gardens, got into the fields, and took him to flight, being very swift of foot, and knowing they had just fired all their pieces. They pursued him, and, loading their muskets as they ran, fired at him again several shot ; but, by good Providence, missing him, the man escaped to the hills, but was heard of no more at his own habitation.

The aforesaid Lieutenant-General Maitland was then an officer among these bloody troops, and was, with some soldiers, quartered in Glasgow ; but, being a man of generous principles, and of too much humanity to be guilty of such things as these, was a great relief to the persecuted people, for he sheltered and protected many who otherwise would have been murdered by the soldiers ; and if he was commanded on the service, which he abhorred so much, viz., to fall upon the poor people in their house or field meetings, would frequently, by trusty messengers, give them private notice, that they might have time to disperse and be gone away, and would often find out some occasion to make his men halt by the way, that his messengers might not come too late.

Yet this compassionate gentleman was forced (much against his will, being under command) to be present at a village where three poor men, weavers by trade, were dragged from their very loom where they were at work, and, without mercy, shot to death. Their names are in the public list mentioned before.

They tell us another story of a soldier, not so divested of humanity as most of them were, and who, meeting a man upon the road, who he suspected was one of the poor outlawed proscribed people, as indeed he was, the man was surprised, and would have got from him, but he saw it was in vain, and yet the soldier soon let him know that he was not very much inclined to hurt him, much less to kill him; whereupon the following dialogue, as it is said, happened between them:

The soldier seeing the countryman willing to shun and get away from him, begins thus—

Soldier—"Hold, sir, ye mon no gang frae me, I have muckle business at you."

Countryman—"Well, what's is your will then?"

S.—"I fear ye are one of the Bothwell-Brigg-men. What say ye to that?"

C.—"Indeed no, sir, I am not."

S.—"Well, but I mon speir some questions at you; and ye's answer me right, ye and I'll be good friends again."

C.—"What questions will ye ask at me?"

S.—"First, sir, will ye pray for the King?"

C.—"Indeed, sir, I will pray for all good men. I hope ye think the King a good man, or ye would not serve him."

S.—"Indeed do I, sir, I think him a good man, and ye are all wicked that wo' no pray for him. But what say you then to the business of Bothwell Brigg. Was not Bothwell Brigg a rebellion?"

(By this time the poor man began to see the soldier was not designing to hurt him, and he took the hint, and was encouraged to answer as he did.)

C.—"I wot not weel what to say of Bothwell Brigg; but, and they took up arms there against a good King, without a good cause, it mun be rebellion, I'll own that."

S.—"Nay then, I hope thou and I'se be friends presently, I think thou'lt be an honest man. But they have killed the Archbishop of St Andrews, honest man. O that was a sore work. What say you to that; was not that murder ?"

C.—" Alas, poor man ! and ha' they killed him ! Truly, and he were an honest man, and they have killed him without any cause. Weel I wot it mun be murder ; what else can I call it ? "

S.—" Weel hast thou said, man. Now I have een but ane question more, and ye and I'se tak a drink together. Will ye renounce the Covenant ?"

C.—" Nay ; but now I mun speir at you too, and ye like. There are twa covenants, man, which of them do you mean ? "

S.—" Twa covenants, say you, what are they ? "

C.—" There's the covenant of works, man, and the covenant of grace."

S.—" Fou fa me and I ken, man ; but een renounce ane of them, and am satisfied."

C.—" With au my heart, sir, indeed I renounce the covenant of works with au my heart."

Upon this dialogue, if the story be true, the soldier let the poor man pass ; but, be the story true or not true, it serves to give the reader a true idea of the dreadful circumstances every honest man was in at this time, when their life was in the hands of every soldier, nor was the consequences other than might be expected on such occasions ; the fields, the roads, the villages, every day bearing witness to the murders that were committed, and to the injuries and abominable things which the poor people suffered from the rage of the soldiers, who were then inhumanely let loose upon them. The following is but a small part of the account of the bloodshed in this manner in one part of the country, and mostly within the year 1685, by which may be judged a little what was suffered from the rising at Bothwell Bridge, which was in 1679, to the Revolution in 1688 :—

Graham of Claverhouse, the same who was after-

wards Viscount of Dundee, and was killed at the flight
at Killicranky, in King William's time, was at this
time a most furious persecutor of these poor people.
It was his rage, in falling upon one of their field meetings, where he met with a repulse, which was the occasion and beginning of the rising at Bothwell, as has
been shewn already.   This man is said to have killed
above 100 men in this kind of cold-blood cruelty, making it his business to follow and pursue poor people
through the whole country, and having at his heels a
crew of savages, Highlanders, and dragoons, whose
sport was in blood, and whose diversion was to haul
innocent men out from their houses, or hiding places,
and murder them.   His companion in this work was
Colonel James Douglas, since called Lieutenant-General Douglas. These two, with their men, killed twenty-
eight men in a very few days, and at several places in
the shire of Galloway, most of them without the least
evidence of their being guilty, all of them without
any legal prosecution, and some without so much as
examination.

At their first coming down they found five men in
several prisons, who had been committed by other
persecutors before their coming.   It seems somebody
had maliciously told this Graham* that they were of
the Whigs that used the field meetings ; upon which,
without any oath made of the fact, or any examination of the men, without any trial or other sentence,
than his own command, his bloody soldiers fetched
them all to Mauchlin, a village where his head quarters were, and hanged them immediately, not suffering
them to enter into any house at their coming, nor at
the entreaty of the poor men, would permit one to
lend them a Bible, who it seems offered it, nor allow
them a moment to pray to God.

Four more men, who were betrayed to him, being

---

* God did not permit him to have time at his death to pray or repent,
but he was killed in the very article of victory.

hid in a house at the Water of Dee, and were at the time his men came praying together, he caused to be dragged just to the door, and shot dead as they came out, without an inquiry whether they were the persons that he came to apprehend. Their being found praying to God was, it seems, sufficient testimony of their party and offence. After this, coming to the same place, at two or three days' distance, and understanding the people of the town had buried the bodies, he caused his men to dig them up again, and commanded that they should lie in the fields. The names of these four were John Grier, Robert Ferguson, Archibald Stuart, and Robert Stuart.

At Camonel, in the county of Carrick, he saw a man run hastily across the street before his troop, and as he might suppose did it to escape from or avoid them, though, as the people of the place related it, the poor man had no apprehensions of them, but as he took all occasions for his bloody design, he commanded his men to shoot this person, without so much as examining him, or asking who he was. The poor man's name was Matthew Mekellwrat.

The same party having intelligence that there were several of the Whigs hid in a great cave among the hills of Glencairn, that the people resorted to them to pray together, and that several women carried them provision and coal to burn to warm them, Colonel Douglas sent a small party, who surounded the hill, and drew five men out of the cave. It seems there had been near fifty there just before having met to pray, but were separated again. Had they been all there, Douglas had not had them so cheap; for, being all armed, it was likely they would have sent him back faster than he came, having but eighteen dragoons with him. These five, however, who, it seems, were betrayed by one Watson,* this Colonel

---

* After the Revolution, this Watson, who betrayed them, was seized

Douglas dragged out of the cave and immediately shot them dead, not giving them time so much as to recommend their souls unto God.

The names of the murdered men were Robert Grierson, Robert Mitchel, James Bennoch, John Edgar, and John Gibson.

The same wretched gang coming to a house where they had been informed one Welsh, a field-preacher, was harboured, or was to be found, they rushed violently into the house, but found—not the man they sought, neither indeed was he there—but they found five men together, with the women and children of the family, all on their knees at prayers; whereupon, without examining any farther, they said it was a seditious meeting which was forbidden by the Council, and thereupon instantly dragged out the men and shot them to death before the door.

John Smith was shot to death by two soldiers at Lismehago. William Skillilaw was shot by one Lieutenant Saunders in the river Air. John Ferguson, George Whitburn, and Patrick Gemmil at Finnick by two soldiers.

That murdering persecutor, Graham of Claverhouse, seeing a man riding by him on the way, called after him, and the man not making an answer nor stopping his horse, Graham caused one of his soldiers to shoot him dead as he rode along; whereas, upon enquiry into the matter, it was found that the poor man was deaf, and could not hear him call to him. The murdered man's name was Robert Auchinleck.

William Adams, at the Wallwood in Kyle, going along the way, and seeing some soldiers at a distance, hid himself in a thicket thinking to shun them, but, being discovered by the soldiers, they instantly shot him, without so much as asking his name, or enquiring after any other guilt than his shunning to meet them.

by some of the relations of these poor men, and put in prison at Dumfries, but they did not put him to death as he deserved.

Captain Douglas seized a tailor and shot him dead, only because he had some small pieces of lead about him such as the tailors put in the sleeves of women's clothes; and another of that persecuting family of the Douglas shot ———— ———— on no other pretence than because he had a flint in his pocket : these things, it seemed, they called ammunition.   At another house he shot a man because he attempted to escape from him, though he had no knowledge of the man or any charge against him.

Several were killed in the dark, being shot by they knew not who, or for what.   The Highlanders shot men for their sport without asking them any questions, and answered that they could not mistake, for all the country were rebels.

Most of these mentioned above were massacred in the year 1685, and in one count, besides many more in all parts of the west country.   The dragoons patrolled all over the country, by night as well as by day, so that the distressed people who lay hid in the mountains could not come down to the houses of their friends in the night, as they usually did for succour, and so retreat again in the morning before day ; but now they got no liberty to come down but at the utmost hazard, so that their wives and children or relations, and sometimes charitable and compassionate Christian friends, went to them to the hills and to the caves and holes in the earth where they were harboured, to carry them necessaries and relief, and without which they must have perished, for mere want of food ; and notwithstanding which they endured in those vast and desolate hills inexpressible hardships, extremities of cold, without covering, without shelter, without fuel in the deepest of winter, and often without food and without light.   A list of threescore and eighteen men by name has been published who were massacred by the persecutors named above, and of whom some of those named here were a part, but the number who were thus hunted down and murdered by the Highlanders and the dragoons in the whole country is not to be reckoned up, and is indeed incredible.

The writer of these Memoirs, having talked with many sober and judicious persons who lived in that part of the country at that time, and were eye-witnesses to much of it, found that they all agreed in this, that many thousands of people perished under the violent hands of these men, besides those killed in the field of battle at Pentland Hills, Bothwell, &c. And one reverend minister of the Church of Scotland assured the writer hereof that, taking in the people who died in prisons and in banishment, there was an account taken of above eighteen thousand people, whose blood these persecutors have to account for, besides the numbers who at the time of the revolution were actually in prisons, in the Isle of the Bass, Dunnotter Castle, Blackness, Edinburgh, and other places, amounting to a very great number.

And yet here it cannot be omitted, that to the honour of the cause these people suffered in, and in justification of the principles which they acted from, we must observe that their number was so far from being diminished, or themselves or their ministers from being discouraged, that on the contrary they increased prodigiously in number, neither were their meetings ever destitute of ministers, nor were they ever so discouraged as to give over meeting for the public worship, resolving not to forsake the assembling themselves together, where they praised God in singleness of heart, and with joy embraced the opportunities, though at the hazard of their lives.

I cannot express this more fully than in the words of the sufferers themselves left upon record by one of their own fellows in affliction, thus, viz. :—" To speak of the numbers," says he, " we must do justice to the miracle of God's working, whereby the very means

T

used to extirpate us from the face of the earth was
by the wise Disposer of all things made to increase
our numbers; for that, albeit they went on for many
years imprisoning, banishing, and butchering our dear
brethren, yet all the prisons they could fill with us,
and all the ships they could freight with us, and all
the gibbets they could hang us on, could never either
exhaust or lessen our number; but the more we were
afflicted the more we grew, and the design to destroy
us, through the mercy of our God, proved always
ruinous to the destroyers; and this must be acknowledged to the praise of God's clemency and the con-
demnation of man's cruelty, that when they had tried
all ways possible to destroy us and root us out from
the earth—after they had hanged, shot, tortured, and
banished for slaves all they could catch of us, they
were further from their purpose than when they
began. Our numbers were not diminished, our meetings for gospel ordinances were not disappointed, but
we enjoyed the administrations in their purity and
power with greater certainty, and met together in
greater numbers than ever, for that our numbers
increased more and more." That this was true their
enemies openly acknowledged, and this enraged the
persecutors so much the more and that to such a
degree that they once resolved on a general massacre
of all together by the troops of heritors, dragoons,
and Highlandmen, who, forming themselves into a
great army, spread themselves from one side of a
whole county to the other, having their men placed
marching single at a great distance, but always one
in sight of the other; so marching forward, every one
straight before him, they by this means searched the
rocks, rivers, woods, wastes, mountains, mosses, and
every the most private and retired places of the
county where they thought we were hidden, so that
it was impossible any thing could escape them; and
yet so true were the mountain-men, as their perse-

cutors called them, to one another, that in all that famous march they found not one man, though many a good man perhaps, with trembling heart and hands lift up to heaven for protection, saw them, and were passed by them undiscovered.

Failing in any enterprise of this nature, and being disappointed in their prey, always redoubled their fury at those who fell into their hands. It was not far from Edinburgh that a field meeting was appointed, and not the minister only but a great many people went out of that city at the hazard of their lives to have been present at it, when on the way they got notice that the appointment had been discovered, and that soldiers were coming to fall upon the people. The faithful spies that gave them intelligence of this did it so timely and so prudently that the soldiers found nobody assembled at the place. But their rage doubling at the disappointment, they fell upon every one they met in their return, and chiefly upon the poor women and maid-servants, charging them with being actually going to the field-meeting, though not present at it. Besides the rudeness and insolence of another nature which they offered to the women, as upon all such occasions was their manner, they carried about thirty women to Edinburgh, and four or five men, where they were put in prison—some in the Tolbooth, some in the Correction-house, though persons of good fashion and families—and of these seven or eight were at several times put to death, principally upon their refusing to renounce the Covenant, and to make declarations condemning their principles, and on acknowledging their being on the way to a meeting. One poor servant-maid, belonging to a citizen's wife of Edinburgh, being with her mistress, and having her mistress's Bible under her arm, was taken by the soldiers, her mistress escaping by running into a stable. The poor maid being examined upon no other suspicion but having the Bible, boldly owned she was going to the field-meeting, but refused to accuse her mistress or any one else, whereupon they threatened her with the torture to make her confess. She answered she was ready to endure torture or death, and talked to them with such presence of mind, such strength of reasoning, and such cheerfulness, as made them both mad and ashamed. They sentenced her to be hanged in the street of Edinburgh, and another young woman with her. She received the sentence with rejoicing, and, lifting up her hands and eyes, gave God thanks that had thought her worthy to suffer for her testimony to the truth of religion and the purity of his worship.

The cruelty of the persecutors was farther remarkable in these poor young women's suffering, that they brought them to their execution with two murderers, viz. two wretches condemned for murdering their bastard children, mixing them together that the common people might imagine they were all guilty of such crimes, or that, at least, they might not be known asunder by the crowd of spectators, but they easily discovered the difference by the manner of their behaviour; while these two appeared with smiling countenances, singing psalms, and in a cheerful, inimitable frame—the others dejected, confused, and, to say all in a word, like what they really were.

It would be endless to give an account of the manner of execution, the behaviour of the suffering people in their imprisonment and at their execution, or the cruelty of the judges in torturing those who were brought before them with that truly barbarous engine for torture, unknown to all the world but to Scotland, called the Boot; by which, the leg being put in, and the wedges driven with a great maul by the executioner, the bone has been entirely compressed, and the marrow of the bone has been seen to burst out through the macerated flesh.

Yet it was not found that any one of those who were thus tortured yielded to the tormentors, either to accuse themselves or betray others.   Mr Hugh Mackail, a young man of about twenty-four years of age, and being what they call a probationer for the office of a minister, but not yet a minister ordained, was licentiate, and had preached some time before the turning out of the Presbyterians at the Restoration : he is an eminent example of this.   His case, in short, is as follows :

Being a young man of pomising parts and great eloquence, he was appointed to preach in the great Church at Edinburgh the Sabbath before the turning out of the ministers ; and his subject, as might be expected, related to the cruel persecutions which the Church of God in all ages had undergone from the enemies of Jesus Christ and his kingdom.   It was suggested that he carried on a parallel between the persecutions of the people of God in the Jewish Church, and those of the people of God in the Presbyterian Church of Scotland.   And it was very particular and surprising to many that heard him, when he told them the Church was persecuted by a Pharaoh upon the throne, a Haman in the State, and a Judas in the Church ; by whom he was supposed to mean King Charles II., then reigning upon the throne, the Duke of Lauderdale, then principal agent in Scots affairs, and the Archbishop of St Andrews, an apostate from the true Church, and then the most false betrayer, and at that time the most implacable persecutor of that very Church which he had before been a member and minister of.

It seems the Archbishop, who was seldom known to forgive any one, had not forgotten this, though it was in the year 1661——four years before.   And it was not many days after his preaching that sermon, that a party of soldiers was sent to seize him ; but he got notice of their design, and conveyed himself away into the west, where he continued retired till the affair of

Pentland, of which mention has been made, when being obliged, as he thought, to join with his brethren in renewing the Covenant, he went to Lanark, where that solemn renewing the Covenant was performed, as has been observed.   When they were defeated at Pentland, it happened this young man was taken and brought in prisoner to Edinburgh.   The Archbishop remembered the sermon and the man, and had his full revenge upon this occasion, as the event showed.   Mr Mackail was not taken in the action, neither was he in it, nor was he taken in the company of any that were in the action, but merely, and unpolitically enough, as travelling on the road.   For the weakness of his constitution having rendered him unable him to bear the fatigues of marching or the rigour of the season, he was obliged to leave the body of men who marched after to Pentland Hills, being no longer able to endure it ; so parting from them at a place called Cramond-Bridge, he was taken by some countrymen who were sent out to stop the passages to prevent the escape of the rebels, as they were then called.

Being taken and brought to Council, he was committed to the Tolbooth, and several times examined, and at length tortured to make him confess himself guilty, which, however, they could not make him do ; the Archbishop of St Andrews being present all the time of his torture, as one of the judges, appointing and directing the same.   A terrible work indeed it was for a Christian Bishop, but very agreeable to the rest of his character, if we may believe what was generally said of him at that time among even indifferent men.

They questioned him likewise upon torture to declare what was the original cause and design of that insurrection.   He answered he knew not any more of it than that it was occasioned by the cruelty of Sir James Turner, who having been resisted by some people who could no longer bear his violence, that resistance having exposed them to the revenge of the soldiers, and the apprehensions of that revenge having made them desperate, that very accident drove them to take arms, as has been observed before in the accounts given of that action.

They were not satisfied with this answer, but pressed him to declare all he knew of that affair; and upon his declaring he knew no more, they ordered him to be tortured. At every blow the tormentors struck, they asked if he would confess; and upon receiving still the same answer, viz., that he knew no more than he had told them, they renewed the torture till he had received eleven strokes of the hangman.

It seems they had been heated the same morning, and their fury increased, by having just before tortured another gentleman, viz., Mr Nicholson of Corsack, in a most terrible manner.

Here, for the information of the English reader, or other stranger to the customs and judicatories of Scotland, it is necessary to note that this examination by torture is always done in the presence of the judges, who order the tormentors when to begin, how long to proceed, and when to stop, and interrogate the sufferer all the time, and in the interval of their blows.

"Mr Mackail," says an author who relates that story, " having before declared ingenuously all he knew, could not be moved by the torture to express any impatience or bitterness, though the torture was in itself very violent and terrible, by reason of the compressure of the flesh, sinews, and even the bones, by the force of wooden wedges driven in with a hammer in a double and unusual measure, even to ten or eleven strokes, with considerable intervals, all of which he sustained most constantly and christianly. But before he received the last three strokes, he protested solemnly in the sight of God, that he could say no more though all the joints of his body were in as great torture as that poor leg; and desired to know what could hinder them to believe one of his profession, who had solemnly declared, as in the sight of God, that he knew no more than he had told—viz., that, to the best of his knowledge, the rising in the West was merely occasional, upon a discontent between the people in the stewartry of Galloway and Sir James Turner, to which every one did run as their hearts moved them when they heard of it.

The violence of this torment threw him into a fever, and yet could not these merciful judges be prevailed with to respite his appearing before them above one day, though two physicians and a surgeon certified his dangerous condition, and he petitioned for a delay on that account. Accordingly the next day he was rather dragged or carried than went to their bar, and was condemned to die ; on the third day after which he was executed accordingly.

There is another of these sufferers who cannot be forgotten when we are recording the zeal of the Church of Scotland's martyrs, who, in imitation of the primitive zeal of the first centuries, offered himself to the sacrifice, without any one laying hand on him. This was James Nicol of Peebles.

He was occasionally at Edinburgh when three of the western people were to be brought to their assize or their trial, for refusing to answer the wicked ensnaring questions so often mentioned in these Memoirs. He went to the Justiciary Court to see them tried. It grieved his soul to see three innocent men delivered, as meek lambs, into the hands of the butchers to be slaughtered. It moved his passion to see the tyrannical behaviour of the cruel judges and persecutors insulting and reviling the sufferers ; and much ado he had, as he expressed himself, to restrain his anger from breaking out upon the spot, and from reproaching them with shedding innocent blood ; but was in part satisfied and appeased when he heard the three sufferers, who were his dear friends and brethren

in the cause of God, answer with such cheerfulness
and courage as put their enemies to shame.

He went from the court, however, grieved in his
spirit, having seen them condemned, and heard the
bloody sentence pronounced ; and that, it being then
about eleven o'clock, they were ordered to be carried
not back to prison, but from the court, where they
received their sentence, to the place of execution.

Mr Nicol, not intending to see the sad sight, ordered his horse to be brought out about one o'clock,
to return to his own house, but was obliged to stop
at the West Port of the city to have his saddle
mended. While he was staying there, he saw the
people running, and, asking what it was for, was told
the three honest men were bringing to the place of
execution, and looking up the street saw them ascend
the scaffold, which was in view of the place where he
stood. This moved him to walk up the Grassmar-
ket to see them die. Now he was on longer able to
contain, being moved with a strong zeal against these
murderers, but he cried out in the midst of the throng,
They had murdered three of God's servants contrary
to their own laws, and in a most barbarous and inhuman manner. Hereupon he was immediately apprehended. This was on the 10th of August 1684. On
the 18th, he was examined before the Council, where
they were astonished to find that he, against whom
they had no accusation, was bold to declare himself
in the most dangerous questions, and rather sought
the martyrdom he expected, than that he would endeavour to avoid what they had to inflict, as the
reader will see by the manner of their interroga-
ting him, and his answers penned by himself as follows :—

" First, I was interrogated by two in a room privately thus — *Ques.* Was you at Bothwell Brigg?
Ans. I am not bound to be my own accuser. I am
not, said one of them, to desire you, but only say

upon you honest word that you were not there.   *A.*
I am not bound to satisfy you, but prove what you
have to say against me, and especially you, till I come
before my accusers.   Well, said he, I am one of them.
Then I answered, I was there.   *Q.* How came you
to rise in arms against the King?   *A.* Because he
has broken the Covenant of the Lord my God.   *Q.*
Was the Prelate's death murder?   *A.* No, it was
not murder.   *Q.* Was Hackston's death murder?
A. That it was indeed.   *Q.* How dare you own the
Covenant, seeing the King gave orders to burn it by
the hand of the hangman?   *A.* Yes, I dare own;
for although ye should escape the hand of men for
so doing, yet ye shall all pay for it ere all be done,
and that to purpose.   As for me, I would not do it
for the whole earth.   Then I was interrogated by
other two, who asked some frivolous questions which
I baffled to silence.   Then I was brought in before
the bloody crew.   What now, sir, said they, do you
own the King's authority?   *A.* I own all things that
the precious word of God owns in less or more, and
all faithful magistrates.   *Q.* But do you not own
King Charles also?   *A.* I dare not for a world, because
it is perjury; for he has unkinged himself in a high
degree, and that in doing all things contrary to the
Word of God, and Confession of Faith, and Catechisms Larger and Shorter.   *Q.* Know ye to whom
ye are speaking?   *A.* I know I am before men.
But, said one of them, ye are speaking to the Chancellor and Members of Council, sir.   But, said I, as
I have told you already that he has unkinged himself, so have you degraded yourselves from being
princes.   *Q.* If the King were here what would you
say, sir?   *A.* I know how I ought to speak to the
King, if he were King.   Sir, is ordinarily said to
him; and so to let you know that I am no Quaker,
or erroneous in any thing, but a pure Presbyterian,
and of a gospel, apostolic spirit, I call you sirs, be-

THE CHURCH IN HER PERSECUTED STATE.   299

cause ye are noblemen by birth, but not because ye
are my judges.   Q. Will ye not say God bless the
King's Majesty?   A. I dare not bless them whom
God hath rejected.   'If any man bring another doctrine than ye have received, bid him not God speed,
nor receive him into your house,' 2 John 10.   And
Psalm xvi. 4, says David, 'Their drink offerings of
blood will I not offer, nor take up their names into
my lips,'—viz., them that hasten after other gods,
and therefore I dare not pray for him.   Q. And will
ye not pray for him?   A. If he belongs to the election of grace, he has a part of my prayers; and also,
if he were a King that had keeped Covenant with God,
I would give him a double share, and make mention
of his name; but he is an apostate.   (So, my friends,
they looked still one to another at every question and
answer.)   Q. How old are you, sir?   A. I am fifty-
one years.   Q. How dare you own the Covenants
seeing we have burnt it by the hand of the hangman?   A. Sir, I dare own them upon all perils
whatsomever to the utmost of my power, all the days
of my life.   And, with that, they smiled and laughed
one to another and to me; and said my days were
near an end.   I said, I am now in your power, but
if ye take my blood, you shall take innocent blood
upon yourselves, as in Jer. xxvi., 'As for me, I am
in your hands; do to me as seems good and meet
unto you.   But know for a certainty, that if ye put
me to death, ye shall bring innocent blood upon yourselves, and on this city, and the inhabitants thereof.'
And as for me, if ye take my blood, it is as innocent
blood as ever ye did take, for I did never wrong any
man to this day.   Q. Do you go to the Church?
A. I went aye to the Church where I could get any
faithful minister to go to; but for your prelates' kirks,
and Baal's priests, I never heard any of them, nor
never intends to do, if I were to live an hundred years.
But, said they, ye shall not live long now, sir.

"Then on Tuesday they called me before them again, being the 19th day of this instant. *Q.* What say ye the day? do ye adhere to all ye said yesterday? *A.* I adhere to all and haill upon all perils whatsomever. *Q.* Do ye approve of Bothwell Bridge? *A.* Yes I do. *Q.* Do you go to the kirk at Peebles? *A.* No; nor never intends to go there, nor no place else which pertains to the perjured prelates. *Q.* Do you own the Covenants? *A.* I adhere to every point of them. *Q.* Do ye own Aird-Moss, Sanquhair, Rutherglen, and Lanark declarations? *A.* Yes I do, because they are agreeable to the Covenants, and work of Reformation. Many more questions they asked which I cannot now particularly remember; but I told them in general, that I was against Popery, Prelacy, malignacy, and profanity, and all that is against sound doctrine, discipline, worship, and government, and all errors whatsomever which are contrary to sound Presbyterian doctrine, be what they will; for there is none other right but erroneous, how fair a face soever they have, which shall be found not agreeable to the apostles' doctrine. And then they read something of what I had said, and questioned if I would subscribe what I had said. I answered, No. *Q.* Can ye write? *A.* Yes, I can write. Then do it, said they. I said, I would not do it at all. Now, my friends, I say these are but part of my interrogations.

"Again I was brought before the justiciary (as they call themselves) on the 20th of this instant, and interrogated thus: *Q.* What now, sir—what think you of yourself the day? *A.* I praise my God I am the same I was. *Q.* What think ye of what ye said yesterday before the Chancellor and the Council? *A.* I hold all, and decline nothing—no not one ace. *Q.* Were ye at Bothwell-Bridge? *A.* Yes, that I was. *Q.* Had ye arms? *A.* Yes, that I had. One of them said, God help you: and I said, I wot none of ye can pray for yourself. Said he, I wish you better nor ye do yourself. But I said, No; for ye would have me disown my great Lord, the King of Zion, and obey man—yea, base men, whose breath is in their nostrils, who give out laws and commands contrary to his. *Q.* How dare ye rise in arms against the King? *A.* It is better to obey God than man, and he is an enemy to God. *Q.* Would ye rise yet in arms for the Covenants against the King's laws, if ye had the occasion? *A.* Yes, that I would—say the contrary who will, upon all peril. *Q.* What think ye of yourself in spoiling the country of horse and arms, sir? *A.* Sir, I had not the worth of a spur whang of any man's, but was mounted of horse and arms of my own. *Q.* Where have ye been all this time? *A.* Sometimes here and there in England and Scotland. *Q.* Whom have ye conversed with? *A.* I was about my business, being a merchant. They said, Ye have been about another business, for ye are found to be a fugitive and a vagabond. *A.* I have been a merchant from my youth. *Q.* But where had you ye chamber in this town? *A.* I had none these several years. *Q.* Where quarter ye in this town? *A.* I have not been much in it these seven or eight years. *Q.* But where was ye the night, and the last night before the execution. *A.* I was not in town; I came but into port just when the first was cast over. Then they looked to one another, and whispered together. But they would fain have had me wronging my landlords in all the parts of the country, and in all burghs; but glory to my Lord, I I have wronged none yet, nor yet hopes to do : for it was ay my care and prayer to God earnestly that I might wrong no man, and that I would rather suffer before any were wronged by me, which he has kept me from this day. Then they read what I had said. *Q.* Wilt ye subscribe what ye have said. *A.* No, no. *Q.* Can you write, sir? *A.* Yes, that I can. Well, said they, write down that he can, but will not. They told me five or six times that my time should not be long, and said to me, will ye have a minister? *A.* I will have none of your Baal's priests."

After these interrogations, and that they had left him for two or three days, on the 22d one brought him the copy of his indictment, telling him at the same time that on the 27th he would receive his sentence, and that he would be carried directly from the bar to the scaffold, which was done accordingly, and where he died with the same resolute undaunted courage that he had behaved with all along.

There was yet another small action in arms, which the writers of those times say little of. They are ashamed to call it rebellion : they would call it a pursuit of murderers ; but the fact was thus. The number of the persons proscribed was prodigiously great, who, flying into dens and holes and caves of the earth, lay concealed in the hills and mountains, from whence, by the vigilance of their enemies, they were frequently dragged out to execution and death, either with or without process, as has been said. Sometimes, as occasion offered, these distressed people would get together, either for their field meetings, or to shift from place to place, as occasion offered for their relief ; and that they might not be a prey to every single soldier or laird that should meet them naked and unarmed, they carried arms for their defence, so long only as they were together, separating again as they had occasion, and then laying by their weapons.

One of these parties, with Mr Richard Cameron, their minister, the same from whom these men were after called Cameronians, having been together some days, but with no other view than their own security as above, were pursued by the dragoons, and being surprized as they were lying down upon the grass for refreshment at a place called Aird-Moss, they were obliged to fight. The dragoons who came upon them were about 120 men, being three troops. The persecuted people were about forty foot indifferently armed, and twenty-six horse. The horse were led by David Hackston, Esq. of Rathillet, a gentleman of a good family, and allied to some of the best families in Scotland. He had been proscribed long before for the killing the Archbishop of St Andrews, though, as has been observed, he was the only man of that company who refused to have any hand in it. Some say he refused because he would not have had him killed, but others say he refused because he formerly had a declared quarrel against him personally, and would not suffer it to be said that he executed his private revenge. Be that as it will, it is allowed by all that he was not an actor in the death of the bishop any way whatsoever, but that being with the persons who killed him, he separated from them, and refused to be concerned in it.

Being forced thus to fight as above with so unequal numbers, Mr Hackston, followed by fifteen horse, charged up to the very faces of the dragoons, and after giving them a fire from their carabines, broke into the body of them, where having showed all the marks of bravery and gallantry possible, being surrounded by numbers and overpowered, the most of them were killed or wounded. Mr Hackston seeing his men broken, fought like a lion, and with a desperate courage made his way quite through the enemy, killing and wounding several of them with his own hand; and being got clear, and without receiving any considerable wound, he made off, but was closely pursued by four dragoons. The goodness of his horse carried him from them, and he was in a fair way to have escaped, when his horse plunged into a bog, from whence he could not get him out. Being thus unhorsed, a dragoon came up to him who knew him, and offered him quarter, which he refused, and fought him with his sword, and would have mastered him, but three other dragoons surrounding him, they knocked him down, giving him several wounds in the head, and so took him prisoner.

Mr Cameron fighting as boldly at the head of the other part of the horse, was killed, and his head cut off and carried with the prisoners to Edinburgh. The foot being rode down by the dragoons and dispersed, fled to the hills. About seventeen of them were killed or taken, and the rest escaped. They carried Mr Hackston, wounded as he was, to Edinburgh, where they led him and three more of the prisoners taken at the same place in triumph through the city on a horse, with his face to the horse's tail, Mr Cameron's head stuck on the point of a halbert being carried before him, and another head in a sack. His examination, his resolute answers, his horrible torture, and his cruel execution, are well known to all Scotland.

He had been several times carried before the justiciary court, as they were called, for he would not call them so, where he refused to answer to any questions whatsoever—declining their jurisdiction, and protesting against their authority. But they resolved to treat him for it in a method which they doubted not would bring him to submit to them, wherein, however, they failed, and were most effectually disappointed; for neither was their threats of torture, the barbarous loading him with irons, who had seven wounds upon him, the refusing to let those wounds be dressed for some time—no, nor at last the torture itself, prevail with him to answer them.

They would have had him confess the murder of the Archbishop, but he would not; then they would have had him deny it, but neither would he do that, but steadily adhered to his protestation—viz., that they had usurped the supremacy over the Church, which belonged alone to Jesus Christ, and established idolatry, perjury, and other abominations; and in confiscating themselves therein had persecuted God's people, and shed innocent blood, and for this reason he would have nothing to say to them, but declared them open enemies to Christ's kingdom, competitors with him for his crown and power, and utterly declined them as judges. This was the substance of his answers upon several times being brought before them, and it is no wonder that they were exceedingly provoked at him, as they soon showed they were.

Upon Friday July 30, being again brought before the counsel, it was asked of him if he had any other thing to say? He answered, That which I have said I will seal it. Then they told him that they had something to say to him, and commanded him to sit down and receive his sentence, which willingly he did, but told them they were all murderers, for all that power they had was derived from tyranny, and that these years bygone they have not only tyrannized over the Church of God, but have also grinded the faces of the poor, so that oppression, bloodshed, perjury, and many murders were to be found in their skirts; upon which he was incontinent carried away to the scaffold at the Market-Cross of Edinburgh, where he died with great torture inflicted upon his body,* nor being permitted to leave any testimony to the world, except what is comprehended in a few missives directed to some of his Christian acquaintances from his prison in the Tolbooth of Edinburgh, which are as follows :—

It is impossible to relate all the particulars of their persecution, either as to the cruelty of the persecutors or the constancy of the sufferers. What has been said will serve to open the eyes of all who are yet ignorant, and to fill every Christian reader with abhorrence of the practices, and of the very names

---

* The cruelty of executing Hackston of Rathillet, besides the torture they before put him to, was indeed unheard of—both his hands being cut off, and after his breast cut open, and his heart pulled out, even before he was dead, as many bear witness who saw him executed.

U

and memories of the persons who exercised such
cruelties on their Christian brethren.

I say brethren, because to the dishonour of the
Protestant name it is said that these persecutors were
called Protestants.

There is but one thing that either ever was or indeed could be said to extenuate the charge, and great
pains has been taken to possess the world with the
notion, viz., that these men were madmen, enemies
to government, to monarchy, and to civil society, that
they denied magistracy itself, as well as the person
and government of the King, and that they were
executed as rebels, not as religious persons.

It is needless to answer to any part of this charge,
the profession of the sufferers at the place of execution and upon all other occasions, against the enemies
they opposed, making it clear that they did not oppose
government or monarchy as such, but wicked, perjured, and persecuting governors. These they did
oppose and declare against as enemies to God and
their country, and as breakers of sacred oaths and
covenants, made both with God and man. These
they opposed, and thought themselves bound in conscience to do so, as being discharged from all civil
allegiance to them, by the breach of their coronation
engagements, and of all religious engagements to them,
by the breaking their solemn oath to God and his
Church, and turning persecutors of that very Church
they had sworn to maintain; and this they did on
the same arguments which justified the revolution,
and on which the Protestant succession of Hanover
is now founded—to wit, of taking arms against perjured princes, who break their solemn compact with
God and their people—renouncing and deposing them,
and excluding both them and their race; and blessed
be God who has given such a testimony in our days
to the memory of his saints, and to the truth of the
doctrine and principles which these faithful martyrs

in Scotland suffered for, by bringing the whole nation, nay, even some of the very persecutors themselves, to take up those very principles with respect to government and obedience, that those suffering Christians died for; and to expel and depose, reject and cast off, that very race and one of those very kings as tyrants and robbers, breakers of their oaths, and injurious to the people, which these good people were persecuted and murdered for rejecting before. And, therefore, even the declaration at Torwood, as it was called, where they excommunicated the King, and which the enemies of these good people pretended to be enthusiastic, develish, rebellious and anti-Christian, and for which said good people were censured even by their brethren who accepted of the indulgences,—I say that very excommunication is expressly founded upon the same grounds as was afterwards the renouncing the King by the revolution, with this difference only that the reasons given by Mr Cargil, Mr Cameron, and the people then called Cameronians in the declaration of the Queensferry, and the excommunication of Torwood, contain all that is understood in the memorial to the Prince of Orange, from the people of Great Britain, to invite him to assist them in arms against the same King, and much more.

To make this clear, I here give you that famous excommunication, pronounced by Mr Donald Cargil at Torwood, anno 1684, and only desire the impartial reader to compare it with the memorials above-named, and see if it be possible for any British Protestant, who owns the justice of the Revolution, to reflect upon the zeal of these people without blushing for himself and the whole nation, that they did not see and abhore the tyranny of those reigns sooner. Then they had joined with these people, instead of censuring their zeal; the Revolution had then been brought about without foreign help at all; the Prince of Orange had then been called over as peaceably as

King George to take possession of the crown, and the blood of near twenty thousand people—who were one way or other murdered or destroyed, by that now abdicated race of tyrants and their bloody administration—had been saved.

What a shame it is to us, and how much to the honour of these persecuted people, that they could thus see the treachery and tyranny of those reigns when we saw it not; or rather that they had so much honesty of principle, and obeyed so strictly the dictates of conscience, as to bear their testimony early, nobly, and gloriously, to the truth of God and the rights of their country, both civil and religious, while we all, though seeing the same things, and equally convinced of its being right, yet betrayed the cause of liberty and religion by a sinful silence, and a dreadful cowardice, not joining to help the Lord, or the people of the Lord, against the mighty,—sitting still and seeing our brethren slaughtered and butchered in defence of their principles, which our consciences told us, even then, were founded on the truth, and by those tyrants who we knew deserved to be rejected both of God and the nation, and who afterwards we did reject accordingly. But to proceed.

As those suffering people are abundantly justified by the practice of the whole nation in the Revolution, so I must add that they are abundantly acquitted of that weak and unjust charge mentioned before, viz. of their being enemies to government, and refusing to submit to lawful authority; by their behaviour in the Revolution; their cheerful joining in it, and their being the first that petitioned the parliament to make the Prince of Orange king and promising all dutiful submission to such a king as they knew would rule in righteousness, and defend, not destroy, the heritage of the Lord. But as this belongs to the next part of this work, I shall refer to the fuller account of their conduct, which will appear in its place.

Here follows an account of the proceedings at Torwood :—

The meeting was in the fields, at a place called Torwood, in the western part of Scotland, the 11th of September, 1688, Mr Richard Cameron, Mr ———, and Mr Donald Cargil, ministers, assisting ; but Mr Cargil preached the action sermon from Ezek. xxi. 25, 26, 27, " And thou profane, wicked prince of Israel, whose day is come, when iniquity shall have an end : Thus saith the Lord God, remove the diadem, and take off the crown," &c. In this preaching he made first a short pertinent discourse on the nature, subject, causes, and ends of excommunication, and declared fully his own motives then to pronounce it, and that it was not from any private spirit, malice, or passion, but conscious of his duty and zeal for the honour of God, and of his Church; after which, he began as follows, viz. :—

" We have spoken of excommunication, the causes, subject, and ends thereof, we shall now proceed to the action itself, being constrained by the conscience of our duty and zeal for God, to excommunicate at this time some of those among us in these lands, who have been guilty of such crimes as renders them the proper subjects of this censure, and especially those who have been authors of the present mischiefs to the Church of Christ, in this nation of Scotland ; and in doing this, we shall give them the ordinary names by which they are called, that it may not be in the least doubtful who we are speaking of, in so solemn an occasion.

" I being a minister of Jesus Christ, and having authority and power from him, do in his name and by his spirit, excommunicate Charles II., King, &c., and that upon account of these wickednesses following: 1. For his high mocking the Majesty of God in that, where he had confessed his own sins, his father's sins, his mother's idolatry, and had solemnly engaged against them in his declaration at Dunfermline, August 16. 1650, and was upon that declaration, and on the conditions thereof, accepted as King. He has broken the said solemn engagement, and returned more avowedly to those sins than all that were before him. 2. For his abhorred perjury* in that, after he had twice solemnly subscribed the Covenant, he most presumptuously disowned and renounced it, causing it to be burned by the hangman. 3. For that he has caused all those laws† for establishing religion and reformation, and which he had engaged in the said Covenant to preserve, to be rescinded, and enacted laws directly contrary, and is still working to set up Popery among us.‡ 4. For commanding his armies‖ to destroy the Lord's people, who were standing in their own just defence of their rights and privileges, and for the blood§ he hath shed by land and by water of the people of God, for the sake of religion and of righteousness, more than all the kings that have been before him in Scotland, the said people being most willing in all other things¶ to render him obedience, if he had reigned and ruled them according to his Covenant and oath. 5. For that he is still an enemy to, and a persecutor of true Protestants; a favourer** and helper of the Papists, at home and abroad, and hath hindered the due execution of just laws. 6. For his relaxing of the kingdom, by his frequent granting pardon to murderers, which is expressly contrary to the law of God, and therefore not in the power of any king to do. 7. His great and dreadful

---

* At the Revolution they charged King James with perjury in breaking his coronation oath, wherein he had sworn to maintain the Church and true religion.
† At the Revolution they charged him with dispensing with the laws, and setting up his arbitrary will in the room of the law.
‡ King James charged with setting up Popery among us.
‖ King James charged with keeping up a standing army in time of peace.
§ King James charged with arbitrary shedding innocent blood.
¶ Mark that, willing to render obedience, &c.
** King James charged with helping and favouring Papists.

uncleanness, adultery, and incest; his drunkenness and dissimulation with God and man, performing his promises where his engagements were sinful, &c.

" By the same authority, and in the same name, I excommunicate and cast out of the true Church, and deliver up to Satan, James, Duke of York, and that for his idolatry, as far as concerns Scotland—for other things I read not—and for setting up idolatry in Scotland to defile the Lord's land, and his encouraging and drawing others to do so.

" Next, in the same name, and by the same authority, I excommunicate James, Duke of Monmouth, &c., for his coming into Scotland upon his father's unjust command, and leading armies against the Lord's people—they being constrained to rise, being killed in and for the right worshipping of the true God—and for his refusing at Bothwell the cessation proposed by others.

" Next I do by the same authority, and in the same name, excommunicate, cast out of the true Church, and deliver up to Satan, John, Duke of Lauderdale, for his dreadful blasphemy against the great God, especially those horrible expressions used by him to the Prelate of St Andrews, in profanation of the holy Word of God, viz., ' Sit thou at my right hand, until I make thine enemies thy footstool;' likewise for his atheistical drolling upon the Scriptures of God in general, scoffing at religion and religious persons, his apostacy from the Covenant and Reformation, and persecuting thereof after he had been professor and pleader for and possessor of the said Covenant, &c.; likewise for his perjury and murder, in the case of Mr James Mitchell;* likewise for his adulteries and

---

* He was one of them in the Council who gave public faith to Mr Mitchell that his life should be saved, if he would confess his firing a pistol at the Bishop of St Andrews, and wounding the Bishop of Glasgow; without which confession they could not have put him to death, notwithstanding which, they not only did make use of that confession to condemn him to death, but made oath before the Justiciary Court upon his trial and torture, that there was no such public faith given.

uncleanness, for his counselling and assisting the King in all his tyrannies, and endeavouring to overturn the true religion ; for his openly gaming on the Lord's Day ; and, finally, for his usual and ordinary cursing.

" Next, I do by the same authority, and in the same name, cast out of the true Church, and deliver up to Satan, John, Duke of Rothes, &c., for his perjuries in the aforesaid case of Mr Mitchell ; for his adulteries and uncleanness, and openly allotting the Lord's Day for the same ; for his openly professing and avowing his willingness and readiness to set up Popery in this land, at the King's command ; and for his barbarous and unheard-of cruelty to that worthy gentleman, David Hackston of Rathillet, whereof he was the chief author, contriver, and commander ; and, lastly, for his ordinary cursing, swearing, and drunkenness.

" Next, I do by the same authority, and in the same name, excommunicate, &c., Sir George Mackenzie, the King's advocate, for his apostacy in turning to a profligate conversation after he had begun a solemn profession of holiness ; for his constant pleading against, and persecuting to death, the servants of God, and alleging and laying to their charge things which in his conscience he knew to be against the word of God, against truth, reason, and the laws of this kingdom ; and, on the other hand, his pleading for sorcerers, murderers, and other criminals, that by the laws of God and man ought to have been put to death ; likewise for his ungodly, erroneous, fantastic, and blasphemous tenets published to the world in his pamphlets and pasquils.

" Lastly, I do by the same authority, and in the same name, excommunicate, &c., Thomas Dalziel of Bins, for his leading armies, and commanding the pillaging, oppressing, and cruelly murdering the Lord's people ; particularly for his commanding to shoot at Post —— Finlay, an innocent person, at New-Millus, without any form of law, civil or military—he not being guilty of any thing which they themselves counted a crime; likewise for his lewd and impious life, led in adultery and uncleanness from his youth, in a contempt of lawful wedlock, which is the ordinance of God; for his atheistical and irreligious life; and, lastly, for his unjust taking away and keeping possession of the estate of that worthy gentleman, William Muire of Caladol, and other injurious deeds in exercise of this power."

After he had pronounced the above sentences of excommunication, he went on to the purpose following. "I think," said he, "none that acknowledge the Word of God, the power deputed to his Church, and the reason and nature of that power, can judge this sentence to be unjust. The pretence of its being informal, without warnings, admonitions, &c., is fully answered, in that those men have placed themselves above the admonitions of ministers, have repelled all due warnings, and wickedly put to cruel deaths the servants and ministers of Christ, who have with freedom and boldness adventured to give them warnings and admonitions, and shut up all access from us that remain to do the like; and as for proof of the fact I have here charged upon them, it needeth not, the deeds being notour and known, and the most of them such as themselves do avow, and to their shame boast of. And as the causes are just, and such as for which the ministers of Christ have in all ages proceeded to the like sentence, so it being now done by a minister of the gospel, and in such a manner as the present circumstances of the Church of Christ, with respect to the present cruel persecution, will admit, the sentence likewise is undoubtedly just also; and there are no powers on earth, either of kings, princes, magistrates, or ministers of the gospel, can, without the repentance of the persons openly and legally appearing, reverse these sentences upon any such account. And as God, who is the author of that power, is the more engaged to the ratifying these sentences, so all that acknowledge the Word of God, and believe themselves subject to his government, ought also to acknowledge them.

" If any shall object, as we hear they do, that these proceedings, though not unjust, are foolish and rigorous, we answer with that word of Scripture, which we have much more reason to use than those of whom it is recorded—Genesis xxxiv. 31, ' Should he deal with our sister as with an harlot ? '   Should they deal with our God as with an idol ? should they deal with his people as with murderers and malefactors ? and shall we not draw out God's sword against God's enemies."

It is true that this action was the execration and aversion of those times, and of the sovereign that then reigned, and to their reproach it will be recorded, that two sorts of people blamed the Cameronians for running that length.   First, Their brethren of the Presbyterian Church, who temporised at that time, and not thinking themselves called to bear their testimony in such a manner against the persecutors ; or perhaps not being able to bear the fury of the prosecution, consented to receive the liberty of their worship by the indulgence of the King and the license of the bishops.   And, thirdly, The good people, as well Dissenters as others in England or elsewhere, who were ignorant not only of what those people suffered, but of the principles by which they acted, and who receiving their information in a partial or imperfect manner from their enemies only, or from the other people who joined not with them, never rightly understood their case, which ignorance, and consequently the prejudices that attended it, remains to this day.

As to the first, God has been pleased to convince most of those people that their suffering brethren were in the right ; and for the information of the second part, these memoirs are written.

I shall close this account of sufferers with two or three remarkable instances, as well of Christian con-

stancy in the persons suffering, as of the account given
by them of the reason of their then bearing their testimony against the power that then ruled.   And the
first is in the death of Mr John Nisbet, who was put
to death at Edinburgh, December 4. 1685, the first
year of the reign of King James VII.

The account of this gallant spirited gentleman
as well as courageous Christian, is thus faithfully
abridged by one of his near relations, who was an
eye witness to his sufferings.

In the year 1664, he had a child born, and refusing to let it be baptized by the parish curate or
Episcopal parson, he had it privately baptized by one
of the outed ministers,—the persecution being then
but newly begun, and very little blood shed on that
account.   The curate being enraged at this, published in his pulpit, that he would excommunicate
Mr Nisbet the next Lord's Day, and had done so, but
that the day before he was snatched away by death
suddenly.   When the persecuted people, in 1666,
met together at Lanark, and received the Covenant
at Lanark, his conscience summoned him to join with
them ; and being known and threatened with death
for that action, was obliged for his own safety to follow those people, and keep with them in arms.   At
the fight at Pentland he was sore wounded, stript as
dead, and left among the slain, but was preserved, and
made his escape.

At the insurrection at Bothwell, he joined with
the same people again, and fought openly and boldly
at the bridge—being not only a zealous Christian, but
a man of great bravery and resolution—as long as any
man would stand, and made his retreat, and escaped
falling into the enemy's hands for that time ; but
being known, was proscribed by proclamation, and a
large reward offered for apprehending him, his estate
and goods seized, and his wife and four children stript
of all and turned out of doors.

In this condition he was one of those who are
described in Hebrews xi. 38, " They wandered about
in deserts, and in mountains, and in dens and caves
of the earth ; of whom the world was not worthy."
And thus he lived, suffering, as we may say, all kinds
of distress, from the year 1679 to 1685, above six
years, not accepting deliverance, that he might preserve to himself the free enjoyment of the gospel
faithfully preached in the fields and hills ; whether
he and a select company, such as he was, came always
well armed, as well to defend themselves as to protect
their ministers and brethren from violence during the
worship of God, as occasion should present.   At
length, being retired to a poor man's house in the
parish of Tinnick, where they had used to be sheltered
in severe weather, it pleased God that they were seen,
and private information given ; so that before they
were aware the house was surrounded, and after a
very desperate resistance, in which he had received
seven wounds, they were all taken.   The lieutenant
of dragoons, who was of his own name, yet insulted
him, and treated him in a most barbarous manner.   First, he took his three friends who were prisoners with him, and shot them dead before his
face ; then coming to him, asked him what he
thought of himself now ?   He replied, " I think as
well of Christ and his cause as ever, and not at all
the worse for what I suffer ; and I only grieve that I
am left, and my dear brethren are gone to heaven
whom you have wickedly murdered." The bloody cruel
wretch replied with an oath, he should not be long
behind them, but he reserved him for worse punishment. He answered, " If the Lord stand by me, and
keep me faithful to death, I care not what sufferings
I am put to endure."   The lieutenant then bound
him cruelly, though bleeding at his wounds, and carried him to Kilmarnock, and from thence to Ayr,
where, by intercession of friends, a surgeon was allowed

to dress his wounds, after which he was carried to Edinburgh. It seems all this was done, that the lieutenant might have the reward published for apprehending him, otherwise he had been shot with the rest.

Being brought to Edinburgh he was brought before the bloody Council, where they asked him the questions following, and received short answers from him, such as barely shewed that he neither expected or sought any mercy at their hands. The questions were thus :—

Q. Was you at the field conventicle at ——— ? [Here they named the day and the place.]

A. Yes.

Q. How many men in arms had you there ?

A. I went there to hear the Gospel preached, and not to take an account of men or arms that might be there.

Q. Which way went you when the preaching was done ?

A. The best way we could to escape your cruelty.

Q. Where keep you the general meetings, and what do you at them ?

To this he answered he was not obliged to give an account, at which one of the council pretended he would do it for them, and made a long speech of what was done (though he gave a false account) at a general meeting near Edinburgh. Then they asked the prisoner if he was not there.

A. No.

Q. We hope you are so much of a Christian as to pray for the King.

A. Prayer is a holy ordinance of God, and we ought to pray for the King as well as for others, but not when every profligate commands us.

Q. Do you own the King as lawful and sole sovereign lord ?

A. He being Papist, and that from his youth, and

a Protestant of the Presbyterian covenanted persuasion, I neither can nor will own him while he remains such. If he repents and turns to God, I shall readily acknowledge him and obey him, and pray for him.

Upon these answers and without any further process they passed sentence of death upon him, which he received, says the relator of this story, not only with Christian submission but with thankfulness—blessing and praising God who had counted him worthy to suffer for his name. During the time of his imprisonment he was used very cruelly, having a merciless weight of irons upon him during the whole time ; yet he declared that he had a constant wonderful inward assistance and support from the good spirit of God, bearing him up under the cross, having both a comfortable assurance of the pardon of his sins, and a full satisfaction of the justness of the cause in which he suffered.

After this we need but conclude this work with an account of the last martyr who suffered in this cause, and this was a godly minister, to leave it upon record that as the first that died was a minister, viz. Mr James Guthrie, so was the last also, viz. Mr James Renwick.

There is another observation on the occasion of his death, viz. that he died the 17th of February 1688, the beginning of the same year of the Revolution, testifying that the Episcopal party never abated or relented—that they were never satiated with blood, but went on as long as they had power, even till they saw the very cloud hovering and the storm ready to break upon their heads ; nor had their thirst of blood been quenched to this day, or as long as there had been a faithful member of the Church of Scotland left alive, had their power lasted ; so that it was the end of their government put an end to their persecutions, and no clemency, pity, or compassion in them ; no such things were so much as named among them.

This observation puts me in mind of a brief story within the compass of my own knowledge of a gentleman who was set upon by a furious mastiff dog. The gentleman defended himself with a sword for some time, but the mastiff, after being very much wounded, got within his point and fastened on his arm. The gentleman being in great distress, and fearing every moment that he would quit his arm and fasten upon his throat, had no other way to master this great dog, but being a large heavy man he cast himself flat down upon the dog with his other elbow lying on the dog's breast, and thus with the weight of his body crushed the beast to death, and upon this he observed that as the dog died gradually under him, so fast and no faster his teeth loosened in his arm; his fury lasted with his life, and both ended together.

The whole story is applicable to the purpose in hand. The Church of Scotland was near worried by this cruel creature called prelacy, and very near she has to being taken by the throat and destroyed. But she fell at last upon the mastiff and crushed him to death; and as he died under her his teeth loosened, his bloody feud abated, and not one jot faster. The persecuting rage of Scots prelacy continued with its life, died when it died, and will revive, if ever it revives, of which we shall see some confirmation in the last part of this work.

Mr Renwick at his death hath this remarkable prophetic expression in his last speech, viz.—Do not fear that the Lord will cast off Scotland, for he will certainly return again, and show himself gracious in our land. This I quote here, though his last speech is also added at large in the next pages: I say this prophetic saying I quote here, because the fulfilling of this prophecy is the subject of the next part.

In this persecution, as has been collected from the accounts, both public and private, above 18,000 people have suffered the utmost extremities their enemies could inflict, of which the following particulars are a part, many of which can be proved even to the very names of the persons, with the places of their abode.

Seventeen hundred have been banished as slaves to the English plantations, besides such as were by order of the council, at the beginning of the persecution, ordered on pain of death to leave their country, which amounted to eighty-seven ; and besides above 750 banished to Shetland, to the Isles of Lewis, Orkney, and other remote places belonging to Scotland. Of these 200 were wilfully and premeditatedly murdered, by keeping them under hatches until they were drowned, when the ship was stranded, and there was time for them to escape, as is observed already.

Eight hundred were outlawed, as we call it in England, about the time of Pentland affair, by the order of the High Commission Court ; and fifty-five eminent persons were pannelled, as the Scots law terms it—that is, were prosecuted absent, and were sentenced to be executed without farther prosecution, when they should be taken, as many of them afterwards were. Among these were ten or eleven ministers, of which notice is taken before.

It is impossible to give an account of those who perished by unjust and tedious confinement in prisons by the barbarity of merciless jailors, stench of close and horrible dungeons and vaults, want of conveniences, crowding thirty or forty into little dark and damp rooms together, lying on the ground, extremity of cold and hunger, weight of chains, bolts, and irons, and the like. Besides this, great numbers, by the unhappy places where they were confined— such as the castles of Blackness, Dunnotter, Inverlochy, and the Bass—and by innumerable cruelties practised upon them in those places, contracted diseases, lost the use of limbs and senses, as sight, hearing, tasting, and some even of their understand-ings, but many more of their lives ; and those who think they have modestly computed the number of these—for an exact account cannot be had—tell us they amount to above 3600, including the 800 and the twenty-seven last-mentioned.

In the several actions, which their persecutors call rebellions, and the skirmishes which on those occasions, as also upon surprises or otherwise, have happened, there has been killed in the field about 560, as at Pentland, Bothwell, Aird-Moss, Queensferry, and other places, in defence of their meetings and personal defence of their lives, besides those who have died of wounds received on such occasions, which are reckoned to be about 120.

Those that have fled from their country into voluntary banishment have been yet a greater number. These made their way into England, Ireland, Holland, Sweden, and to any place whether necessity drove them for safety of their lives, and as opportunity of escape offered,—in which countries they were driven to great distress, such as want, cold, and hunger, having their lives given them indeed for a prey, but being perfectly destitute of friends, shelter, help, or relief, other than what God was pleased to raise them up by his providence and by the Christian charity of foreign Protestants.   The number of these have been estimated by such as think they have made a modest calculation at above 7000.

Of these, that I may do justice to the charity of every man and every sort of men, the cruelty they suffered at home and the extremities they suffered abroad were such as was even detested by Papists themselves ; and some of the suffering people have acknowledged they have met with compassion even among the Roman Catholics, who have expressed their astonishment that Protestants should exercise such inhumanities upon one another.   In England, also, they were often harboured, relieved, entertained, and

x

concealed even by some charitable people who were of themselves Episcopal, and members of the Estab. lished Episcopal Church, but who abhorred the cruelties and inhumanities of the Scots persecutors, and even abhorred the persecution itself.

Of those who went then into voluntary banishment, or, as it may be rather said, fled from the face of their bloody persecutors, very few ever returned again to Scotland, the number of years being such that age, together with the hardship of their sufferings, carried most of them off before the happy time of the deliverance of their country arrived.

Besides these there were abundance of innocent and pious sufferers, who were basely murdered by the soldiers and persecutors upon the occasions, and by the methods of which we have spoken, being generally killed in cold blood without process of law, civil or military, without visible crime, charge, or examination.   Of those the printed accounts tell us the names of seventy-eight murdered by particular persons, and I am well assured there were very many more, and have heard that a person, whom I have not met with, has the names of above 420 more, but that number I do not avouch.

The number really executed, in the pretended course of justice, and by the sentence of the cruel persecutors, and who died by the hangman, as I am credibly informed, is very great ; and I am told that about 362 are to be found on the several books of the justiciary and council courts upon record, besides what were executed by military laws, as they call them, of which no record has been kept.

The numbers of those who perished through cold, hunger, and other distresses, contracted in their flight into the mountains, wandering without shelter or harbour, in dreadful winters, during the long space of twenty-eight years' persecution, and who often came home in such extremities as just to step into their own houses to die, and some times were, even in the article of death, dispatched by the murdering soldiers; these were many thousands, and cannot be calculated, but will certainly make up more than the number of eighteen thousand, mentioned above.

Among these I say nothing of the pillage and spoil of goods, the turning women and children out into the field, in cold and nakedness, after devouring their food, and tearing off the clothes from their backs, of which many perished for want, and by the extremities of the weather.

It were also endless to number the families ruined and reduced to misery and want, which must be the consequence of the plunderings and murders mentioned above; so that it should be wondered rather that any of those people were left, or that there were any found at the Revolution, though, to the honour of truth, it must be owned that at the Revolution their number was found to be greater than ever. Witness their raising a regiment of 800 men in one day, without beat of drum, for the guard of the Convention, and for the service of their Protestant King, which regiment was composed of men, as serious in religion towards God, as resolute in arms for their King and country, and were eminent in the army for preserving the worship of God among them, for which they were called in derision the Psalm-singing regiment.   Their noble Colonel, the Earl of Angus, was killed at the fight at Steenkirk, where the regiment behaved with such gallantry that the King himself gave testimony of their bravery, and is still in being in the army, having lately given another happy instance of their behaviour at Preston, where great part of them were slain, and where, if they had not behaved with an uncommon resolution, the rebels had not been reduced as they were.

All the accounts given of those things are filled with the last speeches of the dying people, which the brevity of these memoirs does not allow, nor the design of them make needful. However, as I promised, I have closed the scene with the dying speech of one Mr James Renwick, whose tragedy closed the persecution; for he was not only the last minister, but the last man they had power to put to death, and it is as follows :—

" Spectators (or if there be any of you), auditors, I must tell you that I come here this to lay down my life for adhering to the truths of Christ, for which I am neither afraid nor ashamed to suffer; nay, I bless the Lord that ever he counted me worthy, or enabled me to suffer any thing for him. And I desire to praise his grace, that he hath not only kept me free from the gross pollutions of the time, but also from many ordinary pollutions of children, and, such as I have been stained with, he hath washed me from them in his own blood. I am this day to lay down my life for these three things. (1.) For disowning the usurpations and tyranny of James, Duke of York; (2.) For preaching that it was unlawful to pay the cess, expressly exacted for bearing down the gospel; (3.) For preaching that it was lawful for people to carry arms, for defending themselves in their meetings for the persecuted gospel ordinances. I think a testimony for these is worth many lives, and if I had ten hundred I would think it little enough to lay them all down for the same.

" Dear friends, spectators, and (if any of you be) auditors, I must tell you that I die a Presbyterian Protestant. I own the Word of God as the rule of faith and manners. I own the Confession of Faith, Larger and Shorter Catechisms, Sum of Saving Knowledge, Directory for Worship, &c., Covenants, National and Solemn League, Acts of General Assemblies, and all the faithful contendings that have been for the work of Reformation. I leave my testimony approving the preaching of the gospel in the

fields, and the defending the same by arms.   I ad-
join my testimony to all that hath been sealed by
blood, shed either on scaffolds, fields, or seas, for the
cause of Christ.   I leave my testimony against Popery, Prelacy, Erastianism, &c.   Against all profanity, and every thing contrary to sound doctrine,
particularly against all usurpations made upon Christ's
rights, who is the prince of the kings of the earth, who
alone must bear the glory of ruling his own kingdom,
the Church, and, in particular, against the absolute
power usurped by this usurper, that belongs to no
mortal, but is the incommunicable prerogative of Je-
hovah, and against this toleration flowing from that
absolute power."

Upon this he was bid have done.   He answered,
" I have near done."   Then he said, " Ye that are
the people of God do not weary in maintaining the
testimony of the day in your stations and places ; and
whatever ye do make sure of an interest in Christ,
for there is a storm coming that shall try your foundation.   Scotland must be rid of Scotland before the
delivery come.   And you that are strangers to God
break off your sins by repentance, else I will be a witness against you in the day of the Lord."   Here they
caused him to desist.   Upon the scaffold he sung a
part of the 103d Psalm from the beginning, and read
the 19th chapter of the Revelation.   And having
thus finished his course, served his generation, and
witnessed a good confession for his Lord and master,
before many witnesses, by the will of God he yielded
up his spirit into the hands of God who gave it, being
the last that sealed the testimony of this suffering
period in a public way upon a scaffold.

PART IV.

THE CHURCH IN HER PRESENT STATE.

~~~~~~~~

We are now happily come to the end of this me-
lancholy part, and the Church of Scotland having now
gone through a long series of trouble and affliction,
began to see a glimpse of that glorious deliverance
which was approaching. The tyrannic and illegal
attempts upon the religion and liberties of the English nation, as well as of the Scots, began to stir up
that nation to think of preserving themselves from
destruction ; and having applied themselves to the
Prince of Orange for assistance, that glorious person
began to listen to their proposal, and to make preparations for his coming into England.

In the deliverance that followed, the Church of
Scotland found her deliverance also ; for, in the death
of civil tyranny, Christian liberty revived.

The history of the coming of the Prince of Orange
to the English throne is perfectly and fully related
in so many histories, is recent in the memory of all
people at the writing hereof, and probably will still
be on so many subsequent occasions preserved to posterity, that, as it does not immediately relate to our
present memoirs, so also I need not enter upon an account of it here, other than what is absolutely necessary to the story I am relating.

It is also well known, that this glorious Prince,
having finished the deliverance of the English nation,
resolved the same should extend to Scotland ; and

that, as it is expressed in his déclaration, religion should be settled in Scotland in such a manner as was most agreeable to the inclinations of the people, from whence, and in the consequence of which, we shall soon see many useful observations most naturally drawn, pertinent to the case now before us, and which I see all have great occasion to make mention of again in the process of these memoirs.

1. But as it has been already made plain in the first part of these memoirs, that the beginning of the Reformation in Scotland and the first Reformers of Scotland were Presbyterian, and that Episcopacy sprung up there but from the degeneracy of the Reformation, so it will, now that the inclination of the people of Scotland ran with an irresistible torrent into Presbyterianism again at the Revolution, as it had always done when it was left in the choice of the people, and that as at the Revolution aforesaid, it was left to the nation by the Prince of Orange, to settle religion in such manner as was most desired by the people, not a dog wagged his tongue against the Presbyterian Establishment, not a mouth gave a vote for Episcopacy ; nor was it so much as named to the King as a question, whether the inclination of the people was for Episcopacy or Presbytery, insomuch that the King was often heard to say afterwards, that he wondered much what was become of the Episcopal party, seeing no man at the Revolution so much as named the word Episcopacy to him, nor had the party any one to speak for them, or one word to speak for themselves.

How they could since that have the face to say, especially as they often did to the late Queen, that they were superior in number to the Presbyterians, and that, if the people of Scotland were left free to vote, they would carry it for Episcopacy—I say, how they could say thus, would be strange to any that did not know how that party have on all occa-

sions made such things their refuge, and the refuge
of their prelatic hierachy; and the author of these
memoirs is thankful, that even at the time they did
so, he had the honour, in behalf of the Church of
Scotland, to let her late Majesty know how untrue
that suggestion was, and to convince her ministry
how grossly those men endeavoured to impose upon
England in that case, as they did, at the same time,
in their boast of the people receiving the English service-book with willingness in Scotland, which her
Majesty was afterwards fully satisfied was a cheat,
and done only to amuse the English clergy, and get
money of them.

2. It is observable in the Revolution, that the
people of Scotland came all into the principles of the
suffering sincere party; the suffering party kept their
own footing, and did not go over to them. Those
that had through fear, or from time-serving principles,
or for want of zeal, or for any other weak reason,
consented, and, as I may call it, taken so low a step
as to accept of licences from God's enemies to serve
Christ—asking leave of men to worship God—a duty
and debt which they had a natural and divine right
to, without bowing the knee to Baal for it—I say,
these, far from justifying or recommending the
practice, openly recognised the zeal, courage, and
sincerity of the sufferers, honoured them for it, and
rather desired to bury their own compliances in silence and forgetfulness than to have it mentioned or
remembered.

3. Now it was seen, and made plain to the world,
that the suffering people in Scotland acted upon no
principles of enthusiasm, blind zeal, or religious frenzy
as their enemies suggested; that they were no enemies to monarchy, civil government, order of society,
and the like, as had been scandalously said; but that
they kept strictly to the rule of God's Word, adhered
to an honest cause, and acted upon just principles;

and when such Kings were called to the throne as
desired to rule for God and the good of the people,
who made the laws of God and man the rule of their
government, and the prosperity of religion, and of
their subjects, the end of it, they knew how to obey,
serve, and defend such princes with their blood and
treasure, as well as they had courage to resist and
reject those who, with the breach of faith, honour,
or constitution, became tyrants and persecutors—
enemies to God and destroyers of men, as their former princes had been.

This is evident by their practice at the Revolution,
in that no sooner was our Prince of Orange landed in
England, and the enemies of our constitution began
to stagger, but these people immediately took arms,
and successfully chased the bloody party out of their
country. But when this was done, what measures
did they take? Did they run into any enthusiasm?
Did they set up King Jesus as a temporal prince, and
the fifth monarchy in his name? Did they preach
the doctrine of dominion founded on grace, or form
schemes of republican government? Did they erect
themselves as tyrants in the room of those they pulled
down, so making the people change their masters,
not their yoke? No, no; they adhered to the legal
constitution of their country; they submitted cheerfully to the return of magistracy and the free course
of the laws of their country; they armed themselves
and came up to Edinburgh at their own charge,
formed themselves into companies—indeed they were
able to have formed a considerable army—and offered
themselves to march to any part of the nation against
the Popish and Jacobite party; and especially they offered, and were accepted, and admitted to guard the
Convention of Estates against the attempt of the
Duke of Gordon, who at that time commanded a
Popish garrison in the Castle of Edinburgh, and
against all of any denomination that should attempt

to disturb them ; and, to the eternal honour of the wild, antimonarchical, enthusiastic, lunatic Cameronians, for so their enemies had called them, they were the first men in Scotland that addressed or petitioned the Convention of Estates to place the crown of Scotland on the head of their deliverer William, which was done accordingly—to the restoring of religion, healing the breaches of Scotland, and the utter confusion of their persecutors, of whom I shall have more to say presently.

I cannot give a better account of this than in their own words : First, of their Declaration, or Memorial of their Grievances, and then their Petition itself. At the end of the said memorial of grievances we have them concluding thus, the repetition of which will appear very pertinent to the case in hand, viz. to prove their willing adhering to legal and religious governors and government. Their words are these—viz. : " We are represented by our enemies as antipodes to all mankind, enemies to government, and incapable of order ; but as their order and cause is, *toto diametro*, opposite to the institutions and cause of Christ, so they must have little wit, and less honesty, who believe and receive those notions, and the reproaches of those who were as great rebels and enemies to the present government as we avowed ourselves to be to the last. Our sufferings for declining the yoke of tyranny and Popish usurpation are already hinted, and are generally known ; and all that will examine and consider our conduct since the King began his heroic undertaking to redeem these nations from Popery and slavery, will be forced to acknowledge that we have given as good evidence of our being willing to be subject to King William as we gave before of our being unwilling to be slaves to King James. Upon the first report of the Prince of Orange's expedition, we owned his quarrel, even while the Prelatic faction were in arms to oppose his coming. In all our meetings we prayed openly for the success of his arms, when in all the churches the prayers were for his ruin. Nay, and note even in the indulged meetings they prayed for the Popish tyrant, who we prayed against, and who the Prince came to oppose. We also associated ourselves early, binding ourselves to promote his interest, and were the first who openly owned and declared our desire to join with him, and this when the others were associating with and for his enemies. In order to make good our declared intention upon the false alarm of Kirkcudbright being burned, we had recourse to arms, and modelled ourselves into a body and into distinct companies, whereby we were in readiness to offer our assistance; and did offer, and had the honour done us to be accepted, and admitted to guard the honourable Convention of Estates against all the attempts of the Popish and persecuting party under the Duke of Gordon, Viscount of Dundee, or other enemies whatsoever; after which, understanding that the Government required the raising forces for its defence against the threatened insurrections and foreign invasions of King James VII., we no sooner heard thereof than we offered ourselves to raise a regiment for his majesty's service, and accordingly made up the Earl of Angus's regiment of 800 men all in one day, without beat of drum or expense of levy-money, having first only concerted and concluded such conditions with the Lieutenant-Colonel Cleland, a gallant gentleman and Christian soldier, as were necessary to clear our consciences, and to secure liberty and safety, viz. :—

"1. That all the officers should be men of conscience, honour, of approved fidelity, well affected, of sober conversation, and such as had never before served the enemy in pulling down that cause they were now to defend.

"2. That the service they should now be employed in, should be under the King's majesty, for defence of the nation, the recovery and preservation of the Protestant religion, and, in particular, the work of Reformation in Scotland, in opposition to Popery, Prelacy, and tyranny."

Upon these terms the regiment was raised, and they offered to complete two or three regiments more, if his Majesty had occasion. " But," says the same memorial, " before we offered to be soldiers, we first made an offer to be subjects ; and because we did not look upon ourselves as subjects to the late King, who treated us as enemies, we made therefore a voluntary tender of our subjection to our deliverer in a peculiar petition, the tenor whereof follows :

" To the meeting of the Estates of the kingdom of Scotland, viz., the noblemen, barons, and burgesses lawfully called and chosen, now assembled at Edinburgh, for establishing the government, restoring and securing the true religion, laws, and liberties of the said kingdom :

" The humble petition of the poor people, who have suffered grievous persecution for their religion, and for their revolt from and disowning the authority of King James VII., pleading for devolving the government upon the Prince of Orange, now King of England,

Sheweth, &c.,

[Waving, for brevity sake, the long introduction and recital of the sufferings of Scotland, under the reign and tyranny of King James the VII., they go on thus :]

" We prostrate ourselves yet under the sorrowing smart of our still bleeding wounds at your honours' feet, who have a call, a capacity, and we hope a heart, to heal us ; and we offer this our petition, enforced, and conjuring your honours to hearken to us.

" By all the formerly felt, presently seen, and for the future feared effects and efforts of Popery and tyranny.

" By the cry of the blood of our murdered brethren.

" By the sufferings of the banished free-born subjects of this realm, now groaning in servitude, being sold into slavery in the English plantations of America.

" By the miseries that many thousands, forfeited, disinherited, harassed, and wasted houses and families have been reduced to.

" By all the sufferings of a faithful people, for adhering to the ancient covenanted establishment of religion and liberty.

" And by all the arguments of justice, necessity, and mercy, that ever could join together to begin communication among men of wisdom, piety, and virtue.

" Humbly beseeching, requesting, and craving of your honours, now when God hath given you this opportunity to act for his glory, the good of the Church, of the nation, your own honour, and the happiness of posterity. Now when this kingdom, the neighbouring, and all the nations of Europe, have their eyes upon you, expecting you will acquit yourselves like the representatives of a free nation, in redeeming it from slavery, otherwise inevitable, following the example of your renowned ancestors, and the patron of the present Convention and Parliament in England. That you will proceed without any delay to declare the late wicked Government dissolved, the crown and throne vacant, and James VII., whom we never have owned, and resolved, in conjunction with many thousands of our countrymen, never again to own, to have really forfeited and rightly to be deprived of all right and title he ever had or could ever pretend to have thereto, and to provide that it may never be in the power of any succeeding ruler to aspire unto, or arise to such a capacity of tyranizing. Morever, since anarchy and tyranny are equally to be detested, and the nation cannot subsist without a governor;* as

* Note here the justice of their principles as to government, and how entirely free they are from all that they have been charged with, as to refusing lawful subjection to just powers, or being of Commonwealth principles, enemies to Monarchy, and such like.

also that none can have a nearer right or fitter qualifications than his illustrious highness the Prince of Orange,* whom the most high has singularly owned and honoured to be our deliverer from Popery and slavery. We cry, therefore, to your honours, and crave that King William, now proclaimed King of England, may be chosen and proclaimed also King of Scotland; and that the legal authority may be devolved upon him, with such necessary provisions and limitations as may give just and legal securities for the peace and purity of religion, the stability of our laws, privileges of Parliament, and liberties of the people, civil and ecclesiastic, and may thereby make our subjection both a clear duty and a comfortable happiness."

[Here they enlarge upon the King's being obliged to profess and preserve the pure religion and the work of Reformation, and conclude thus:]

"Upon such terms as these, we render our allegiance to King William, and hope to give more pregnant proofs of our loyalty to his Majesty in adverse as well as prosperous providences than they have done or can do, who profess implicit subjection to absolute authority, so long only as providence preserves its grandeur.

"May it therefore please your honours," &c.

From this time forward till the Union, we scarce ever heard of the Cameronians. Their separation before was evident from just reasons, their not complying with indulged liberty, accepting that from their enemies which was their native right, and by which they must recognise the right and superiority of Episcopal jurisdiction, which they abhorred—this was all founded on conscience and in just exceptions; but when upon

---

* Here it is evident they preserved the principles of the Crown's lineal descent, as well as that of a monarchical government, and perhaps were always as true to the doctrine of hereditary right as they who have made such great stir about it, could do.

the Revolution, and upon King William's establishing their ancient liberty, and that Episcopacy was deposed, as we shall see presently. They appeared to be all one united body of Presbyterians, one Church, under one religious government and administration, the same in opinion, the same in doctrine, discipline, worship, and government, having fewer breaches, fewer divisions, fewer fallings off to a differing opinion, than any Protestant Church in the world.

It remains then that our memoirs give a brief account of the restoration of the Church upon this great turn of affairs, and this shall be done so concisely, and with such regard to what has been made public already on other occasions, that I hope none shall think their time lost in looking back, or think the relation a vain repetition.

According to the prayer of the above petition, King William was declared King of Scotland, the crown was tendered to him, and accepted by him in form, in conjunction with Queen Mary. The act of tender, the claim of right, the King's acceptance, with his Majesty's letter to the meeting of Estates concerning his accepting the crown, and the remarkable oaths taken by the King and Queen on that occasion, are all to be found in the Collection of Public Acts of Scotland, vol. iii, p. 147, 153, 156, 159, 187. As soon as these things were done, the Convention of Estates were turned into a Parliament, and from thenceforward began to act as the public Legislature of the nation. I say no more of the particulars, because they are to be found in all the histories of that time; but it is to our present purpose to note that therewith persecution entirely ceased, Episcopacy sunk into its primitive state of obscurity, the persecutors fled on all hands from justice, the banished and proscribed, such as were left alive, returned to their families, friends, and native country. Religion now began to hold up its head, the godly persecuted ministers and people shewed their faces, and possessed the seat of their enemies.

The first act of Parliament (after that for turning the Convention into a Parliament, and another to recognise the King's authority) was the act for abolishing Episcopacy. This makes it abundantly clear that the general bent and inclination of the people was for Presbytery, and that Episcopacy was their aversion ; for that the very first act after consti<sub>tuting the civil Government was this of abolishing the lesiastic Government—I say the first, because as there were but two acts which passed before it, one for turning the meeting into a Parliament, the other for recognising the King's authority—it is evident without these they could not have acted at all, and therefore the act for abolishing Prelacy may be said to be the first act they made, after the power of acting was confirmed.

The act for abolishing Prelacy is very remarkable, and cannot be omitted without manifest defect in our work. It is as follows :—

" Act for Abolishing Prelacy, July 22d. 1689.

" Whereas the Estates of this kingdom in their claim of right, of the 11th of April last, declared that Prelacy and the superiority of any office in the Church, about presbyters, is and hath been a great and insupportable grievance to this nation, and contrary to the inclination of the generality of the people ever since the Reformation, they having reformed from Popery by presbyters, and therefore ought to be abolished. Our sovereign lord and lady the King and Queen's majesty, with advice and consent of the estates of Parliament, do hereby abolish Prelacy and all superiority of any office in the Church of this kingdom above presbyters ; and hereby rescinds cases, and annuls the 1st act, 2d sess., the first Par. Cha. II. ; and the 2d act, 3d sess., 1st Par. Cha. II. ; and the 4th act, 3d Par. Cha. II.; and all other acts, statutes, and constitutions, in so far allanerly as they are inconsistent with this act, and do abolish Prelacy, or the superiority of church-officers above presbyters; and do declare that they, with the advice and consent of the estates of this Parliament, will settle by law that church government in this kingdom which is most agreeable to the inclinations of the people.

This was a short session, the meeting requiring nothing of public business at that time but those three necessary acts. They met again in April, and then the second act passed was to do justice to the poor persecuted suffering ministers who had been driven out by the fury of the late times. By this act all the ministers who had been so driven away, or, as the law expresses it, thrust from their churches, from the 1st of January 1661 to that time, should be forthwith admitted and allowed free access to their churches, from which they were so thrust out, that so they might presently exercise their ministry in their several parishes without any new call, and the present incumbents are ordered to give place to them, and remove themselves.

This was not persecution, as some would have stiled it, but restoring the persecuted and removing intruders, for they were no other; and this was previous to any church settlement, because it was no more than putting the injured men into possession of their legal right. All this while Episcopacy held its possession in general, though its government was dissolved.

But the fifth act of the same session of Parliament laid the axe to the root of the tree. This was that famous act entituled "For ratifying the Confession of Faith and settling Presbyterian Church government." The law itself is too long to be reprinted here; it is to be found in the Collection of Acts, vol. iii. page 206 to 234.

As the government of the Church was now restored, so were her judicatories of course, and at this time

Y

began the first free General Assembly, which for eight and twenty years had not been seen in Scotland. It is needless here to enter into the detail of the acts of assembly, which are all to be found in the registers of the Church ; it is enough to our purpose to record that now the Church was restored to the full and free exercise of her just and legal authority, the judicatures were erected in their proper places, such as kirk-sessions, presbytery, synod, and assembly, and all ecclesiastical justice ran in its proper channel.

Before I go on to what has since happened, in consequence of this revolution in the Church, it will be necessary to say something here to that challenge which some have been very forward to bring against the Church of Scotland, as if she were also of persecuting principles, and had exercised the same coersion in point of conscience in her turn which she had condemned in others. This they have carried on even to the charge of cruelty and persecution in the treatment and usage of the Episcopal ministers who were dispossessed by those two acts, viz., of abolishing Prelacy, and settling Presbyterian church government.

This charge consists of two parts, in clearing up both which the honour and character of the Church of Scotland will not only be vindicated, but the injustice and indeed the ingratitude of the Episcopal people, who have brought this charge, will very much appear, and a quite contrary behaviour will be made out to have been the practice of the present government.

1. The first respects the conduct of the people when they took up arms in a tumultuous manner at the beginning of the Revolution.

2. The next respects the judicial proceedings against the Episcopal party since, in both which there needs no more for the vindication of the Church than that the truth of fact should be impartially stated.

As to the first it is true, that as soon as the news

came to Scotland that the Prince of Orange was landed with an army in England, and that King James was not able to maintain his ground—the people of England inclining to a general revolt—the people in the West of Scotland, for they were the first, ran immediately to arms, and declared for the Prince of Orange. This was done with so universal a resolution, and the consternation the other people were in at the general face of things was such, at the same time, that there was no capacity or even disposition to oppose them.

In this general defection from the Government, the western people not only took arms, as is said, but ran in a tumultuous manner, first upon the Church affairs, for there it was that the oppressions of the former times had been most sensibly felt. In this first fury it cannot be wondered that they dispossessed the Episcopal ministers (curates, as they called them) of their Churches, and, restoring the old worship, caused their own banished persecuted ministers to come and preach among them; but the nature of all such rabbles considered, and above all the sufferings and provocation of those poor people, and of which I have given some account, being duly weighed, it must be confessed to be wonderful that any kind of violence was forborne: not that I allow it was just to have committed them; but how could less have been expected from a people so treated as they had been, when they were thus perfectly let loose to their own resentments.

Yet we do not find that the utmost violence complained of amounts to any more than an over-hasty turning the said Episcopal ministers out of the parsonage houses, which it was their opinion were unlawfully possessed, and some injurious hurrying their goods out with them, and this but to a few; but as to any personal injury, such as wounding or killing of any, I do not find that any such thing is charged upon them.

On the other hand, when we reflect how many must be among those rabbles who had suffered deeply in the persecution I have spoken of, who had lost fathers, mothers, children, husbands, wives, and the dearest of remoter relations in that persecution, and could not be without the warmest resentment; add to this, that some of those ministers or curates who they were then dispossessing had dipped their hands too much in the persecution of those poor sufferers; I say, if these things were duly considered, what can be said but that it was next to miraculous that an ungoverned multitude, left to the full vent of their own rage, and that rage grounded upon such just provocation, should have left any of them alive; and I cannot think it any breach of charity to say, it is very probable had the parties been changed it would have been quite otherwise.

And though any tumultuous violences are not justifiable in a civilized Christian nation, yet the conduct of these people at that time, with their provocations and circumstances considered, is a great testimony of the moderation of the Presbyterians in Scotland. The Scripture makes this an extraordinary case, 1 Sam. xxiv. 19, "If a man find his enemy, will he let him go well away?" Yet when the Presbyterian people in Scotland had their enemy in their hands, for so at this time they had, they left their revenge to Him to whom vengeance belongs; and contenting themselves with putting it out of the power of their enemies to do any more mischief for the time to come, they meddled not with punishing them for what was past.

But supposing those rabbles did commit some violences, as to plunder, and as to personal rudeness to the ministers, &c., who they turned out, which yet I have not met with any account of, this is fully answered in a book formerly written on that subject, in these words:—

" What's this to the Church ? It might be done by Presbyterians of the Church, but it can never be said it was ever done by the Presbyterians as a Church. It was done by no act of the Church, no, nor of the Government ; nor did either the Church or the Government ever approve, justify, or employ any of the persons. * * * 'Tis true, there was no public punishing the actors, neither did the Government in England punish, neither was it a time to punish those excesses ; and particularly the Government in England thought fit, by Parliament, so far to bear with them, as to stop all process against trespasses, &c.

" There is also another unhappy circumstance that so effectually clears the Church of this charge, that I cannot but wonder the party could ever make use of it as an argument, or bring this matter of rabbling into the charge, and that is, that these tumults, plunderings, and driving away the Episcopal ministers were all done and over before there was any such thing as a Presbyterian Church, I mean established, or in any power to act as a judicatory, or as a body ; so that to charge the Church with this, is like indicting a man for a murder committed before he was born."*

This, I think, may serve to clear up the first head —viz., the conduct of the rabble, &c.

I come next to the general proceedings of the Church of Scotland as a Church after their restoration, or new Establishment. How they were settled by act of Parliament has been already observed. It remains to enquire how they acted when settled, and whether either the civil government or church government can be justly charged with persecution.

" It could not be expected but that, upon the Revolution, the prelatic tyranny would fall with the

---

* Presbyterian Persecution, p. 9, 10.

regal; and, were it worth examining into, it would be easy to prove there was an inevitable necessity it should do so, they being so effectually supported one by another, that they could not but stand and fall together.

"That the conjunct tyranny of both Church and State had treated the Presbyterians with such an impolitic fury, as must imply they had not the least apprehension of being ever pulled down again by them, is very evident from the particulars which make up the former part of these memoirs." But to return to the history.

The bishops being deposed, and the Presbyterian government and discipline restored in the Church, the first thing the Assembly went upon was to consider of planting ministers in the vacant churches; for it could not be but that in eight and twenty years of cruelty and blood which they had suffered under, and which I have given some account of in these memoirs, a great number of the ancient ministers were fallen; besides that, even the length of time would, by the course of nature, carry a great many off the stage. And so it was, even to such a degree that it was at first not very easy to find ministers to supply churches from which the Episcopal ministers or curates were necessarily to be removed.

And here again the pretence of persecution is brought as a plea against the displacing those incumbents who would not qualify themselves according to law, but neither will it hold in this case neither. (See the words of the same author upon the same subject, where he gives the following brief history of the first step taken in this case :)

The government, says he, was no sooner established by the Revolution, and the Kirk restored to her judicatorial authority, but her several courts, as session, presbytery, synod, and assembly, took their courses, and began to act.

By the first act of Parliament for settling these matters, past June 7. 1690, intituled, " Act ratifying the Confession of Faith, and settling Presbyterian Church government," it is ordained "That the General Asembly, the ministers and elders, should have power to try and purge out all insufficient, scandalous, and erroneous ministers, by due course of ecclesiastical process and censures." But this act no where empowered them to censure any who were not insufficient, scandalous, or erroneous, though they would not take the oaths to the government. So that by this law the Church could not be capable of persecution.

It may be objected here, that to be episcopal might be adjudged erroneous by this judicatory, and so come under the Church censure by authority of this act.

To this it is replied—*First*, In fact no man was ever since the Revolution deposed by the Church merely for being episcopal, nor was any process ever commenced against any man on that foundation.

Secondly, It was particularly declared by the first General Assembly after the Revolution, viz., in the sixth session, in the year 1690, " That this Assembly will depose no incumbents simply for their judgment anent the government of the Church, and urge reordination upon them." Vide Index to the unprinted acts of the Assembly, sess. 6, 1690.

In the same Assembly, in their instructions given to their Commission, which was to sit during their recess, we have these words :—

" That they be very cautious of receiving informations against the late conformists, and that they proceed in the matter of censure very deliberately, so as none may have just cause to complain of their rigidity ; and that they shall not proceed to censure, but upon relevant libels and sufficient probation." Act 15th, sess. 26th, Assembly 1690.

Again, lest the Presbyterians should be rash and severe, the Commission is empowered as follows :—

" That if they shall be informed of any precipitant procedure of the Presbyterians in such processes, to restrain them." Vide the same act as above.

If, then, they were thus moderate even in scandalous things, and declared against proceeding in cases merely episcopal, where shall we find the article of persecution ?

It is true that in the year 1693, an act of Parliament was made to deprive all such ministers as would not both swear to the government, and acknowledge the Church government also, and the Confession of Faith. But the occasion of this act is visible to all that know the affairs of that time, viz., that it was passed to satisfy the minds of the people, who were exceedingly disturbed at the Churches having been insulted in the Assembly 1692, by a general formula, procured by the Episcopal clergy, together with their appeal to the King on a refusal ; and the Assembly being abruptly dissolved, or dismissed *sine die*, which put the nation into a very great ferment.

Yet, even upon this act, I may challenge the Episcopal clergy to show me one minister that ever was deposed for not acknowledging the Church, if, at the same time, he offered to acknowledge the government and take the oaths ; and they have been often challenged on this head. And to confirm this lenity of practice by a law, that famous act of Parliament was made in the year 1695, wherein taking the oaths to the government is made the only and fully sufficient qualification, and all ministers that would so qualify themselves are continued ; as may be seen at large by the act, intituled, " Act concerning the Church, anno 1695."

This very act of Parliament, if I were to go no further, effectually clears the Church of Scotland from the charge of persecution ; since it is plain there was no religious tenet in dispute, but a civil question of owning or not owning the government.

It was by this act of Parliament taken quite out of the power of the Church to depose any man merely for being episcopal in principle, or for refusing to own the Presbyterian Church. Nay, the Episcopal clergy, who, by virtue of this act, remain in their livings, many of them to this day refuse to acknowledge the Church, to submit to any of her judicatories, or to join either in discipline or worship.

How impossible it is then to be true that the Presbyterian Church has been guilty of persecution, I leave to any impartial reader to judge; adding withal what was published in the same case, viz., that there was at the time of the Union one hundred and sixty-five Episcopal ministers then possessing churches and stipends in Scotland by the lenity and forbearance of the government, who had no other qualification required of them than the taking the oaths to the government, and were not bound to, neither did they comply with or submit to the Presbyterian Church; and a list of their names has been published, and of the parishes in which they reside. Nay, in several parishes where these Episcopal ministers are incumbent, the Presbyterians are at the expense to have a minister of their own, whom they maintain, and who preaches in a meeting-house at their own private expense. Take the case in the words formerly published thus.

It would be pleasant for people who charge the Church of Scotland with persecuting the Episcopal clergy, to go to some of these parishes and see this uncouth jest, where the persecuting established Church is fain to submit to a meeting-house, and the persecuted Episcopal clergymen insults them from the parish church, and keeps both the pulpit and the stipend in spite of them all. Here is the Established Church turned Dissenter, and the Dissenter made the incumbent; the persecutor become persecuted, and, *per contra*, the persecuted made the persecutor.

Thus the Church has re-obtained her establishment, and here she may be said to be arrived at the full extent of her militant state, flourishing in peace and the wounds of her afflicted state healing apace.

It remains as a proper close to this work, that something should be said concerning this despised persecuted Church in general; a body of Christians placed thus, as it were, in the remotest part of the world, in whom, however, God has been pleased so eminently to appear, and for whom to do such great things as has been here related.

Now she enjoyed her full establishment, I mean just before the Union. After the Union, no attempt that Episcopacy could make upon her could overthrow her settlement without overthrowing at the same time the whole constitution of Great Britain. What attempts have been made upon her during the interest which her enemies had in the administration at the latter end of the last reign, have rather scratched her face than touched her vitals, and have rather shewed their design than their power. Whether she will obtain that justice to have those injuries redressed now the whole government is restored, I cannot yet say, nor does it relate to the present part of this work.

Her government, discipline, and worship, are established now by treaty, and have the assent of an Episcopal Church and nation as a sanction to it. The act for her security is incorporated into, and made a part of, the Act of Union; and the establishing the Church of Scotland is there called the establishing the true Protestant religion.

I know but two things which the Church of Scotland can be said to complain of, or to ask more than was at this time granted to her; and those, there is some reason to fear, she never will obtain; but as they are not essential to religion itself, I shall not lay too great a stress upon them.

1. That the revenues of the Church, I mean of the archbishops and bishops, deans, chapters, &c., when they were deposed and Episcopacy abolished, were not appropriated to the uses of the Church, as indeed they ought to have been, but divided, like the spoil of the Revolution, among the nobility and gentry. Had this been done, there had been a fund for the service of the Church, which would have been sufficient to have answered several wants, which, in default of this supply, she feels the effects of, viz. :—

1. There had been a supply for supporting students in the colleges for the study of divinity, and to have enlarged the stipends of the regents or tutors in the said colleges, which were at that time very low, and not suitable to the labour and application requisite in those offices. The latter was so evident, that the late queen was pleased to add considerably out of her own purse, as an increase of salary, amounting in the whole, as I have heard, to about £300 per annum.

2. There had been a fund to increase the stipends of ministers in remote parishes, where they were too small, to encourage the incumbents and support their families in waiting upon their work.

3. There would have been a fund to have bred up ministers to act as missionaries for the Highlands, to study the Irish language, and qualify themselves to go into the remotest parts to instruct the poor ignorant families of the Highlanders, and to support them in such a work—a thing attempted since the Union, by a general subscription for the propagating Christian knowledge, but I do not find the success answers the goodness of the design.

4. There would have been a fund to have answered the common incidents of the Church, such as sending up ministers to London to solicit redress of grievances, upon any occasion, and for every public transaction with the Court. Or, which were very desirable for

the maintaining an agent constantly at London to take care of their interests, to present their addresses, recommend their concerns, and, in a word, to manage their affairs; all which they are now obliged either to want assistance in, or the ministers who do come up as agents on extraordinary occasions are obliged to bear their own charges, which is a hardship many of them may not be very well furnished to bear.

2. Another thing they complain of, is the want of the sanction of civil power to enforce ecclesiastic discipline and censure; for want of which obstinate offenders are often encouraged to stand out in scandal and in wicked practices, and refuse to submit to the sentences of the Church, however just, righteous, and moderate. This is one reason why the nobility and gentry very often live in defiance of ecclesiastic judicatures and process, even in the professed and avowed commission of flagrant crimes, such as blasphemous swearing, open drunkenness, fornication, and even adultery itself; whereas, were the civil magistrate obliged to assist in the execution of Church sentences, no man would then be above reproof and punishment in just cases.

But as I said before, these things do not at all break in upon the Church, either in her doctrine, or in the liberty of her worship; they may, indeed, affect the establishment of her discipline, though not much, so that by the Treaty of Union it is to be hoped her last struggle with Episcopacy is at an end, and she may now be able to say that not only she is arrived to her full-grown state, but that the continuance of it is secured to her people and their posterity.

This brings to my mind a reproach usually cast on the Church of Scotland by her enemies, or rather it may be called an insult, viz., that Presbytery was often hatched in Scotland and nursed up, but was never major—never came to be of age—alluding to a young man who, though carefully brought up, dies before he attains to the age of one and twenty. But that jest will serve them no longer, seeing it is now eight and twenty years since the Revolution and since the passing of the act for abolishing Episcopacy, and yet presbytery not only remains, but seems to be in a better and more probable way for duration than it ever has been since the Reformation.

It might be proper here to say a few words by way of observation concerning the present state of the discipline of the Church of Scotland, which was confirmed also at the time of the Union, and indeed I cannot refrain it for two reasons:

1. That I think it is a debt due to the Church herself, which I find suffers innumerable unjust reproaches, and is contemptibly thought of not among her enemies only, but even among those in England whose interest as well as principles ought to move them to inform themselves better concerning her, and who, being better informed, ought to do more justice to those who so well deserve it at their hands.

2. That she may be a pattern to all the several sorts of Protestants in Britain, and may show them by her example not only what the blessing would be of an established well executed discipline in a national church, and of a laborious well regulated clergy, but also how easy it is to attain to it.

I shall not examine into the discipline of the two national churches in this island, in order to compare them, to recommend one of them as better than the other. But for their due emulation this I may say, that supposing the rules of their discipline equally good, yet no man will deny two things.

1. That the Church of England's discipline is the most neglected, the execution of it the most encumbered, and the prosecution made the most difficult and tedious, as well as expensive and chargeable to the prosecutor, of any Protestant Church in the world.

2. That the Church of Scotland's discipline is the

most exact in form, the most easy and cheap to the
prosecutor, and the most punctually and strictly executed, without partiality, bribery, or any sort of corruption, as also without a tiresome, tedious, and
dilatory proceeding, of any church discipline in the
world.

Some of the consequences of this are these :—

1. The ministers (for they are as much subjected
to the discipline of the Church as the people, and
perhaps more) are daily and duly enquired into as
to their conduct, and fail not to be censured if they
give occasion of scandal in the severest manner ; and
in this censuring of the ministers in Scotland, it is to
be particularly observed that ministers have there a
severity used with them, if they offend, which the
common people have not, and which perhaps no ministers in the world but these are subject to, viz.—
that if a minister falls into any scandalous crime, for
which he is deposed, he is deposed for ever.   A private man is received again, after scandal given, if he
repent and give satisfaction, but a minister never.

[Note, upon repentance and making public acknowledgment to the satisfaction of the Church, he shall
be received again to communion as a fellow Christian,
but as a minister he is perfectly useless, and never can
be reponed.

Note, also, that this severity is not by the law of
discipline, but the practice and usage of the Church,
and the people will never hear or receive such a man
as a minister.

Note, thirdly, that the happy consequences of this
severity, and which must be mentioned to the honour
of the Church of Scotland, is, that there is not a
minister now preaching and exercising the office of a
pastor in the whole Church of Scotland who can be
charged with any immoralities or scandalous behaviour except such as are under prosecution for the
same.]

Could this be said of the Church of England, or could it be said that all due care, as far as her own laws would allow, was taken to bring it to this, what a new face would there be of religion in this part of the island !

2. The people are restrained in the ordinary practice of common immoralities, such as swearing, drunkenness, slander, fornication, adultery, and the like. As to theft, murder, and other capital crimes, they come under the cognisance of the civil magistrate, as in other countries. But in those things which the Church has power to punish, the people being constantly and impartially prosecuted, they are thereby the more restrained, kept sober and under government, and you may pass through twenty towns in Scotland without seeing any broil or hearing an oath sworn in the streets ; whereas if a blind man was to come from thence into England, he shall know the first town he sets his foot in within the English border by hearing the name of God blasphemed and profanely used, even by the very little children in the street.

Another thing I cannot omit, in which the constitution of the Church of Scotland is singular and differing from her neighbours, and this is, that not the least room is left here for the popular charge of priestcraft, with which the Deists, Atheists, and profane people of this age charge the ministers of the Gospel of all persuasions, alleging that all they do is either under the awe of the great ones to pursue their interest and livings, or with wheedling and delusion to win upon the poor to make a profit of them.

To the honour of the Church of Scotland, her ministers are so stated as that—1. They are under no influence, awe, or command from the great ones— for the stipend or salary of the minister depends not upon the lord or patron, but is settled by Parliament, to be paid duly by the heritor or person who receives the tithes; and if he refuses or delays, the minister may demand it of his tenant; so that the ministers are wholly independent of the gentry, how much soever the poor people are in bondage to them.

2. As they can lose nothing by the anger of the gentry, they can get nothing by favour of the commonality; and this is very remarkable that no fees, no perquisites, no advantages are made of any kind by the minister in his parish of or from his people. He receives nothing for burials, marriages, baptisms, visiting, or any other thing belonging to his office as a minister—so that he has nothing to wheedle the people into or for. On the contrary, as he presides in his kirk-session or vestry, he is rather a magistrate or inspector over the lives and conversations of his parishioners, than a tool to please and cajole them, that he may get money by them, as is too much the case in England, and in other countries also.

This power of the minister in his parochial jurisdiction is that upon which Mr Lauder,* in that famous and yet unanswered book of his, argues, that a private parish minister in Scotland is a complete diocesan bishop, according to Cyprian, and according to the Scripture institution of a bishop, presiding in judicature over his flock or diocese, being vested with the power both to censure and absolve; and that the government of the Church of Scotland by kirk-sessions, presbyteries, synods, and general assemblies, is really and properly Episcopal government, to all intents and purposes, as the government of the Church was Episcopal in the third and fourth centuries.

3. The office of a minister in the Church of Scotland is a quite different thing from the office of a minister in England—that is to say, as it is now executed, either in the National Church or among the Dissenters; and it may be said without an hyperbole,

---

* Vide Lauder, Ancient Bishops Considered, cap. viii. page 31ʳ,

that were the ministerial office subjected and discharged in England as it is in Scotland, in that
laborious, self-denying manner, and under such small
encouragements, thousands of the clergy, I dare say,
would wish to have been brought up mechanics rather
than parsons, and scarcely a man that had any temporal estate to subsist on would take the fatigue of
the gown upon him. Here are no drones, no idle
parsons, no pampered priests, no dignities or preferments to excite ambition, no pluralities and curacies
to encourage sloth, no authority or power over one
another to gratify pride, no exemption from the laborious part, or excuse for not performing it.

Every minister in Scotland preaches twice a-day,
and lectures upon or expounds a chapter, or part of
a chapter, before the morning sermon, except only
where in some large parishes there are assistants or
colleagues allowed. Every minister is bound by his
office to visit every family in his parish ministerially,
and at least once a year to examine every examinable
person in his parish. Every minister is obliged, in
conjunction with his elders, who, with the minister
compose the kirk-session, to take cognisance of and
hear all complaints against the morals of every person in his parish, and proceed judicially as the case
shall require. Every minister likewise is obliged to
visit the sick in his parish whenever they send to
him; nor is that an easy work in the country where
the parishes are large, and the villages included in
them remote from one another.

Whoever considers the office of a minister in Scotland, how faithfully the ministers there execute it,
how constantly they preach, how painfully they study,
how diligently they examine, how duly they visit,
will easily account for that weak scandal that our
people in England raise upon them—viz., that we
see none of their writings. And I shall add to it,
what a worthy and reverend divine of the Church of

z

England said on occasion of that reflection—viz., that if our ministers, as well of the Church as the Dissenters, would study more, preach more, visit, comfort, examine and instruct their people more, though they wrote less, it would be better service to the Church, and they would more deserve the name of gospel ministers.

There are many other laborious things which the ministers of the Church of Scotland go through, and which ministers in England know nothing of; such as their managing the parish charity, keeping the treasure for the poor (for there are there neither church-wardens nor overseers), their travelling to reconcile breaches and heal divisions among their people, their expensive journeys monthly to the Presbyteries, half-yearly to the Synods, and annually to the General Assemblies, and the like; all which serve to make it true which was said by an impartial enquirer there, viz., that the life of an English porter was easy compared to that of a Presbyterian minister in Scotland.

Yet all this is supported and discharged with such courage, such temper, such steadiness in application, such unwearied diligence, such zeal and vigour in the work, that our English sermon-readers know little of—not having the same support, and I fear not the same spirit to carry them through. In a word, as they have a work which human strength is hardly sufficient to discharge, so they have a support which human nature is not capable to supply; and I must acknowledge that there seems to be such an appearance of the spirit and presence of God with and in this Church, as is not at this time to be seen in any Church in the world.

Farther, as there is among the ministers a spirit of zeal, and an earnest devoting of all their powers, faculties, strength, and time to their work, so the people's part is in proportion equal. Their taste of hearing, their affection to their ministers, their subjection to be instructed, and even to discipline, their eagerness to follow the directions given—those are things so visible in Scotland that they are not to be described but admired.   To see a congregation sit with looks so eager, as if they were to eat the words as they came out of the mouth of the preacher; to see the affection with which they hear, that there shall be a general sound of a mourning through the whole church upon the extraordinary warmth of expression in the minister, and this not affected and designed, but casual and undissembled.

And one thing, as a hint to English hearers, I cannot omit, viz., that in a whole church full of people, not one shall be seen without a Bible—a custom almost forgotten in England.   On the other hand, in a church in Scotland, if you shut your eyes when the minister names any text of Scripture, you shall hear a little rustling noise over the whole place, made by turning the leaves of the Bible.   Nay, if a blind body be at the church, they will have a Bible, which they will give to the person next to them to fold down the texts quoted, that they may cause somebody to read them to them when they come home.

There are many more circumstances in which I might show the Church of Scotland to be happily distinguished from most, if not all the other Protestant Churches in Europe, but the particulars are too many.

I wish I could have had room in these memoirs to have set down the heads of their discipline, which we call in England the Canon, but it is too long.   What has been said, as it is impartially sincere, so though short in particulars, is sufficient to let you know what a Church she is, and what a flourishing and glorious state she is now in.   The glory be to Jesus Christ, the eternal King and only Head of his Church, for ever and ever.   Amen.

APPENDIX.

STATE OF THE CHURCH SINCE THE UNION.

As these memoirs were written soon after the Union between England and Scotland was finished and ratified, so the period chosen for the last part was proper to the time, but no less than nine years having passed since that time, and before the publication hereof, it is requisite that some notice should be taken of what has happened in that time, and this the rather because some depredations have been made upon the established liberties of the Church of Scotland since that time, and some attempts, even besides the open rebellion of the Jacobites, in order, if possible, to pull down her fences and lay open her enclosure, that Jacob might be given to the spoil, and Israel to the robber.

But that providence which has so eminently guarded the Church of Scotland in so many dangers, has delivered her from this also, and now she sees herself again free from farther invasion.

We have seen in the accounts passed on what foot of establishment the Church stood soon after the Revolution, and how she went even till the Treaty of Union, neither is there any thing in her history which requires particular notice during that interval of time. Farther, it is observable, that the Church being effectually restored as before, and enjoying an uninterrupted prosperity, there remained nothing to be done in her behalf, at the time of the Treaty of Union, but to preserve her, as she was in the full enjoyment and security of her doctrine, discipline, worship, and government.

For this reason, when the treaty began it was laid down as a fundamental, that the Commissioners on either side should have no power to enter into any conferences upon the ecclesiastic settlement of either nation; for as there was no view or design, or indeed possibility, of bringing the two Churches to unite, so to agree at first that both should remain just as they were was the only method to put the treaty in a way of being finished; the want of such a preliminary having been the only reason why all other attempts for a union had proved ineffectual, and come to nothing.

The Church then having no room to apprehend that her constitution should come to be debated in this treaty, had nothing left to do but to bring her security to be one of the articles of the union, and so bring the Episcopal Church of England not only to recognise her establishment, but to engage the whole nation and power of England to support and maintain it.

And this alone made the Union be acknowledged to be serviceable to the Church of Scotland, for otherwise it must be allowed that it had been a dangerous thing for the Church of Scotland, which was the weaker, to join and incorporate her civil power, which was her defence, with the English, which was the stronger; but now the security, liberty, and establishment of the Church of Scotland being twisted with the English constitution, and built upon the same foundation with that of the Church of England, it becomes invulnerable, unless we shall suppose the whole ecclesiastic and civil constitution of Great Britain should suffer a convulsion, and be overturned and destroyed.

Nor had the Church of Scotland so good a security for her establishment before, her nobility and representatives being not the best friends to her constitution, often offended at the severity of her discipline, and, in part, debauched from her principles by the levity and fashion of the court; and it was more than probable that, in time, they might have given a blow to the constitution of the Church, which now it is for ever out of their power to do.

It is true, that there is not one ounce of good will the more between the two Churches for this Union; nor can I say that the English Church has not shown her teeth on several occasions since that. The Scots Episcopal clergy have met with encouragement in their insulting the Church of Scotland, as in the case of Mr Greenshields, who set up a meeting-house in the teeth of the magistrates of Edinburgh, and vilely insulted them when they touched him on that head, telling them he was a member of the Church of England, and appealing from them to the House of Lords.

But, after all, as the government were convinced that the Episcopal men were in the wrong, and that they could not support the design, so the man had some money given him to withdraw, and the case was dropt as quietly as they could, and with that just caution with which wise men generally drop a thing they are ashamed of.

Nor can I say that even the Union itself has been so sacredly observed on the English side as the case of the Church of Scotland required, or her privileges so well preserved as they had reason to expect, from the good words which were given them at the time of the treaty. Witness the several attacks made upon them in the affair of patronages, the Yule vacance, and the imposing oaths upon the ministers inconsistent with their principles—things of which all I shall now say is, that as they were done in a reign which did several other things which the present reign disowns and declares against; so we have great room to hope, and the Church of Scotland to expect, that those impositions and infractions of the treaty will be repealed, and that she shall have more justice for the future.

The Church made what struggle they could at that time against the passing of the bill for restoring lay-patronages. The agents they employed here were heard by their council; and, considering how much was said against it, and how little was or could be said for it, it was thought very unaccountable that such an act should pass at all, but it must be placed to the account of the times. And whoever reflects upon the persons who managed the affairs of Scotland, and had the power at that juncture, will find the necessity they were in of gratifying the Episcopal party. Their advocate then was the Earl of Mar, the same who has been since their champion, and who was then Secretary of State; it was no wonder then that the Church had as little favour in every thing that was moved against her, or wherein her interest was concerned, as if she had been an enemy; nor was it in the power of the few gentlemen in England who were sensible of the injury, and would have served her at that time to do any thing for her.

However, a long defence of her privileges was published and delivered to the members of Parliament, and was handsomely spoken to in the house; and the Church had this satisfaction, that her cause was lost by numbers, not by strength of reasoning or of right.

It would be too long to insert here the tedious account published on that occasion by some who showed their good-will, rather than capacity, to state the case; but the true state of the case, as it was presented to the House of Lords by the three ministers deputed by the Church for that purpose, cannot but be proper to publish, because it gives the Church's plea in her own words, and is as follows:—

" To the Right Honourable the Lords Spiritual and
Temporal in Parliament assembled ; the humble
representation of William Carstairs, Thomas
Blackwell, and Robert Baillie, ministers of the
Church of Scotland, concerning the Bill for re-
storing Patronage, now depending before your
Lordships.

" It is with all humble duty and submission represented unto your Lordships, that this depending bill
seems to be contrary to the present constitution of
our Church, so well secured by the late Treaty of
Union, and solemnly ratified by the acts of Parliament in both kingdoms. That this may be more clear
it is to be observed, that from the first Reformation
from Popery, the Church of Scotland hath always
reckoned patronage a grievance and burden, as is
declared by the First and Second Books of Discipline,
published soon after the said Reformation, since which
time they were still judged a grievance, till at length
they came by law to be abolished.

" These patronages having been restored with Episcopacy, in the years 1661 and 1662, did continue to
the year 1690, that Episcopacy was abolished and
Presbyterian government again established ; and
though the act of Parliament 1690, resettling Presbyterian Church government, was founded upon the
act of Parliament 1592, which bears a relation unto
patronages, yet the said act of Parliament 1690,
doth expressly except that part of the old act, and
refer patronages to be thereafter considered, which
accordingly was considered in the same Parliament,
1690; whereby it is plain, that the abolition of patronages was made a part of our Church constitution,
enacted by the act 1690, and that this act 1690, with
all other acts relative thereto, being expressly ratified, and for ever confirmed by the act for securing
the Protestant religion and Presbyterian government,
and ingrossed as an essential condition of the ratifica-

tions of the Treaty of Union past in the Parliaments of both kingdoms; the said act abolishing patronages must be understood to be a part of our Presbyterian constitution, secured to us by the Treaty of Union for ever.

Yet it is to be particularly considered, that the same Parliament, 1690, was so tender of the civil rights of patrons, and so sincerely desirous only to restore the Church to its just and primitive liberty of calling ministers in a way agreeable to the Word of God, that they only discharged the patrons' power of presenting ministers to vacant churches; but as to any thing of their civil rights, did make the condition of patrons better than before, not only by reserving unto them the right of disposal of vacant stipends for pious uses within the paroch, but also for giving unto them the heritable rights of the tythes, restricting the minister, who formerly had the said right to stipends, much below the value of the said tythes, notwithstanding which advantageous concession to the patrons by the Parliament, this bill takes back from the Church the power of presentation of ministers without restoring the tythes which formerly belonged to her, by which the patrons come to enjoy both the purchase and the price.

" This being then the true account of our legal settlement as to this matter, it appears to be evident that the restitution of patronages, as to the point of presentation, can only gratify a few; while, on the other hand, it must necessarily disoblige a far greater number that are now freed of that imposition; and, indeed, it cannot but seem strange that this bill should be so much insisted upon, when there are so many patrons, and those, too, of the most considerable in Scotland, that are against such a restitution.

" It is also apparent that Presbyteries must come under many difficulties and hardships as to their compliance with this innovation, and that many contests, disorders, and differences, will probably ensue betwixt patrons, presbyters, heritors, and people, besides the known abuses wherewith patronages have been attended even in their most settled condition, whereof many instances might be given, especially, that thereby a foundation was laid for Simoniacal factions betwixt patrons and those presented by them; and likewise ministers were imposed upon paroches by patrons who were utterly strangers to their circumstances, having neither property nor residence therein.

" It is therefore, with all submission, expected from your Lordships' justice and mature deliberation, that a bill, as we humbly conceive, so nearly affecting the late Treaty of Union in one of its most fundamental and essential articles, respecting the preservation of the rights and privileges which our Church at that time was possessed of by law, for the security of which the Parliament of Scotland was so much concerned as not to allow their commissioners to make it any part of their treaty, but reserved it as a thing unalterable by any judicature, deriving its constitution from the said treaty, shall not be approved by your Lordships, especially while the nature of the treaty itself shows it to be a reciprocal transaction between the two nations.

" W. CRASTARES.
" THOS. BLACKWELL.
" RO. BAILLIE."

Before the Commons, as has been said, they were heard by counsel; but all was to no purpose, the bill passed; and which is worse, we do not see the Church of England, or even the gentlemen in the Parliament of Britain, who were actually against the bill at that time, equally solicitous to restore the Church now to the privileges which she lost then, how unjust soever the taking them away has been.

Indeed, we find the Commission of the Assembly very earnest to solicit the redress of those grievances, and not without hope that it shall be effected ; and therefore, even while this was writing, two ministers, viz. Mr ——— Hamilton, professor of Divinity in the College of Edinburgh, and Mr William Mitchell, one of the ministers of Edinburgh, are deputed by the said Commission to attend the sitting of the approaching Parliament, to get, if possible, redress of the Church's grievances, and a repeal of those acts which passed in the preceding reign in their prejudice.   The acts are particularly—

1. The act for restoring Patronages.
2. The for tolerating Episcopal meetings.
3. The act for the Yule vacance ; that is, for keeping Christmas.

If those three acts are obtained, the Church will then be restored to her full lustre and authority, and it is hoped will never more have any occasion to complain of being oppressed.

FINIS.

NOTES BY THE EDITOR.

Page 5.—"*It began to reform from Popery in the year 1557.*"

This was the year in which John Knox was invited to return to Scotland, by the Earl of Glencairn and others, who pledged themselves to uphold the reformed religion at the hazard of their lives and fortunes. In December of this year also, the first Covenant was subscribed at Edinburgh, by a considerable number of the nobility and gentry, the chief of whom were afterwards called the Lords of the Congregation. In this interesting document, the subscribers bind themselves "to maintain, set forward, and establish, the most blessed Word of God and his congregation, and to labour to have faithful ministers," whom they promise to maintain, nourish, and defend, "at our whole powers and wairing of our lives against Satan and all wicked power."

Page 13.—"*However, to make up the matter as well as they could, they made another image to sit in the pageant.*"

Calderwood says, "an idol was borrowed from the Grayfriars; a silver piece of James Carmichael's was laid in pledge."

This, and some of the circumstances subsequently narrated, occurred the year after the subscribing of the first Covenant, though, from the text, the reverse would appear to have been the case. The error, however, is one merely of dates.

Page 16.—"*Soon after this they sent their proposals to the Queen Regent by Sir James Sandilands of Calder, which contained in short these particulars.*"

Under the first particular it should have been mentioned that they craved the liberty of reading the Scrip-

tures in the vulgar tongue. The third particular mentioned is not expressly stated in the petition of the
Reformers. Perhaps, however, our author was right in
inferring that the Reformers asked the choice of their
own ministers from the following clause in the petition,
in which they ask, "that the grave and godly face of the
primitive Church may be restored, ignorance expelled,
that true doctrine and good manners may once again
appear in the Church of this realm."

Page 18.—" *They came there with such attendants, and so
numerous,*" &c.

The ministers did not appear at Stirling to answer the
citation. The diet against them was deserted, and a promise given to Erskine of Dun that their trial should be
postponed. They were, notwithstanding, outlawed for
non-appearance.

Page 27.—" *October* 17. 1559, *they appointed the reformed
ministers to preach publicly in Edinburgh.*"

John Knox was chosen by the people of Edinburgh to
be their minister on the 7th July 1559, and immediately
entered upon his labours amongst them.

Page 30.—" *Mr Willock first gave his opinion.*"

The opinions of Knox and Willock on this subject are
given more at length by Calderwood, but the statement
as quoted from Spottiswood in the text is substantially
correct. We presume no one, now-a-days, will venture
to dispute the soundness of the judgment pronounced by
the two divines; and the question regarding the policy or
prudence of their intermeddling with such an affair of
State will be easily resolved : 1st, By considering that
they were appealed to, and their judgment asked by the
counsel of State, and 2d, That the matter referred to the
ministers was not so much a question of politics as of
religious obligation. The Reformers, as God-fearing
men, wished to know whether, in accordance with the
obligation to obey magistrates laid down in the Bible,
they might, under any circumstances, resist their commands. The object was to define the limits of the magistrate's authority and of the subject's obedience, and this
came properly within the sphere of a minister's duties.

Page 36.—*" She asked pardon of all she had injured, and died very Christianly."*

In her death she appears to have maintained the same hypocrisy and inconsistency which had characterized her reign. She told Willock her belief that there was no salvation, but in and by the death of Jesus Christ. After his departure she sent for a priest to administer extreme unction.

Page 40.—*" An act for abolishing the jurisdiction and authority of the bishops."*

This statement is apt, as it stands, to be misunderstood. The act referred to prohibited any subject of Scotland from making suit to the Bishop of Rome for title or investiture; and also prohibited any bishop within the realm using any jurisdiction by authority of the Bishop of Rome.

Page 43.—*" It was then moved in the Assembly that the Queen might be desired to ratify the Book of Discipline."*

The Book of Discipline was not under consideration of the first Assembly at all. It was agreed to and subscribed by the members, and by a larger portion of the nobility in January following. It was not proposed to make application to the Queen for its ratification till December 1561, at the third General Assembly.

Page 47.—*" The Queen married the Lord Darnley in July 1564."*

The marriage was solemnized on the 27th July 1565. It is right to mention also, as qualifying the immediately subsequent statement in the text, that Murray, and others who were opposed to the Queen's marriage, were summoned to the court, and, on their non-appearance, were outlawed. It was in consequence of this step, on the part of the Queen, that they took up arms.

Page 63.—*" The Church had been now fourteen years in her first struggles with Popery, and had enjoyed her assemblies twelve years."*

If we date from the martyrdom of Patrick Hamilton (and, after his death, the struggle with Popery never ceased till that monstrous system of superstition was overthrown), we shall find that the contest had lasted nearly forty years. Hamilton was martyred in February 1528 ; the Acts of Parliament establishing the "true evangil" were passed in 1567. At this period the Church had not enjoyed her assemblies for twelve years. The first General Assembly was convened on the 20th December 1560.

Page 67.—" *The Bishop of Dunkeld was actually deposed by the Assembly.*"

The Bishop was not deposed this year, but threatened with suspension from his office, unless he should, within forty days, pronounce the sentence of excommunication against the Earl of Athole. Neither was the Superintendent of Lothian censured by this Assembly. In 1576, the Bishop of Dunkeld was declared to have forfeited his office for dilapidation ; and the same year the Superintendent of Lothian was censured for the cause stated in the text.

Page 83.—" *Mr Melville himself declined the jurisdiction of the Council.*"

It is necessary to qualify this statement. Melvile's doctrine, as asserted in his declinature, was, that for what he uttered in the pulpit he should be tried, *in the first instance,* by his ecclesiastical judges. He claimed no exemption from liability to trial and judgment for offences chargeable against his conduct as a citizen and a subject.

Page 94.—" *There were two Assemblies in the year* 1587, *but the latter was convened extraordinary.*"

This latter assembly, which was instrumental in forming the general bond against Popery, was convened in 1588.

Page 112.—" *The Commission of the last Assembly was sitting at that time.*"

The Convention at Falkland was held in August. The commissioners of Assembly, with several others of the ministers, having learned that the Popish lords had returned, were incited, by the imminent danger, to hold a meeting at Cupar in September following. They sent to the King at Falkland, the two Melvilles, with Patrick Galloway and James Nicolson. James Melville was not chosen as their speaker because he was first in the Commission, but because, as himself says, " he could propone the matter substantiously, and in a mild and smooth manner, which the King liked best."

Page 114.—*" That he have a negative voice in the Assembly."*

The desire of the King was that no act of Assembly should be held valid, unless ratified by him in the same way as acts of Parliament.

Page 127.—*" The next year finished the work,"* &c.

The King did not obtain his object at the conference, as would be inferred from the account in the text. The conference was broken off by him in anger and disappointment. It was in the Assembly at Montrose, 1600, that his schemes were forced upon a reluctant Church, under caveats which were never observed.

Page 151.—*" The Council instead of shewing any concern,"* &c.

The Council did shew not a little concern. They published a protestation two days after the petition was laid before them, setting forth that the charges regarding the Service Book extended no farther than the purchase of that book. They at the same time sent a report to the King of the state of affairs in Scotland, leaving it to his Majesty to determine what should be done to mitigate or allay the ferment. The proclamations of the Council, removing the courts to Linlithgow, &c., were not issued until after instructions to that effect had been received from England.

Page 157.—*Accordingly, they began to lay taxes,"* &c.

It is rather remarkable that our author should have omitted all mention of the Assembly 1638, its important acts, and the results to which it necessarily led.

Page 161.—*" I have only to conclude this part with saying, that, from this time to the restoration of King Charles II.,"* &c.

The Church of Scotland under the Commonwealth did not enjoy her full liberties. Her Assembly was forcibly dissolved by Cromwell, and prohibited from again meeting.

2 B

Page 203.—" *One Mr Porterfield.*" &c.

As there were several gentlemen of the name of Porterfield implicated in the persecution of the times, it is perhaps necessary to state that the gentleman referred to in the text was John Porterfield, laird of Ducall, in Renfrewshire. He was accused of not hearing the curate of Kilmalcom. For refusing to take the oath of allegiance without explanation he was fined £500 sterling, and confined to Elgin, as stated in the text.

Page 204.—" *Four poor men of the parish were hereupon convened before them,*" &c.

The narrative of this transaction by Wodrow is different in several particulars from that given in the text, and is more likely to be correct. On the day named for Mr Scott's induction a country woman desired earnestly to speak with him, and " in her coarse, rude way pulled him by the cloak, praying him to hear her a little. Whereupon, not like one of Paul's bishops, who were not to strike, he turned and beat her most cruelly with his staff. This treatment provoked two or three boys to cast some stones at him, which touched him not, nor any of his company. This was presently found to be a treasonable tumult, and the sheriff and country magistrates thereabout fined and imprisoned some of them. This, one would think, might have atoned for a fault of this nature; but our high commission behoved to have those criminals before them; so four boys, and the woman, with two brothers of hers, of the name of Turnbull, are brought into Edinburgh prisoners. The four boys are brought before the court and confessed that upon Scott's beating the woman, they had thrown each their stone. The commissioner told them hanging was too little for them. However, the sentence of this merciful court was, that they should be scourged through the city of Edinburgh, and burnt in the face with a hot iron, and then sold as slaves to Barbadoes. The two brothers are banished to Virginia for no other crime I can hear of but protecting their sister. The poor woman was ordered to be scourged through Jedburgh."

Page 230.—" *There had been a meeting in the fields in Nithsdale,*" &c., to Page 194.

There is strong internal evidence that tradition had

added not a few embellishments to the story as received
by our author. Of the same incident we have the following account in Wodrow. "Out of the multitudes who were
cast in prison in Dumfries, many parcels were sent in to
Edinburgh, as the managers saw good, where they were
banished, transported, or executed, if they were not prevailed upon to make some compliances to save their
lives. About this time, nine prisoners were ordered in
to Edinburgh under a guard of twenty-eight soldiers.
Some of their friends who were upon their hiding in
the country about, getting notice of this, resolved to do
what they could to rescue them, and chose the narrow
path of Enterkin in the road from Dumfries to Edinburgh
as the most convenient place for their purpose. There
they posted themselves in the best manner they could;
and when the prisoners came up, two and two tied together
upon horses, they demanded them; they were answered
with a volley of shot, which they returned and scattered
the guard, and unloosed seven of the prisoners and took
them with them. One of the soldiers was killed, and several of them wounded." The above narrative of Wodrow is taken from an account written by one of the prisoners. That of Defoe, must have been taken from the
traditionary recollection of the event in the country.

Page 245.—" *About* 300 *of them having received a general
sentence of transportation,*" &c.

Wodrow says 257.

Page 249.—" *In this our zeal, and fortified with such considerations as these, five men of our number,*" &c.

Wodrow gives the number as nine, others mention the
names of twelve. The gentleman for whom they lay in
wait, was William Carmichael, whom Wodrow designates
as a bankrupt merchant, and who had been guilty of great
cruelties against the Covenanters in Fife.

Page 253.—" *They knew that these persecuted people,*" &c.

The principles here set down as characterizing the whole
body of the Presbyterians, were held in their full extent
by a comparatively small portion of them.

Page 262.—*" The censure of such, therefore, was of no value to them, and they insisted upon the right they had, to declare their revolt from their allegiance to King Charles II.," &c.*

Our author in this part of his narrative, represents the Presbyterians as far more generally involved in the proceedings referred to, than was actually the case. The first document in which these views were broached, was an unsubscribed and unfinished paper, called the Queensferry paper; and, probably, expressing the views of only one or two persons. Even the Sanquhar declaration, in which allegiance to the Sovereign was renounced, was countenanced by very few. When it was read at the Cross of Sanquhar, only about twenty persons appeared in support of it. Cameron and Cargill were almost the only ministers concerned in it.

———

Page 293.—*He got notice of their design, and conveyed himself away into the west, where he continued retired till the affair of Pentland."*

Wodrow says, " he went abroad and accomplished himself in travelling some years." The conclusion of his last speech as given in Naphtali, though well known, may be here given. It affords the most sublime instance we know of martyr heroism, and Christian joy. "And now, I leave off to speak any more to creatures, and turn my speech to thee, O Lord. And now, I begin my intercourse with God, which shall never be broken off. Farewell, father and mother, friends and relations; farewell the world and all delights; farewell, meat and drink; farewell, sun, moon, and stars. Welcome, God and Father; welcome, sweet Jesus, the Mediator of the new covenant; welcome, blessed Spirit of grace, and God of all consolation; welcome, eternal life; welcome, death. O Lord, into thy hands I commit my spirit; for thou hast redeemed my soul, Lord God of truth."

CPSIA information can be obtained
at www.ICGtesting.com
Printed in the USA
BVHW081806220819
556561BV00019B/4311/P